The New Reality

The New Reality

The Politics of Restraint in British Columbia

Edited by

Warren Magnusson
William K. Carroll
Charles Doyle
Monika Langer
R.B.J. Walker

New Star Books
Vancouver

Copyright 1984 by The Committee on Alternatives
for British Columbia

First Printing September 1984
1   2   3   4   5   88   87   86   85   84

Canadian Cataloguing in Publication Data

Main entry under title:

The New Reality

ISBN 0-919573-34-7 (bound).—ISBN 0-919573-35-5 (pbk.)

1. British Columbia - Economic policy - Addresses, essays,
lectures. 2. British Columbia - Economic conditions - 1945-
- Addresses, essays, lectures. 3. British Columbia - Politics
and government - 1975-   - Addresses, essays, lectures.
I. Magnusson, Warren, 1947-
HC117.B7N48 1984   330.9711'04   C84-091434-2

Publication of this book was financially assisted by the
Canada Council and by the Government of British
Columbia through the British Columbia Cultural Fund
and Lottery Revenues.

Printed and bound in Canada
by Gagne Printers, Louiseville, Que.

New Star Books Ltd.
2504 York Av.
Vancouver, B.C.
V6K 1E3

Contents

Preface

THIS BOOK IS THE FIRST result of an ongoing programme of research and education concerning B.C. public policy being conducted by the Committee on Alternatives for British Columbia. The Committee was formed in December 1983 by University of Victoria faculty and professional staff who were concerned about the B.C. government's "restraint" programme. Its members are of diverse views. The Committee is not affiliated with any other organization, and does not speak for the University of Victoria as such.

The editors thank everyone who worked to a tight schedule to bring the book to completion. We received valuable secretarial and research assistance from many people, and owe special thanks to Mollie Arnold, Marion Babity, Doris Lam, Barbara Millward and Chris Morry.

Individual essays in the book are the responsibility of their contributors. The editors have sole responsibility for the book as a whole.

1983

May 5   Social Credit re-elected.

July 7   Government introduces budget and 26 bills.*

July 8   400 provincial government employees receive pink slips effective October 31, 1983.

July 11   B.C. Federation of Labour President Art Kube announces formation of Operation Solidarity.

July 14   Human Rights Branch director Hanne Jensen fired. Government announces elimination of Branch.

July 15   B.C. Government Employees Union members picket government offices throughout the province.

July 23   20,000 demonstrate at B.C. Place in Vancouver in support of economic, democratic and human rights.

July 27   25,000 gather on lawn of provincial legislature; it is the largest political demonstration in Victoria's history.

Aug. 10   40,000 rally at Empire Stadium in Vancouver.

Sept. 19   Government begins all-night sessions to force legislation through. Closure invoked for first time since 1957.

Oct. 6   Opposition Leader Dave Barrett forcibly ejected from legislature and banned for rest of session.

Oct. 11   Closure used a record ten times to cut off debate on Bill 3.

Oct. 15   60,000 march past Social Credit convention to Queen Elizabeth theatre in Vancouver in largest demonstration against ''restraint'' package.

Oct. 20   Premier Bennett goes on television to announce adjournment of House for ''cooling off'' period.

Oct. 28   Operation Solidarity announces programme of escalating strikes beginning with BCGEU.

Nov. 1   BCGEU strikes.

*For details see Appendix A, page 281.

Events, 1983-84

Nov. 8   Education sector workers, including teachers, go out.

Nov. 10   Crown agency employees go out.

Nov. 13   BCGEU concludes a tentative two-year master contract; Jack Munro, regional president of International Woodworkers of America, works out details of "Kelowna Accord" at Premier Bennett's home.

Dec. 1   B.C. Federation of Labour annual convention reaffirms support for Solidarity; 700 delegates march to government offices to demonstrate support for Solidarity Coalition.

1984

Jan. 3   Government announces layoff of 300 to 400 public employees by March 31.

Jan. 10   Operation Solidarity announces province-wide job action to be held in abeyance, following local school board decisions to rescind or reduce planned layoffs.

Jan. 30   Legislature re-opens.

Feb. 1   12,700 pulp and paper workers locked out.

Feb. 20   Government introduces 1984/85 budget, cutting funds to all ministries and eliminating grants to students. Plans announced to fire 2,000 public employees by March 31.

Mar. 19   500 delegates to B.C. Teachers' Federation annual convention vote to remain in Operation Solidarity.

Mar. 30   Government introduces back-to-work legislation for pulp and paper workers.

Mar. 31   2,000 rally in Vancouver to protest the new budget.

Apr. 2   Pulp companies lift their lockouts, pulp workers strike.

Apr. 10   Labour Relations Board forces pulp workers back to work.

May 16   Legislature adjourns for summer having given royal assent to several bills, including new Labour Code (Bill 28) and Human Rights Act (Bill 11).

Introduction

THE EVENTS OF 1983 are still fresh in the minds of most British Columbians. In May, the Social Credit government and Premier Bill Bennett won a third term of office, unexpected even by themselves. In face of a New Democratic opposition still widely associated with the "financial mismanagement" of the early 1970s, Premier Bennett promised a continuation of the policies of moderate restraint his government had thus far followed. In his acceptance speech on the night of the election, he even held out an olive branch to thousands of public sector workers who had campaigned against him. It seemed, despite the disappointment of the NDP, that life would continue much as before.

It did not. When Bennett's cabinet assembled at an Okanagan retreat before the opening of the new legislative session, it was briefed by Michael Walker of the Fraser Institute, a right-wing "think-tank" once regarded as part of the lunatic fringe of Canadian politics. Walker emerged smiling from the session. A few weeks later, the cabinet stunned the province with a budget and a package of legislation unprecedented in Canadian history. It marked the beginning of the New Right reaction in British Columbia.

The budget did more to proclaim the objective of "restraint" in public expenditures than to implement it. Thanks mainly to increases in health and welfare costs that the government could not easily control, spending rose by more than 12%. Attacked were a host of small spending items associated with "liberal" and "socialist" aims — to provide extra help for the poor, the handicapped and the socially disadvantaged; to protect the rights of tenants, consumers and workers; to provide what was once called a "liberal" education; to protect the environment; etc. These cuts, which even cumulatively had little effect on the provincial deficit, were in line with the basic thrust of the government's legislative programme — a package of legislation apparently designed to get the people off the backs of business.*

It was remarkable how many different groups the government managed to offend at once. At the core of the opposition was the labour movement. Basic union rights in the public sector were undercut by the government programme, and there was every reason to believe that private sector unions would be next. The unions had good grounds for opposing the government before it went any further, and unlike most groups they had formidable resources at their disposal. Although the strong and militant labour movement in B.C. had not always enjoyed good relations with the NDP or other progressive groups in the province, the government's programme made every oppositional group look to labour for support and leadership: the Solidarity Coalition was born.

People from all sorts of groups, and from all parts of society joined in Solidarity. They were united by

* The legislative package of July 7, 1983 is summarized in Appendix A on page 281.

their belief that only a massive show of strength could deflect the government from its regressive course. Although people's concerns were diverse, they could sense their common interest in defending the system of social welfare and the set of human rights that had been developed since the Second World War. The Bennett government was trying to turn back the clock, to rid the province of the rights and services that set it apart from Alabama and the Philippines. By ridding business of social responsibilities, the government apparently hoped to make the province the centre of an economic boom. Its opponents were not prepared to surrender so much for a doubtful economic "recovery."

Like many people in the province, we were shocked by the government's programme. As the weeks went by, what at first appeared a random assault on everything associated with liberalism and social democracy took on an insidious logic. It was a logic made familiar by Margaret Thatcher and Ronald Reagan: the brutal logic of the New Right.

Two things were especially frightening about it. The first was that it made a sort of sense, in terms not of an enlightened humanism, but of the requirements of capitalism and those who profit from it. What Bennett was doing, what Thatcher had done, and what Reagan had done, *would* serve the interests of big business by making it easier for multinational corporations to adjust to what some have called "the third industrial revolution." It would also make us all more malleable subjects of international capital. This was frightening enough. More frightening still was the fact that so many people accepted it all as a rational necessity, an inevitable response to the "new economic reality."

This situation was reminiscent of the 1930s — and not only because unemployment had risen to Depression levels. In the 1930s, millions of Europeans responded to the tough new policies of a new brand of leader, policies that promised an end to the softness of the 1920s and a return to the harsh struggle of the past, policies that would deal with what was *then* a new economic reality.

The genial style of Ronald Reagan marks a contrast to the strutting of the fascist heroes of the 1930s, but behind the facade is the same iron determination to fashion a new order. Reassured by the genial smile, people respond to that will and to the rough measures of Reaganomics.

Poor Bill Bennett is hardly in the same league: more like some Balkan potentate of the 1930s than a great master of events. But those who live in the Balkans must suffer their fate, and that fate for us is the local version of the politics of the New Right.

So far, the left has stated no clear alternative to these rightist politics; it seems as confused and disorganized as it was in the 1930s. There is, understandably, still the call for "revolution" from the extreme left. Accompanying this small voice are the groans of an ailing social democracy. These are cries not only of confusion and anguish, but of betrayal, for the liberal/social democratic left committed itself to the welfare state and Keynesian economic management on the understanding that the other side was also committed. This was the great compromise that would put an end to class struggle and a beginning to the end of ideology. Words like "revolution" would be put aside, and in return left and right together would commit themselves to managing the mixed economy and extending the benefits of social welfare to everyone. But now the deal is off. What is to be done? Something must be done to save the threatened rights and services which until now have meant a better life for large numbers of people. What can we do?

We can express our anger. That was partly what the strikes and demonstrations of last year were about. But there is more to what happened, and to what we are doing here, than that: we are searching for a way to stop the Social Credit government's backward shift to a grimmer and more repressive society. The first step is to know what has been done to us, to know what we have lost. That is what we can explain here. The next step is to develop a strategy of response. That strategy is not yet clear to us, but we hope that this book will aid in the struggle to discover it. What we ourselves have learned is reflected in our concluding essay, but there is much more to be said, much more to be done.

Part I
The Political Economy
of "Restraint"

Introduction

THE CLAIM THAT *a policy of "restraint" is essential for economic recovery in British Columbia recalls the old medical practice of bloodletting. A severe economic crisis has been diagnosed. The prescription, we are told, is massive cuts in human rights and social services, and the bleeding of human resources and aspirations. This harsh course of treatment promises future health for the provincial economy in return for some short, sharp surgery on the lives of the people who live here. Yet while this policy is reminiscent of ancient quackery, it is seemingly justified in hardnosed economic terms. It is to the economic issues, therefore, that we turn first.*

While we can readily acknowledge that something is wrong with the world economy in general, and with it the economy of British Columbia, this does nothing to justify either the present B.C. government's diagnosis of the economic crisis or its policies. There is, to begin with, a considerable discrepancy between the more obvious problems that confront the B.C. econ-

omy and the questionable analysis and rhetoric through which the government has been able to persuade so many people of the inevitability of its own specific version of "restraint". This discrepancy is the major focus of the opening chapter by Pat Marchak.

The economic theories that the government uses to justify its policies are, to say the least, highly controversial. John Schofield argues that Keynesian policies of mild fiscal stimulation offer a much more appropriate guide to economic recovery than the crude monetarism so popular with the New Right. The force of this argument is increased considerably through the careful demonstration by Gideon Rosenbluth and William Schworm that the government is seriously exaggerating the seriousness of the structural deficit in the B.C. budget.

In fact, the underlying theme that emerges from these essays, a theme which is taken up more explicitly by John Malcolmson, is that current policies of "restraint" have less to do with simple cutbacks demanded by a period of general scarcity than with a fundamental restructuring of the B.C. economy. As amendments to the Labour Code also indicate, this restructuring involves a reduction of public sector power and the enhancement of private investment and accumulation. The formula of "restraint" both mystifies and justifies a programme that has more to do with dubious political and ideological motivations than with hard economic necessities. The ideologues of "restraint", like the barber-surgeons of an earlier age, offer remedies that are more dangerous than the disease itself.

The four chapters in this section, while sharing a common indictment of the economics of the "restraint" programme, suggest two different views of the current economic crisis. Schofield, Rosenbluth and Schworm present an orthodox Keynesian perspective, arguing that the crisis is illusory, and that a fiscal policy of mild stimulation is the appropriate response to the immediate economic recession. Marchak and Malcolmson, on the other hand, suggest that the government's programme is an understandable though deplorable response to a global economic crisis that has, among other things, led to a collapse of forest revenues. However misguided, this response appears to reflect a recognition of new economic forces that cannot be met with orthodox Keynesian policies alone.

In our view, B.C. has no fiscal crisis. There is, however, a serious global economic crisis which has clearly worsened the structural problems that already exist in the B.C. economy, Not only has the government's fiscal policy had, and will continue to have, a depressive effect on the provincial economy in the short term, but its investment strategies will increase the structural deficiencies of the B.C. economy. If our standard of judgement is the welfare of the provincial economy as a whole, then the government's economic policy is clearly senseless in both the short and long terms. The need for alternative policies, drawing on both Keynesian traditions and on more creative and democratic responses to the global economic crisis, is urgent. Current policies only make sense from the point of view of the minority of people in this province who stand to gain through enhanced private investment and accumulation. It remains an open question whether the government sees itself as the servant of this minority, or is so caught up in its own rhetoric that it cannot see the implications of its own actions.

The New Economic Reality: Substance and Rhetoric [1]
Patricia Marchak

A MAJOR CHANGE is occuring in the world economy. The extreme right would have us believe that only one response — theirs — is possible. That is untrue. What we are going through in British Columbia is not inevitable or necessary, and does not lead to better things in the future. But to move in new directions and take control of our own corner of the earth we need to have a firm understanding both of the way the world economy is shaping our lives and the nature of the Socred rhetoric that masks the economic realities.

The central fact about British Columbia is that our resources have been exploited by more advanced industrial societies, and that the wealth created from those resources has not been invested in secondary industries here. We have always been a resource hinterland or peripheral state, first to Great Britain in the fur trade, then to the United States while it was the dominant world industrial power, and now to both the United States and Japan. These more advanced nations use many other regions in their quest for economic supremacy, but they can use places like B.C. only because our governments have been willing to make it easy for them to do this. During the entire post-war period our provincial governments have voluntarily accommodated the resource companies from other countries and have done nothing to encourage local manufacturing or genuine development. It is for that reason that we are so weak now in the face of a shift in world economic power.

The Changing World Economy

What Premier Bennett calls "the new economic reality" is a bundle of technological changes such as microelectronics, robotics and biotechnology that make some of our current ways of producing goods obsolete. Implementing these new technologies is an expensive process, and causes a drop in investor's profits. Companies that cannot afford them are taken over by those which can. The take-overs are also expensive and eat into immediate profits. During this process of retooling and take-overs companies decrease their demand for raw materials and labour. As well, they call on governments to help them purchase the new tools and expect governments to worry about the displaced labour.

This new economic reality is in many ways a replay of the process that occurred between about 1910 and 1935. Then, too, the accumulated technological changes associated with mass production, assembly-line mechanization, oil and hydroelectric fuels, steel and chemicals created an economy in which many small and even some large companies went bankrupt, and the survivors borrowed heavily from public taxes to retool their expanded businesses. Capital was gradually redirected toward new industries, but labour and community organizations were still attached to the old, more rural forms. The 1930s was almost literally a period of closing down for renovation, renovation which was completed during the Second World War.

One big difference between the 1930s and the 1980s is that the new techniques which emerged then and which dominated the next three decades required labour. The assembly lines needed large numbers of workers in single urban locations, and the resource industries needed many workers in the mines and forests. The growing bureaucracies established by world-wide companies to sell their new products needed large numbers of clerical and administrative workers. The continuing effort to develop new products required scientists and technicians. Since these workers had first to be educated and trained, there was an increasing demand for teachers. Thus, though mechanization displaced many skilled and unskilled jobs, it also created new labour demands.

The technologies which replace simple mechanization today are not labour-intensive. In some industries human labour can be replaced altogether. This displacement hits unskilled manual workers, skilled manual workers, clerical workers, teachers and lower- to middle-level administrators. As jobs are automated or become obsolete, a long list of other jobs associated with them is affected. The outcome of the present changes in technology will include a very much-reduced demand for labour not just right now while the retooling is taking place, but in the long run as well.

The mass production process depended on one other large factor: ever-increasing markets. These existed in post-war Europe and North America, but these regions today are no longer hungry for what they produce: they are already saturated with consumer products.

An important feature of the 1930s revolution was that it provided the basis for the welfare state. In part this occurred because an economist, John Maynard Keynes, was able to persuade the American government that an industrial society could be pulled out of a recession by spending public funds on job creation projects. During buoyant times, he argued, the public purse should tax heavily enough to put capital aside for this purpose. In this way, workers have enough money to buy consumer goods, and their purchases provide the stimulus for economic growth.

In addition to putting this theory into practice and discovering that it was true, governments throughout the industrial world responded to the demand from the growing corporations to provide a ready labour supply in the places where it would be most useful. They also responded to the demand from growing unions to provide aid to workers displaced by technological change, laid off during seasonal or other low-market conditions, or otherwise forced into unemployment. The welfare state was a response to the kinds of labour demands and needs created by the changes of the 1930s and the post-war industrial expansion.

The welfare state required labour for its administration. The public sector provided the education, skill training and basic maintenance for the labour force. In addition, the state provided a wide range of services to corporations as they became integrated and global. Women, who were pushed out of the workforce at the end of the war, were reinducted with the post-war expansion. They provided the pool of appropriately skilled workers for the public sector and the clerical staff for the private sector at a cost far below the wages of men in industrial production.

With expansion in the role of government, the same process as had occurred earlier in the private sector was re-enacted in the public: unionization and demands for higher wages. What was in part an effort to close the wage gap between men and women increased the cost of the welfare state. This cost was covered mainly by taxes on workers' incomes, which was possible only if a majority had paid work. Corporate taxes throughout the post-war period have been proportionately lower than individual taxes, and they have actually declined as a source of income for governments.

Unemployment began to rise in North America in the 1970s. Some of the reasons were the increase in fuel costs, the saturation of markets for consumer goods, increased competition for remaining markets from the European Economic Community and Japan, and the effects of the renovations to industry which Bennett calls the "new economic reality."

B.C.: A Peripheral State

These events affect all the industrial market societies and are not peculiar to Canada or British Columbia.

Where B.C. differs is in its extreme dependence on the export of raw materials, particularly wood products, to the United States and, more recently, Japan. During the prolonged period of economic expansion in the United States between 1945 and 1970, with forest products in strong demand for housing and newsprint, the region became a wealthy but not industrially diversified area. Lumber and pulp were the major products of a lush forest. The mills were owned mainly by American and central Canadian firms. Very little manufacturing either of the major resource or any linked products occurred within B.C. Investors continued to add new pulpmills, heavily subsidized by both levels of government, and by the mid-1970s pulpmill capacity was much greater than the resource could sustain. It was also greater than market demand.

Dealing first with the problem of market demand, the excess capacity of B.C. pulpmills is part of a world excess capacity, meaning there are simply too many suppliers of a resource for the demand. In addition, the demand itself is declining, not only for pulp but also for lumber. Radio and television are supplanting newspapers, changes in housing construction materials have reduced demands for construction lumber, and pulp-quality timber is now being grown in sufficient quantity in the southern climates to serve many buyers who previously bought from Canadian mills.

The mass production of lumber and pulp ravished the forest. Even during the period of high demand, reforestation and forest nurturance were low priorities in provincial budgets and company planning. The Social Credit government saw its job as providing the conditions suitable for outside businesses — long-term forest tenures, very low resource rents, and no requirements for capital investments in secondary industries.[2] In return it got American forest and mining companies which shipped an unfinished product to their parent firms or United States markets, and which invested profits in manufacturing in their home territory. These provided employment in B.C. resource regions, but they did not create the industries that would allow B.C. to become a developed and more self-sufficient economy. Nor did they sustain the forest on a long-term basis. Forests are potentially renewable, but renewal by nature takes centuries; renewal by humans requires investments which companies make only if they are sure of their future markets. The B.C. government did not require the firms to replenish in sufficient quantity, and it did not sufficiently fund the Forest Service so that it could do the job.

For the Social Credit government, this was the path of least resistance. As long as somebody wanted the trees and there were enough of them, things looked rosy. It was only when some of the American companies with plants on the coast began to move out of B.C., and when U.S. market demand dropped sharply, that the reality started to show through. British Columbia was for a while a rich periphery, but a periphery none the less. And peripheries are just regions with nothing to keep them going when the centre stops wanting their products, or finds it more profitable to invest elsewhere.

The current reorganization of the B.C. economy involves some basic changes in the forest industry and a turn toward Japan.

In the forest industry, because they have depleted much of the coastal forest or because other investments are now more profitable, several American companies have sold out their holdings in B.C. Some other companies, owned by both Americans and Canadians, are close to bankruptcy and may well end up selling their properties to the survivors of the current depression. The stronger companies — operating mainly in the interior of the province and owned by American companies or American/Japanese partnerships — are seeking ways of increasing their control of the remaining timber in B.C. and elsewhere. If they can persuade foolish governments to give them public lands (or sell these at nominal prices), that would suit them very well. The age-old method companies have used to persuade fools to give up something valuable is to threaten to pull out if conditions are not met. Such threats are always most terrifying when there is a recession or depression and the government is both frightened and incompetent.

The Social Credit response to current problems in the forest industry is to gut the Forest Service, to reduce rather than increase funding for reforestation, to reduce funding for research and development, and to talk about the need for "privatization" of our forests. The industry points to the terrible state of public lands and claims that if these were privately owned they would be properly reforested. All of this paves the way for giving up what little control the public has left of the timber that once blanketed the entire province.

As well as seeking more control of the remaining timber, companies are changing their production methods and their labour demands. One of the

newest mills, Quesnel Forest Products, has the latest
technology and can operate with a small number of
workers. It has managed to obtain a non-union
labour force. Other companies that stay in B.C. will
use it as a model.

Japanese investment in B.C. resources has
increased steadily over the past few years. The
Quesnel mill, for example, is co-owned by Japanese
and American companies.[3] American companies
usually attempt to control majority shares or else
fully own subsidiaries in Canada, but Japanese companies have a different approach. Manufacturing
companies which require resources form consortia,
usually with some Japanese government participation
as well, and these put only enough capital into
resource companies in Canada (and elsewhere) to
ensure their own supplies. Where possible, they
invest in various companies around the world, oblig-
ing these companies to compete with one another for
contracts to supply the Japanese investors. Thus coal
producers in south-eastern B.C. compete with producers in the north-east, Australia, the U.S. and
elsewhere.[4] Very few of the construction and other
contracts in the Northeast Coal development benefit
B.C. companies, despite enormous subsidies from
the public purse.[5]

There is nothing in the present Japanese policies
which substantiates the expectation that B.C.'s geographic location on the Pacific Rim will induce
Japanese "high tech" companies to establish assembly operations here if provided with enough low-
wage labour and public subsidies. Although the
present anti-labour policies and high unemployment
rates will lower the wage structure in B.C., there is no
particular geographic advantage enjoyed here and
cheap labour is already in plentiful supply in the
Philippines, Singapore, Hong Kong and elsewhere.
The Japanese want our resources, not our impoverished workers.

Canadian bankers and industrialists will not be

standing up for the workers or for our natural
resources as these changes occur. At the moment they
are more concerned about the cost of technological
change and of capital itself. When resource companies are reorganized, there will be fewer of them
and each will control much more of all the assets and
markets, but they will produce their materials with
less labour. They want to be free to reorganize labour
around their new and expensive plants. How can they
do this without meeting the demands for consultation
with unions? The all-too-obvious answer is to starve
the unions and break their control of the labour
supply.

Prolonged and debilitating unemployment, blamed
on the unions, is the means of creating a cheap
labour force in B.C. and clearing the way for private
investors to do what they will with remaining
resources and industrial plants.

One hears that B.C. employers are unhappy about
the "way" the Social Credit government is going
about this task, but one doesn't hear that they are
unhappy it is being done. The government is method-
ically establishing new ground rules which dramatically cut the bargaining capacities of unions, the rights
of organized labour to be consulted about technological change, and the wages of labour.

The major budget cuts are in the avenues of
upward mobility for workers and their children:
public schooling, higher education, day-care, voca-
tional training, access to health care, housing subsidies and unemployment insurance. Meanwhile, the
educational channels for the wealthy are being
improved, with greater injections of public funding
into private schools, management training, and
selected areas of professional education. The net
effect is the creation of an elite with privileged access
to employment and economic power, and a stiffening
of class lines reinforced by an ideology which blames
the poor for their poverty.

"Downsizing" the public service weakens the

groups most likely to oppose a new socioeconomic hierarchy while it increases the likelihood that such a hierarchy will be created. Educational policies recently imposed on public schools, colleges and universities reduce the range of opportunities for young people and discourage the next generation from assessing critically and intelligently their own situation. They will learn no more than is necessary for serving the corporate structures: basic science, basic literacy, basic mathematics. What they will not learn is how to read through propaganda, how to analyze their own society, how to engage in political action, how to listen to music or enjoy poetry, how to develop their logical and intuitive capacities for living a full life. This was precisely the nature of the education system in Orwell's *1984*. These changes are not caused by a fiscal crisis;[6] they are caused by the Socreds for the purpose of reducing the bargaining power of labour.

Social Credit Rhetoric

The "new economic reality" is indeed world-wide, and the similarities between the Social Credit ideology and those of the Conservative government in Britain and the Republican government in the United States are not coincidental. In all societies where the basic premises of capitalism are accepted, where labour is a commodity sold like all others and granted no more respect than clothespins and television sets, there are similar pressures to assign greater degrees of the total wealth to private capital and smaller degrees to labour, and to do this under the shield of an ideology which justifies privilege and tells workers that their failure to move up the snakes and ladders game is due to their lack of productivity.

But even so, the particular rhetoric of the Social Credit government is what we are obliged to hear in B.C. The ideology of this government is promoted in words such as *restraint, incentives, productivity, efficiency, downsizing, privatization, free enterprise, high technology, the new economic reality* and *our international competitive position.*

These words tap our emotions and have connotations quite separate from their formal definitions. Take for example the word *restraint.* On the surface it appears to be about the budget. But the word itself has emotional connotations entirely divorced from fiscal measures. It means discipline and the curbing of excesses. It may mean a more puritanical sexual code, women playing traditional motherly and wifely roles, and men being unchallenged heads of families. It may mean obedience by children to adults, by workers to employers, by students to teachers — in short, a more authoritarian society. It may mean the establishment of rules for everyday behaviour, rules that all are expected to observe so that everyone knows what to expect and how to behave. And while it may mean obedience, it hints at courage and will-power, at bravely taking control of one's life and accepting responsibility for one's own success — or other people taking responsibility for their own failure.

For some part of the population, especially in the upper middle class, the past two decades have brought affluence but also personal dislocations and sometimes tragedies. Women experimented with liberating options, and permissive childrearing turned out to have impermissible results. The success of "remake yourself" cults and authoritarian substitutes for religion such as Amway and EST, attest to an unease with affluence too easily achieved. There seems to be a strong undercurrent of guilt, and it leads to a resurgence of puritanism. *Restraint* — just the word, just the emotional connotations — catches that sentiment. Moreover, and most significantly, it catches it while serving the economic interests of these groups; indeed, they are encouraged to feel that they are courageous members of a revolutionary force in history. They have the chance to be born again without any serious inconvenience.

Added to the imagery of the word *restraint* is the analogy of the household budget. It is a false analogy. If a household maintains a mortgage on domestic property it is not then in a state of fiscal crisis; it goes into a crisis only when its members quit earning incomes and cannot pay the mortgage. The actions of this government are analogous to the head of a household demanding that all its members quit their jobs, then blaming their lack of productivity for incapacity to pay the mortgage. Even so, the analogy captures the fear workers have, their insecurity, in the face of unemployment and mounting debts.

Fictional enemies have been added to increase the sense of urgency by describing the cutbacks in public service employment as reductions in abuses, reductions in soft sinecures, reductions in tenure, and reductions in costs that come out of taxes. This ignores the fact that the reductions are not only of employees, but also of the services those employees performed. Those services were the means by which a civilized society educated its workers, ensured access to the legal system, provided health care for citizens, aided families in distress, prevented child abuse and many other evils which, when unattended, lead to far more costly social expenditures and a much less humane environment. But when the worker in the private sector is suffering from a real economic crisis there is a vulnerability that can be tapped, a willingness to believe that others are somehow causing this (the cost of public services) and a sense of justice which decrees that others (in the public service) should suffer equally.

In this rhetoric, restraint is linked to privatization and "free enterprise". At the economic level, privatization means socializing the costs while privatizing the profits of public services. Subsidies to private companies will take the place of government administration. The privatization of such services as forestry, government computer services, tourist magazines and vehicle inspections will provide comparable employment simply because these services can increase profits for private capital. The privatization of care services is not likely to lead to such profits, and the private sector is unlikely to jump at the chance to take over rape centres, homes for those who are both chronically ill and impoverished, or transition homes and aids to battered wives and abused children. In other words, privatization has two quite different meanings: one meaning is more profit for private capital; the other is more domestic and voluntary work for those persons who are obliged to drop out of the labour force when both jobs and essential services disappear.

There is an even more sordid twist to the privatization process in education funding. Funds allocated by the federal government for health care and higher education have been used by the provincial government to pay for such extravaganzas as B.C. Place, Expo 86, Northeast Coal, ski resorts and B.C. Rail — all of which will increase the wealth of a few at the expense of many. Provincial funding for public schools has been similarly diverted to these other projects, not one of which will improve B.C.'s "international competitive position" or provide long-term benefits for the labour force.[7]

Free enterprise is a particularly complex concept. On the surface it means "no government intervention in the marketplace," but it also implies the existence of a large number of freely competing companies whose fate hinges entirely on their capacity to please customers who make free choices between them. Since the marketplace is in fact dominated by giant corporations whose monopolistic practices (together with government supports) have eliminated both free competition and free choices by customers, the phrase obviously has another meaning. This meaning becomes clear when one understands the word "free" to mean "private".

We also hear about "deregulation" and "getting government off our backs." This really means that private capital will be rid of regulations that oblige them to pay for pollution controls and health and safety measures; to be subjected to public inquiries and commissions; to pay union wages and engage in negotiations with unions; to report to government auditing boards or agencies concerned with collecting information on the economic life of the province; to adhere to non-discriminatory employment practices, anti-combines legislation or other inhibitions against monopoly; in short, to accept reciprocal obligations to the society off which they earn their profits.

The words *incentives*, *productivity* and *efficiency* have honourable histories in the English language, and are respectable concepts within our still largely puritan culture. But within the rhetoric of neo-conservatism, these words also mask new realities. *Incentives*, for example, refers to an increase in competition for scarce jobs. *Productivity* refers to the substitution of machinery for labour without obligatory consultation with labour or compensation for lost jobs; alternatively, increases in the number of hours worked for the same wage or increases in the range of tasks required by fewer employees per establishment. *Efficiency* has no reference at all to what may be the best ways to employ a population as new technologies are introduced; it refers instead to whatever increases profits for private companies without increasing labour costs.

Downsizing has nothing to do with feather-filled quilts. It means reducing the number of union workers in the public sector, particularly in those areas concerned with increasing equality of access to education, social goods and social services. But what are the connotations? The word suggests the cutting out of *unnecessary* services, redundant and costly employees, of trimming and slimming Jane Fonda-style. Those services the government considers necessary are not trimmed. They include the services to private capital by an increasingly centralized government.

High technology apparently means anything not made out of wood. Judging from the stated programme of the government, this magic phrase includes particularly the assembling of products manufactured elsewhere but brought into B.C. duty-free. The chances of becoming a "high tech" region would be much improved if labour would sell itself at half price. Perhaps this is what Patrick McGeer means when he states that B.C. could become "an intellectual Philippines".[8]

Two words have disappeared from the government's language. One is *unemployment*, the other is *democracy*. The omission of *unemployment* is a means of neglecting the consequences of "down-sizing", "restraint" and "privatization".

The B.C. unemployment rate is now substantially higher than rates elsewhere in North America. Small business bankruptcies are triple the national average and continue to spiral upward when they are declining elsewhere. Even such establishment newspapers as the *Globe and Mail* attribute this to B.C.'s "restraint" measures. One of their columnists recently noted that "class warfare used to be a joke in this province. In the spring of 1984 no one is laughing."[9] Yet the 1984 budget forgets to mention this problem. *Unemployment* becomes one of those words that are quietly dropped from the conversation even though the facts to which they refer stubbornly refuse to go away.

The omission of the word *democracy* is a radical shift. Liberal ideology of the past 30 years has advanced a version of the state as an instrument of majority interests, as government for all the people. This was consistent with the development of the welfare state, the Keynesian compromise between the demands of capital and the needs of labour.

The Social Credit ideology does not advance this version; indeed, it comes very close to advertising itself as government for special interests. Some might argue that the substance is much the same under either rhetoric, but that is not the case. The legitimation of capitalism under the phrases of liberal democracy *has* affected the way in which our society operates, what it expects and demands of governments, and how governments mediate between capital and labour.[10] To delete the ideology of democracy is to provide the ground for deleting the forms as well. In fact, the entire legislative package and budgets give rise to the suspicion that the intention is precisely to abandon democracy along with the welfare state.

Truths and Half-truths

The basic ideological premise of this government is that the solution to the economic crisis lies in the reassertion of vigorous capitalist production and markets. From there the government makes its argument that the only way B.C. could possibly respond is by reducing the wages of its employees, thus reducing the cost of government. This is stated for example in Premier Bennett's speech of March 30, 1984 in the phrases "we are moving into a new economic reality" and "our industries must be free to compete." It is set out at length, as well, in the 1984 budget speech:

> Two years ago, British Columbia was facing a major economic crisis, caused by a shift in the world economic environment. No longer could we increase wage levels and public expenditure, while expecting the world to go on buying our products. We had to recognize our place in a changing world economy and adapt to circumstances beyond our control. . . . employees must continue to be flexible, seeking wages and working conditions that reflect their shared interest in productive and competitive enterprises. [We

must] respond to the demands of the world
marketplace and become more and more productive at doing what we do best.[11]

The government's pronouncements contain a series
of half-truths.

The half-truth is that a shift in the world economic
environment is in progress. The omitted truth is that
B.C. has been developed as a resource periphery and
is now well on the way to being an underdeveloped
province at the mercy of international corporations
seeking low-wage labour.

The half-truth is that public expenditures increased
over the post-war period. The omitted truth is that it
is no longer in the interests of international capital to
have a population fully employed at reasonable
wages, and that is partly what the public expenditures
were designed for.

The half-truth is that there is a world market. The
omitted truth is that it is not a free-enterprise,
competitive market in which nice little companies sell
their goods and services; it is a world economy
dominated by giant firms in every industrial sector,
backed by their home governments which in the best
of times use tariffs, subsidies and sanctions to ensure
the dominance of their economies over others, and in
the worst of times send in the army.

The half-truth is that the new economic reality will
fundamentally alter the way we work and live. The
truth is that the new reality is tied as firmly as ever to
the old structure of private capitalism and external
control of peripheral economies such as that in
British Columbia.

The half-truth is that we have indeed done what we
do best — exported our raw materials. The truth is
that the private companies and investors have not
ploughed back into the economy the wealth we have
produced so that we could not survive in better ways
than by exporting nature's bounty. And the B.C.
government has never called them to account, never

developed its own industrial strategy for economic development, never even charged sufficient rent for the resources so that they might be renewed.

But the central half-truth is that there is nothing we can do about it other than adjust by downsizing governments, reducing education, decreasing general welfare, and privatizing crown agencies and services. What this government means to say is that, given its ideological premise that private control of the economy is appropriate and "good", this is all it can think of by way of solution.

The full truth is that there are many alternatives and they include taking our economy into our own hands, decentralizing a substantial range of decision-making powers, increasing access to information, and providing genuine incentives, not to foreign capital for cheap-wage assembly plants and subsidized resources, but to communities and local groups to produce goods we now import and to produce manufactured products out of the resources we now export. They include mariculture, fish farming on an extensive scale around our bountiful coastline which is now needlessly depleted of sufficient wild fishstocks. They include reforestation and year-round nurturance of the forests, with the development of a genuine log market and reduction of long-term tenures to a few giant corporations. They include enrichment and extension of education so that our children are able to develop viable and environmentally sound industries in the future.

At the very least they include the Keynesian solution for the short-term crisis: use of public funds to employ workers rather than establish monuments and subsidize coal companies. More significantly, though, they include a new set of priorities which rest on the premise that economies are developed to serve the people who live in them, not the other way round.

Those who are opposed to the priorities of this government and the private interests that it represents need to come to grips with the rhetoric. The words *restraint* and *privatization* may be two-edged swords if taken seriously by the opposition. The opposition might, for example, call on the government to restrain itself, and to privatize the costs of technological change for the corporations; or they might demand that the children of the rich be restrained from accepting public subsidies for their education and health, that the "communications" department of the government be downsized, or that the legislature become productive.

What will not succeed for the opposition is a nostalgia for the way things were. The prolonged boom really is over, the United States is no longer the world's uncontested economic leader, the robotics and telematics technologies are not passing fads, and existing industrial empires do not need either a welfare state or a large active labour supply. There is a great need for an opposition which poses a clear alternative to multinational capitalism. We may acknowledge the change in economic reality, but use the occasion of capitalism's reorganization to loosen its grip on both our economy and our understanding of the world.

Change, according to Premier Bennett in his March 1984 speech, "is here to stay," by which *he* apparently means "once we've changed things to what we want, there will never be change again." But change, as history demonstrates, is constant: beyond the Social Credit ideology, beyond the "new economic reality", there is a future. It will never again be the 1950s, but it need not continue to be the 1980s either.

Recovery Through Restraint? The Budgets of 1983/84 and 1984/85
John Schofield

THE PRIMARY goal of the restraint programme introduced by the B.C. government — like that of the Thatcher and Reagan administrations — was to reduce the weight of government in the economy and to stimulate the growth of private enterprise. Neither the costs of recession nor any of the costs associated with re-ordering priorities were of major concern. The programme was motivated by the New Right's ideology of anti-collectivism, a fervent hostility toward the state, and a belief in the virtues of rugged individualism.

According to this New Rightist viewpoint, substantial government intervention in society jeopardizes individual liberty, which is assumed to be the supreme social value. If individuals are free from coercion by the state or by other individuals, they will respond by pushing themselves to the limit to the advantage of both themselves and of society as a whole. Unless public sector economic activity is reduced, so the argument goes, and unless government protection for

groups of individuals who might interfere with entre-
preneurial freedom are also reduced, we slide inevit-
ably down what Friedrich Hayek termed the "road to
serfdom" that takes us to the socialist state.[1] Only
when the frontiers of the collectivist state are rolled
back will each individual's dynamic energies be
released to bring ultimate prosperity for all. The
underlying judgement is that these long-run advantages will outweigh any costs created by the
roll-back.

All major elements of the government's programme are readily understandable in the context of
this set of beliefs. New laws making it easier to lay
off public service workers obviously make it easier to
reduce the size of the government. Deregulation with
respect to human rights, employment standards,
consumer services, tenancy arrangements, regional
planning and motor vehicles inspection also helps to
"downsize" government, loosens government constraints on individual employers, producers, landlords, developers and motorists, and weakens the
countervailing influence of various groups on private
capital. Privatization of social welfare, legal and
other services further contributes to government
"downsizing" and directly expands the private sector.
Centralization of authority regarding school board
budgeting, hospital board planning and course planning in colleges and institutes prevents school, hospital and college boards from offsetting the provincial
government's determination to control public spending. Public sector wage controls also help to control
public spending and benefit the corporate sector, and
are designed to provide a standard for private sector
wage restraint. A high rate of unemployment reduces
the market power of labour, as will recent modifications to the B.C. Labour Code. Even concern
expressed about the size of the budget deficit can be
seen as a justification for limiting public sector
growth as much as a response to worries about the

provincial credit rating or the debt burden being imposed on future generations.

This programme depends fundamentally on nothing more than an act of faith. Furthermore, the case against the more traditional approach of fiscal stimulation as a means of economic recovery remains unproven. To make matters worse, this programme of spending restraint not only involves the reordering of spending priorities, but also creates its own serious costs.

Recession and Restraint

The year 1982 saw the onset of the worst recession since the 1930s in Canada and the western industrial world. Following modest increases in economic activity of about 1% in the major capitalist economies in both 1980 and 1981, a fall of about 0.5% was recorded in 1982.[2] More people were out of work in these countries in 1982 than in the Great Depression. In Canada the decline in real national product from the level of the previous year was around 5%, the rate of capacity utilization in the manufacturing industry plummeted from 79% to 67%, and the average unemployment rate reached 11% of the labour force. In the first half of 1983, the monthly unemployment rate in Canada varied between 11.7% and 13.9% of the labour force.

The most important causes of the recession were the policies of monetary and fiscal restraint pursued by governments in an attempt to combat the inflation which built up during the international oil price shock of 1979-1980. From the point of view of the B.C. economy, which is heavily dependent on export sales in U.S. and Canadian markets, the recession was largely attributable to restrictive economic policies in the U.S. and Canada.

The effects of the recession on the B.C. economy were particularly severe. The province's unemployment rate, 6.5% and 7% in 1980 and 1981, jumped to 12.1% in 1982, when the national average was 11%; in the first half of 1983 the province's unemployment rate hovered between 13% and 16.1%.

The recession also had a marked effect on the finances of the provincial government. Reduced demand for the natural resource products of the province led to lower prices and lower government revenues. By 1982/83, provincial natural resource revenues had fallen catastrophically, to an estimated $544 million from the 1979/80 level of $1,319 million.[3]   At the same time, reduced levels of economic activity in general, together with the accompanying reduction in incomes, led to lower revenues than in the previous year from income taxes and the retail sales tax. Moreover, the need for welfare support payments increased. The result was that in October 1982, for the first time ever, the government broke with its "pay-as-you-go" philosophy, seeking authority to borrow short-term funds to finance the maintenance of government services. By the middle of 1983, a budget deficit of $1.6 billion was being projected. It was against the foregoing background that the government in B.C. presented its 1983/84 budget and associated legislation of July 1983, following this in February 1984 with a budget for 1984/85 which reinforced the restraint thrust of the first phase of the programme.

The claim that spending restraint by government was the key to economic recovery flies directly in the face of the corpus of well-tested principles used to guide economic policy in the post-war period. These principles demonstrate, among other things, that during a recession, when demand for goods and services is too low to generate full employment of available resources, the government can boost demand, either by reducing taxes to stimulate private expenditures or by creating demand for goods and services directly through its own expenditures on public works and government services. The government, in other words, can increase a budget deficit or reduce a budget surplus to stimulate a sluggish economy.

It was this simple principle of fiscal policy, enunciated by John Maynard Keynes in the 1930s, which led western economies out of the Great Depression (largely through huge government expenditures on armaments for World War II) and which, along with monetary policy (manipulation of the money supply), allowed governments to combat recessions and to promote sustained economic growth through the early and mid-1970s. Thereafter, succumbing to the cajolery of the New Right, some governments developed a reluctance to observe this principle. In fact, provincial Social Credit administrations had always remained skeptical of it, preferring the "balanced budget" philosophy prevalent before Keynes's ideas were known. As we moved into the 1980s, Premier Bennett found himself fully in step with the new mood when he offered the unsubstantiated assertion that "no government can spend its way to prosperity."[4]   The watchword, he said, had to be "restraint".

The Case For Restraint: A Critique

The B.C. government's case for "recovery through restraint" rested on the notion of creating business confidence by limiting government intervention in the economy. As the government explained, "A favoured investment environment is being created. . . by demonstrating that B.C. has the resolve to control the size of government and limit future tax increases."[5] In other words, evidence that the forces of anti-collectivism were firmly in control and determined not to impose an undue tax burden on businesses and individuals would stimulate private investment in the province and hence promote economic development. Legislation to weaken the labour movement and to reduce protections for consumers, tenants and other interest groups was a further step in the creation of an attractive environment for private capital.

The government bolstered its case by suggesting that, given a projected budget deficit of unprecedented magnitude, it had no choice but to pursue a policy of restraint; fiscal expansion would increase the deficit still further and add to the mounting provincial debt. In B.C., where the conservative practice of balanced budgeting is widely accepted as the yardstick of good management in government, there was concern that the size of the provincial debt already impaired the credit rating of the provincial government in international capital markets and bequeathed a heavy burden to future generations. Deficit financing can also have undesirable consequences for interest rates and the rate of inflation, although in the context of a depressed provincial economy as we had at the time of the budgets these effects are unlikely to be very serious.

The possibility of these latter effects should be recognized, but there are reasons to believe that the problem of the deficit was exaggerated. First, if budget balance is achieved over the longer term, there should be no cause for great alarm concerning a current deficit. The fact is that, on projected Statistics Canada figures, the 1983/84 deficit was lower than the combined surpluses of the previous three years.[6] Second, a deficit is magnified by recession itself as a result of reduced government revenues and increased welfare payments. This means that an increased deficit need not be indicative of financial irresponsibility on the part of government if it results from a fall in economic activity, and in such circumstances it should not be particularly damaging to the credit rating of the government. Third, inflation overstates the real size of the deficit — the year-to-year change in outstanding debt in constant dollar terms — and hence the real burden of the debt on future generations.

A fourth reason for doubting that the problem was as severe as was claimed is that the projected deficit of $1.6 billion in the 1983/84 budget was undoubtedly based on questionable estimates. Pointing to the inconsistency between falling income tax revenues estimated in the budget and a forecast of rising provincial product, economist Leonard Laudadio has made a forceful case that the projected deficit must have been exaggerated if the forecast of provincial output and income was correct.[7] Another study estimates that correction for unrealistic forecasting and for items omitted in the B.C. budget, but included in Statistics Canada accounts of provincial expenditures and revenues (for example, revenues from such special funds as the Workers' Compensation Board and the Medical Services Plan, which are in principle no different from taxes) could have more than halved the deficit for 1983/84.[8] Finally, it must be remembered that the tendency in budgeting is to err on the conservative side anyway. In fact, skepticism about the earlier estimates was confirmed by the revised official estimates of February 1984 which reduced the projected deficit for 1983/84 to $1.3 billion.[9]

Apart from the reasons advanced by the B.C. government itself, a number of other arguments for restraint have been made by various economists. These arguments, which have been implicitly accepted by the B.C. government, include the notions that the economy is self-regulating and does not require government stimulation to promote recovery; that, in any case, fiscal expansion as a means to recovery is self-defeating; and that expansionary fiscal policy merely creates greater inflation, which is viewed as society's primary economic problem.

The argument that the economy is self-regulating finds its roots in the classical theories of political economy of the 18th and 19th centuries. These assume that in the event of recession and mounting unemployment, prices, interest rates and real wages (purchasing power) will eventually fall, leading to an increase in the demand for goods, services and labour (that is, an increase in output and a reduction in unemployment). There is thus no need for stimulative intervention by the government. Indeed, in the modern version of this theory, intervention is seen as likely only to make matters worse because of the problem of getting the timing and magnitude of corrective measures just right.

But the original notion was never proposed as anything more than a long-run tendency and, as Keynes observed, in the long run we are all dead. In practice, problems of pressing importance cannot be put off to the long term. Furthermore, as Keynes also made clear, prices and wages are not easily reduced, due to institutional arrangements, so that the economy may get stuck in an "underemployment equilibrium", a position of less than full employment.

Monetarists also maintain that the Keynesian approach of fiscal expansion is self-defeating in terms of influencing real output and employment. There are two strands to this argument. The first concerns the effect of expansionary policy on interest rates; the second, its effect on expectations and inflation.

Regarding interest rates, it is argued that expansionary policy will increase real rates, thus dampening expenditure by businesses and consumers and thereby inhibiting recovery. This is the so-called "crowding out" problem: any increase in the government deficit causes increased government borrowing and hence increased demand for available savings (loanable funds), leading to higher interest rates and the "crowding out" of private borrowing. Private sector economic activity consequently falls below the level that would have otherwise occurred. However, the "crowding out" problem can be exaggerated during a recession when demand for loanable funds is limited. Moreover, Canada experiences one of the higher personal savings rates in the western world (around 10% of personal disposable income) so that the availability of loanable funds tends not to be as serious a constraint in this country as it might be elsewhere. Nor is it as serious a problem today as it was in the late 1950s when the savings rate was around 5%.

There are three hypotheses regarding the effect of expansionary policy on inflationary expectations and inflation. The first is that it is impossible over the long term to reduce unemployment below its so-called "natural" level, i.e., that minimum rate consistent with non-accelerating inflation. Any attempt by government to reduce unemployment below this level is supposed to fuel expectations of higher inflation. As workers and sellers adjust their behaviour to these expectations, wages and prices move up, leaving the real wage unchanged and employment, as determined by the real wage, at its allegedly "natural" level.

However, recent estimates put the "natural" rate of unemployment at around 6% or 7% of the labour force in Canada,[10] well below the average rate of around 13% during 1983 in B.C. Consequently, the B.C. government could have adopted an expansionary fiscal policy without running immediately into the "natural" rate problem.

A second hypothesis has to do with what are termed "rational expectations". This is the idea that people form expectations of future economic events "rationally" — on the basis of the best economic theories and econometric evidence — so that, except for random errors, they behave as if they have perfect foresight. Thus, if the money supply determines the price level, as monetarists assume, and if government deficits are presumed to be financed sooner or later out of newly-created money, expansionary fiscal policy creates expectations of future inflation. In turn, this causes economic agents to adjust their charges by the full amount of the expected monetary change in order to protect themselves against anticipated price increases. Any nominal increase in output resulting from the policy is, therefore, offset by higher prices, and no real increase in output occurs. Only in the event that government activity is unexpected or unnoticed can there be any influence on real output. In a less extreme version of the hypothesis, in which expectations are "rational" but reactions are lagged, real effects may occur, but in the short-term adjustment period only.

It is easy to question the realism of the strict "rational expectation" model. In practice, people lack the complete degree of information assumed in the model, and in any case there is disagreement among economists about which theories should form the basis of expectations. Moreover, even if economists could agree on the correct theories, it seems implausible to assert that people behave as if they are just as well informed.

A third hypothesis suggesting that expansionary policy may be self-defeating is that, if it fuels inflationary expectations and thence actual inflation, it may damage business and consumer confidence and inhibit private sector spending. It would be surprising, however, if fiscal action, particularly at merely the provincial level, would have led to a marked effect on inflation, given the wide margin of spare capacity in the economy in 1983. Furthermore, a moderate degree of inflation has traditionally been thought to stimulate private spending as a result of higher anticipated future costs.

A final argument in favour of restraint as a means to recovery is that any recovery strategy which fails to combat inflation is unacceptable because inflation is the primary economic problem. Regardless of whether or not inflation causes recession, it is seen as having over-riding adverse consequences, particularly if it gets out of hand. Its redistributive effects between different groups in society can be pernicious to the extent that it is not fully anticipated, or if anticipated, not adequately taken into account in contract arrangements. In these circumstances, its effects can lead to social and political tensions. Inflation can also jeopardize the external value of a country's currency.

This argument is also questionable. For one thing, it downplays the economic and social costs of recession: the foregone output and income, the personal strain of involuntary unemployment, and the increased incidence of social problems which result. Furthermore, given the fact that there is so much spare capacity in the economy, it is unlikely that a degree of fiscal expansion at the provincial level would have led to serious inflation.

The Costs of Restraint

There is a widely-held view that, despite the rhetoric, the budget for 1983/84 was not really one of restraint, given that government expenditure was projected to rise by 12.3% and the nominal deficit was placed at an unprecedented $1.6 billion.[11] However, once the effects of recession and inflation are taken into account, the real impact of the budget will be more contractionary than the published figures indicate. Certainly, in relation to the kind of budget needed to lift the economy quickly out of its most serious recession since the 1930s, the initiative of July 1983 fell well short of requirements. The facts are that the provincial unemployment rate at the end of 1983 still stood at over 14%, new construction expenditure in the province was even lower in real terms in 1983 than in 1982, and business failures in 1983 were almost 25% up on the figure for 1982.[12] Furthermore, the government plans to reduce the deficit to $671 million in fiscal 1984/85 and to eliminate a large proportion of government debt, mainly by diverting funds away from current expenditures into debt repayment. There can be little question about it: while the 1983/84 budget may not have been totally restrictive, restraint is the order of the day.

Furthermore, it is also clear that the restraint programme has involved a re-ordering of spending priorities on the part of the government. In broad terms, the shift of emphasis has been away from the human resource areas of health, education and social services, toward infrastructure developments designed to facilitate long-run economic growth through the private sector.

It is useful to distinguish between the short- and long-term effects of this programme. In the short term, unemployment and the rate of business failures will be higher than they otherwise would have been, while the level of output and income will be lower. One reason for this is the negative impact on demand that lower government spending has. Another reason is the shift of spending emphasis away from labour-intensive programmes toward infrastructure projects on which a greater proportion of initial outlay flows out of the province for the purchase of capital equipment and is not, therefore, available for re-spending within the province. A third reason is that private spending will have been depressed as a result of the dampening effect on business confidence through the creation of a climate of social and labour unrest, and a dampening both of consumer and business confidence because of the failure to alleviate the recession. Only if the economy were already bursting to exceed full capacity would the restraint programme have involved no lost output or income.

The immediate costs of restraint, it should also be said, will tend to be borne disproportionately by certain segments of society: namely disadvantaged people dependent on government services. Insofar as expenditure restraint deepens and prolongs the recession, the long-term costs will be borne by marginal groups in the labour force — young people and older women — who suffer the highest rates of unemployment; and by particular regions where local economies are least diversified and hence most vulnerable to economic downturn.[13]

In the longer term, the programme of restraint could erode the productive capacity of the economy so that, to use a variation on an old refrain, short-term pain may lead to long-term pain. Expansion in the ability of the economy to produce goods and services and hence income over the long term requires growth in the quantity and improvement in the quality of human, capital and natural resources. While the B.C. government may believe that its programme will stimulate private sector activity as the basis for development over the long run, there is a danger of lasting damage to the productive fabric of the economy.

For example, the current high rate of unemployment which implies some loss of work habit and experience on the part of the labour force, together with the enforced cutting of health and educational programmes, could impair the quality of human resources and hence their productivity in the long term. The closing down and scrapping of plant, and the lost investment spending deterred by the post-budget climate of social and labour unrest, means that the stock of capital goods available for long-run growth will be lower than it would otherwise be. In turn, the rate of technical change, which as embodied in new capital goods represents quality improvement, is likely to be lower to the extent that spending on new capital goods is slowed up. As far as natural resources are concerned, cutbacks in the financing of forest management and salmonid enhancement programmes could reduce the volume of timber and fish available for harvesting in the long term. And as the evidence from such countries as Sweden, Austria and Japan makes plain, an important ingredient in the recipe for sustained economic success is trust and co-operation between competing interest groups, notably capital and labour; this may have been lost for a long time in British Columbia.

Apart from the immediate loss of output and the possible long-term impact on growth prospects, certain budgetary costs may turn out to be higher than would otherwise have been the case. As a result of privatization, for example, legal service costs may rise through higher billings. There is no doubt that welfare support costs, as well as the budgetary costs of such matters as crime and family breakdown, may be increased to the extent that poverty and unemployment are greater than they might otherwise have been. It is also possible that current neglect of social problems due to expenditure restraint could lead to higher costs later for health, welfare and judicial services.

Finally, various less tangible social costs can be expected to increase as a result of both the deregulation component of the programme and the effect of the programme in deepening the recession. The loosening of planning controls, for example, could lead to environmental damage. With the abolition of the Rentalsman's Office and the Human Rights Branch and Commission, substantial costs of delay could be imposed in the court system. As a result of allowing poverty and unemployment to remain high, personal costs of stress and despair, and the related social costs of crime, ill health and family disruption — partly borne by government itself — will mount.

The Case for Measured Fiscal Stimulation

It has been suggested that we cannot afford to leave the economy to the dubious, long-term possibility of self-recovery, that the alleged constraint on fiscal stimulation imposed by the budget deficit appears to have been exaggerated, and that the harmful effects of stimulation on interest rates, inflationary expectations and inflation would not

have been serious. Thus a measure of fiscal stimulation could probably have been applied without great
danger. No more than a controlled measure of
expansion is being suggested here, for the budget
deficit and other possible disadvantages of stimulation do have to be recognized. It is also stressed that
action at merely the provincial level could not be
expected to have eliminated entirely the effects of
recession. With some careful stimulation, however,
the situation could have been eased. Instead, additional costs have been created and still others are in
prospect.

The anti-collectivist response to that position, of
course, is that the benefits of reduced government
influence and greater individual freedom outweigh
the costs of restraint. But to the mind which is not set
against state intervention for ideological reasons, the
alternative budget strategy of measured fiscal stimulation, without the kind of priority re-ordering which
has occured, would have caused no concern.

The Illusion of
the Provincial Deficit*
Gideon Rosenbluth
and William Schworm

IN THE LAST two provincial budgets drastic cuts in spending have been justified by the claim that fiscal restraint was necessary to save B.C. from economic disaster. As the budget speeches have pointed out, the world recession caused both a decline in provincial revenues and an increase in the persons receiving welfare payments. At the same time, a rising medical fee schedule and higher hospital costs resulted in higher expenditures on health services. Hugh Curtis, the minister of finance, has concluded that B.C. must either raise taxes or cut expenditures. The alternative of running larger deficits was rejected.

But the claims about the harmful effects of deficits are not valid in B.C. today. There are sound economic reasons for running a deficit during a recession. In

* A somewhat longer version of this paper was issued as "British Columbia's Budgets and the Need for Restraint," Paper No. 84-8 of the B.C. Economic Policy Institute, May 1984.

fact, there is no *structural* deficit in the B.C. provincial budget and, in spite of the recession, a cyclical surplus is likely in 1984/85. The financial condition of the B.C. government is one of the best in Canada. Although the recession has caused severe economic difficulties for B.C., there is no financial justification for the policy of restraint.

The Dangers of Deficits

That deficits should be avoided is regarded as self-evident by many people. But it is not by any means self-evident. Given that revenues vary over the business cycle, balancing the budget year-by-year would mean that expenditures would fluctuate from year to year because of factors outside of the province's control. Such a policy is simply bad management. No successful business operates by adjusting expenditures to meet revenues on a short-term basis. A sensible fiscal policy would be to fund worthwhile programmes in a deficit year, either with funds carried over from previous surplus years or with borrowing to be repaid in future surplus years. Spending levels should be kept reasonably stable, but should be allowed to vary when economic conditions affect the need for social service and welfare payments. Revenues will change annually according to provincial, national and world-wide economic conditions. The surpluses and deficits incurred over time by this fiscal policy should be managed by a sensible asset and debt policy.

An argument frequently made against government deficits is that they tend to raise interest rates, thus "crowding out" private spending on new capital equipment and so, indirectly, restricting the growth of output. This argument does not apply to British Columbia, where both the government and business borrow at interest rates determined in the large North American capital market. The additional financial borrowing resulting from an increased B.C. government deficit does not have a large enough impact in this market to affect the cost of credit to borrowers.

Another argument is that government deficits contribute to inflation which, in addition to its other undesirable effects, also leads to the "crowding out" of private spending. But in B.C.'s open economy and with the present high unemployment rate this is not likely to happen. A larger government deficit would provide a stimulus to the economy and lead to greater demand for goods and services, both directly, and indirectly, through spending by those who receive payments from the government or are relieved of taxes, so that their spending capacity is not reduced. In B.C.'s open economy much of this increased spending, though by no means all, "spills out" to the rest of Canada, the United States and elsewhere. The remainder increases employment and output in the province. Given present conditions of unemployment and unused capacity, it does not raise prices.

These effects were in fact acknowledged in the July 1983 budget by the appropriation of $415 million, about one third of the deficit, for the express purpose of creating jobs. "This employment stimulation initiative meets the commitment, made earlier this year, to provide a major expenditure injection for creation of immediate employment relief," the government stated in the budget speech.[1] There appears to be some inconsitency between this initiative and the statements in the same speech that "we cannot spend our way out of the recession"[2] and that "we cannot significantly affect the health of our economy by spending or consuming more ourselves."[3] On the contrary, the fact that the health of the economy did not improve greatly can be attributed in part to the fact that government expenditure did not increase *enough*.

Another reason for the aversion to deficits is the fear of "living beyond our means." A family, business or government that spends more than it takes in must either be running down its assets or going into debt. No one's assets are infinite, and in any case running down the assets means that less income will be available in the future. Going into debt leads to interest charges. If a government borrows from its own residents, interest payments are a transfer from taxpayers to debt holders and there is no net drain of payments from the economy. In British Columbia's open economy, however, it is true that a large proportion of the interest payments go ·to other regions of Canada and abroad, and thus represent a loss of income to B.C.

The fact that interest payments are a burden does not mean, of course, that one should never go into debt. It makes good business sense to go into debt to finance an expansion if the return is expected to exceed the interest charges. Households increase their welfare by making use of credit and it is sensible to incur debt if the benefits expected from consumer goods bought on credit exceed the benefits lost by having to pay interest charges. Buying a car to get to work is an example of this. Similarly, governments should not shy away from debt if the benefits expected for the economy exceed the benefits lost by having to pay interest.

Of course, continual large deficits should not be incurred, because this would cause a continual accumulation of debt by the province. If the debt becomes too large, the loss of income caused by interest payments can be an excessive burden in future years.

These considerations suggest that whether a deficit is good or bad depends on the answer to some questions: can the current deficits be financed by previous surpluses? If not, can current deficits be financed by borrowing without imposing an undue burden on the economy in the future? Is the deficit one of a long series of deficits that is resulting in a continually increasing debt, or is the deficit preceded and followed by surpluses that can be used to balance the budget over a reasonable number of years? Only by answering these questions can one determine if a deficit is part of a programme of sound financial management.

The importance of these questions was recognized in the 1984/85 budget speech when Finance Minister Curtis distinguished between the *cyclical* and the *structural* parts of the deficit — that is, between the part that results from a temporary recession and the part that reflects long-term, built-in conditions. Only the latter, he indicated, was a matter of concern.[4] Deficits that only appear at the bottom of the business cycle (i.e., in a recession) help to stabilize employment and output, and do not build up the level of indebtedness if offset by surpluses achieved in better times. When there *is* increasing debt, the important question is whether interest payments constitute a growing burden on the economy. If they are rising, but not increasing as a proportion of the area's total income or output, there should be no cause for concern.

A final reason governments worry about deficits is that potential lenders may worry about them, so that too many deficits of too large a size may impair a government's credit rating and thus make it both more expensive and more difficult to borrow in the future. To judge whether this should be a source of concern one must look at the government's balance sheet, its assets and liabilities, financial and real, as well as its actual and potential revenue base as determined by total income and output of the economy. We will have to investigate whether B.C.'s deficit is cyclical or structural.

The Deficit in B.C.

Answers to questions about deficits, assets, liabilities and net indebtedness are not simple because of the variety of methods used to measure each of these items. There are no simple answers to questions about which transactions, assets and liabilities should be included, and how they should be included, in a financial statement. We first examine the Consolidated Revenue Fund, on which the budget is based, to see if there is any evidence of a structural deficit that might justify the draconian measures of the last two budgets.

One way of searching for a structural deficit is to examine the cumulative average of surpluses and deficits over a period of years. If there is a structural deficit, this cumulative average over several cycles should settle down to a run of negative numbers. Surpluses and deficits as recorded by the government's present accounting system are shown in column 1 of Table 1. They show a cyclical pattern of surpluses in periods of growth and deficits in periods of recession. The cumulative average in column 2 is simply the average surplus (or deficit) of all the years on the table to that point. It turns negative in 1975/76 and 1976/77, reflecting the deficits of 1974/75 and 1975/76, and then remains steadily positive until 1982/83 when it is about the same as it was in 1975/76.

This was the statistical record available when the 1983/84 budget was prepared. There is absolutely no evidence of the steady run of negative numbers that would characterize a structural deficit. And yet this budget and its successor were rationalized by asserting the existence of a serious structural problem. Was there a sudden change in the economic structure in 1982 or 1983? There is no evidence of this.

The high level of the cumulative average deficit for 1983/84 and its projected high level for 1984/85 reflect three things. First, we are in the midst of the worst world-wide depression since the 1930s, and a cyclical deficit is greater when the cyclical depression is greater; second, the provincial government's budgetary policies have aggravated the depression in British Columbia; third, government expenditure

Table 1. The Size of the B.C. Deficits—$ Millions

Year*	B.C. Public Accounts		Adjusted Public Accounts		StatsCan Financial Management System		StatsCan National Income Accounts	
	1. Surplus	2. Cumulative Average	3. Surplus	4. Cumulative Average	5. Surplus	6. Cumulative Average	7. Surplus	8. Cumulative Average
1972	97	97	106	106	128	128	104	104
1973	146	121.5	242	174	240	184	267	185
1974	(10)	78	27	125	17	128	116	162
1975	(410)	(44)	(166)	52	(460)	(19)	(142)	86
1976	97	(16)	163	74	161	17	58	81
1977	205	21	304	113	233	53	393	133
1978	271	56.6	287	138	204	75	379	168
1979	542	117	657	203	593	140	475	206
1980	(257)	76	(213)	156	144	140	159	201
1981	(184)	50	(100)	131	560	182	364	217
1982	(984)	(44)	(954)	32	218	185	224	218
1983†	(1307)	(150)	(1307)	(79)	(1229)	67	N.A.	N.A.
1984†	(671)	(190)	(201)	(89)	N.A.	N.A.	N.A.	N.A.

* Year is fiscal year beginning April 1 of designated year for B.C. Public Accounts, Adjusted Public Accounts, and the Financial Management System figures and is calendar year for the National Income Account figures.

† Estimated.

Sources:

Cols. 1-4—*B.C. Financial Statements for the Fiscal Year Ended March 31, 1978*, pp. A11-A13; *B.C. Public Accounts 1982/83*, pp. B21, B24; *B.C. Budget 1984*, p. 20.

Cols. 5-6—Statistics Canada Cat. No. 68-205 and 68-207, various issues, Table 7 and computer print-outs.

Cols. 7-8—Statistics Canada Cat. No. 13-213, *1967-82*, Table 3.

figures include transfers to extra-budgetary units of the government (such as the transfer to B.C. Rail mentioned below) and other items that reflect the disposition of savings rather than expenditure. We now turn to these accounting problems.

Not all components of the provincial government are included in the budget accounts, and therefore these accounts do not give a true picture of the transactions between the government and the private sector. For example, a deficit can be created in the Consolidated Revenue Fund by transferring funds to crown corporations, even though taxes, etc. received from the private sector exceed payments for goods and services and transfers to the private sector. Second, a deficit can be created by including in expenditures items that fall into none of the above categories, such as loans to the private sector, revaluation of assets, and distribution of assets.

Column 3 of Table 1 represents a rough attempt to estimate the deficit after adjustments for these problems. It deducts from the deficit (or adds to the surplus) investments, advances and grants to crown corporations, other investments and advances, and asset revaluations and asset distribution associated with the BCRIC disaster. The cumulative average of the adjusted surplus is shown in column 4. Every year up to and including the 1982/83 fiscal year shows a cumulative average surplus. Thus the correct reading of the statistical record confronting the government when it embarked on the 1983 budget exercise should have been that the B.C. economy had a structural tendency to generate surpluses.

In 1983/84 the severe depression would have produced a large deficit for just about any fiscal policy. If the spending cuts had not been made, the deficit would have been larger by perhaps one or two hundred million dollars. The statistical record suggests that a larger deficit in 1983/84 would not have been a matter for concern from the point of view of long-run fiscal soundness.

In the 1984 budget, $470 million of the projected deficit of $670 million represents a transfer to B.C. Rail in order to reduce the latter's debt. That is a discretionary intra-governmental transfer which could easily have been deferred and should be ignored when thinking about the province's structural revenue base and spending needs. When it is deducted, the projected deficit is reduced to $200 million. This is well within the range of the government's record of errors of estimate. The 1984 budget figures show that in the 1983 budget revenue was underestimated by nearly $300 million. Thus it is quite possible that the actual deficit for 1984 is close to zero. Again, there is no evidence of a structural deficit.

The suggestion that the government finances of British Columbia contain a structural surplus rather than a deficit is strengthened when Statistics Canada's figures on the B.C. economy are examined. Columns 5 to 8 of Table 1 show provincial government surpluses and deficits for Statistics Canada's Financial Management System and on a National Accounts basis. The first adds to the budget the accounts of certain government agencies such as the Workers' Compensation Board and the Medical Services Commission. It also adopts somewhat different accounting conventions, in particular the consistent exclusion of loans and debt repayment from expenditure. Like the province's budget figures, it excludes crown corporations selling goods and services to the public. The National Accounts series is based on the same set of government agencies but different accounting conventions regarding transactions in capital assets.

Both sets of accounts show consistent surpluses for British Columbia until the 1983 depression. For the Financial Management System, the cumulative average shows a surplus for every year including 1983. These figures reinforce the conclusion that there was no financial crisis facing the B.C.

Table 2. Provincial Surpluses (Deficits) by Province—$ Million

A. Financial Management System

Fiscal Year Starting April 1	B.C.	Alberta	Saskatchewan	Manitoba	Ontario	Quebec	Atlantic	All Provinces*
1972	128	(24)	32	33	(344)	123	(89)	(163)
1973	240	254	95	7	(321)	210	(55)	398
1974	17	860	191	(35)	(730)	272	(155)	382
1975	(460)	709	121	(80)	(1440)	(283)	(320)	(1752)
1976	161	942	51	(59)	(1025)	(332)	(254)	(506)
1977	233	1928	4	(259)	(1465)	(59)	(276)	111
1978	204	2836	130	(64)	(1212)	(445)	(429)	1022
1979	593	1780	81	(22)	(685)	(513)	(177)	1051
1980	144	3982	232	(149)	(446)	(1509)	(261)	1982
1981	560	2147	479	(251)	(617)	(748)	(299)	1306
1982	218	2938	(157)	(343)	(1562)	(1766)	(701)	(1382)
1983	(1229)	(52)	(99)	(611)	(2754)	(1205)	(871)	(6820)

B. National Accounts System

Calendar Year								
1973	267	35	97	(33)	(232)	(153)	(60)	(102)
1974	116	664	150	(63)	(193)	110	(81)	652
1975	(142)	698	53	(92)	(1441)	(638)	(180)	(1756)
1976	58	1050	25	(99)	(1296)	(1022)	(247)	(1543)
1977	393	1484	58	(63)	(1110)	(1403)	(58)	(734)
1978	379	2384	110	(104)	(1310)	(606)	(63)	749
1979	475	1447	184	(79)	(735)	(1273)	(138)	(131)
1980	159	2941	260	(139)	(1080)	(2458)	(159)	(429)
1981	364	3110	271	(236)	(1137)	(2179)	(440)	(204)
1982	224	3163	116	(360)	(2538)	(2047)	(525)	(1950)

* Includes Territories

Sources: A. Statistics Canada Cat. No. 68-207 and Computer Print-outs.
           B. Statistics Canada Cat. No. 13-213, *1967-82*, Table 3.

provincial government at the time of the 1983 budget.

Table 2 compares B.C.'s surpluses with those of other provinces in Canada, both for the Financial Management System and the National Income accounts. Only Alberta and Saskatchewan have a comparable record of surpluses. Ontario and the Atlantic provinces (with the exception of one or two Atlantic provinces in one or two years) have a consistent record of deficits. Manitoba and Quebec match this record, except for some surpluses shown by the Financial Management System from 1972 to 1974.

The statistical record thus shows that British Columbia was in a better position than any other province except Alberta to counter the severity of the 1983 depression by an expansionary fiscal policy. Yet although the 1983 budget earmarked some funds for job creation, the general thrust of this budget, and even more so the one that followed, was toward spending cuts unparalleled by the other provinces.

The Burden of the Debt

Might the spending cuts of the last two budgets have been required by the growing burden of interest payments on the provincial debt? In a sense this question has already been answered. The record up to 1983 shows, on the average, surpluses rather than deficits, hence a decline rather than a growth in net debt. The effect on interest payments is, however, blurred by changes in the interest rate, so that it is better to look at interest payments directly. The provincial government can be both a borrower and a lender, so that it both pays and receives interest charges. If it borrows in order to lend, as it has done from time to time, interest payments and receipts cancel, and there is no burden on the taxpayer. To gauge the burden of interest payments one must therefore look at the net excess of interest payments over interest receipts.

Up to and including the fiscal year 1982/83, British Columbia's interest receipts exceeded its payments. The situation was reversed with the large deficit of 1983/84, and net interest payments are forecast in the budget to rise substantially in 1984/85. As a drain on provincial revenues they are, however, still extremely small, amounting to 1% of provincial revenues (not including interest receipts) in 1983/84 and projected to rise to 2% in 1984/85. In relation to total provincial economic activity they amount to about 0.2% of gross domestic product in 1983/84 and 0.3% in 1984/85.

Current and projected interest charges therefore do not constitute a large burden on provincial revenues or the provincial economy, and a less restrictive fiscal policy would not have encountered any significant obstacles on this score.

B.C.'s Ability to Borrow

Finally, can the dramatic spending cuts we have witnessed be justified by the need to maintain a good credit rating for the government? Considering the eagerness with which the world's lenders have advanced funds to Mexico, Brazil, Argentina, Poland and other countries on the verge of fiscal collapse, it is hardly likely that provincial deficits even twice or three times as large as those of the last two years would have seriously impaired B.C.'s ability to borrow. The difference between a good and a less-good credit rating means at most a quarter of a percentage point on the interest rate.

But would the credit rating have been any worse if B.C. had run a larger deficit? A counter-cyclical fiscal policy would have led to a larger deficit but would also have led to more employment, real output, and a higher growth rate. In determining the credit-worthiness of B.C., lenders do not simply consider the government's current budget, but also the economic prospects of the entire economy, both private and public sectors. These prospects would have been better with a larger deficit.

A major item in determining the financial status of the B.C. government is the record of assets and liabilities. Lenders want to know whether there is adequate equity — the excess of assets over liabilities — to make the loan safe. Since the government not only borrows on its own account but also guarantees the loans of crown corporations, lenders would presumably like to see a balance sheet consolidating the accounts of the government and its crown corporations. The closest we can get to this is the consolidated balance sheet published in the provincial *Public Accounts* in which the accounts of the government are consolidated with those of *some* crown corporations, specifically those serving government departments or implementing government programmes. In addition, the government's net equity in crown corporations selling goods and services to the public is taken into account. The resulting "taxpayer's equity", the excess of assets over liabilities, and its year-to-year change is shown in Table 3.

It is possible that the government was concerned about the recorded drop in taxpayer's equity (row 4) of Table 3 from $1.4 billion in March 1982 to less than one tenth of this amount in March 1983. This record, however, is based on an accounting practice that ignores most of the real assets owned by the government and its crown corporations. This omission can be partially corrected by using the values of fixed assets (at original cost less estimated depreciation) given in various notes in the *Public Accounts*. When these are added, the revised figures of taxpayer's equity are given in row 7 of Table 3. The drop between 1982 and 1983 looks considerably less dramatic — about 20%. Moreover, the net equity of nearly $4 billion at March 31, 1983 seems enough to

Table 3. **Taxpayer's Equity, Province of British Columbia, Consolidated Statement – $ Million**

	Fiscal Year Starting April 1			
	1982	1981	1980	1979
1. Taxpayer's Equity at Start	1357.8	1498.5	1710.4	1256.8*
2. Add Excess of Revenue Over Expenditure	(1218.3)	(335.9)	(353.3)	503.5
3. Add Change in Equity in Commercial Crown Corporations	(22.9)	195.1	141.4	(49.9)
4. = Taxpayer's Equity at Year-end	116.6	1357.8	1498.5	1710.4
5. Add Net Fixed Assets of Consolidated Crown Corporations	905.3	765.3	602.3	512.9
6. Add Estimated Net Fixed Assets of Government Departments†	2900.0	2900.0	2888.7	2601.9
7. = Revised Estimate of Taxpayer's Equity at Year-end	3921.9	5023.1	4989.5	4825.2

* Estimated. Differs from reported figure of 1255.2 owing to changes in accounting practice. See *Public Accounts 1981/82*, p. C 8.

† Figures for 1981 and 1980 are reported in *Public Accounts 1980/81*, p. C 17 as "recorded on a memorandum basis in the Consolidated Revenue Fund." Figures for 1983 and 1982 are rough minimum estimates based on the data for 1981 and 1980.

Source: *B.C. Public Accounts, 1982/83, 1981/82, 1980/81.*

sustain a large volume of borrowing. Owing to the rise in market values in recent years, the recorded values of the fixed assets are undoubtedly too low.

Even adding these estimates of the government's fixed assets gives a very incomplete picture of the province's credit-worthiness because the government's most valuable asset is omitted: its power to collect taxes. As we have seen, even when output and employment are impaired by depression, financing of the accumulated deficits would require only 2% of provincial revenues.

There is nothing in the provincial government's balance sheet or its capacity to obtain revenue that would justify concern for its credit rating and consequent expenditure cuts. There are, however, aspects of the province's financial position not reflected in this balance sheet that a lender might want to consider. The risk involved in the province's guarantee of the debt of "commercial" crown corporations (whose accounts are *not* consolidated with the government's in Table 3) depends on how one evaluates the commercial prospects of these corporations. On March 31, 1983 the guaranteed debt of these "commercial" crown corporations amounted to $8,860 million, most of it accounted for by B.C. Hydro ($7,661 million) and B.C. Railway ($877 million).[5] It is possible that a lender might entertain doubts about the commercial soundness of these two enterprises in view of repeated discussions in the media concerning Hydro's tendency to build dams we don't need and the doubtful prospects of B.C. Rail's new Tumbler Ridge branch line. It is not surprising that the government wants to replace outside borrowing for the Tumbler Ridge branch line, estimated to have cost $455 million, by "contributing equity capital financing as permitted by economic conditions. The province will recover a portion of these costs from revenue generated by this project [Northeast Coal]."[6] And if the revenue is not forthcoming, the province can follow the time-honoured practice of writing off losses in B.C. Rail. During the 1979/80 fiscal year the provincial government wrote off $186 million in B.C. Rail debts; later it wrote off another $45 million.[7]

Until the taxpayers' money has replaced the funds borrowed for the branch line, the government will provide "annual grants equivalent to the amount of interest charged by the Railway to its operations." But the government's guarantees to B.C. Rail (or, more accurately, its creditors) in connection with Northeast Coal go further:

> The Railway will incur in relation to this project, the cost of additional coal related rolling stock and equipment as well as the cost of upgrading other facilities and improving lines in addition to the Tumbler Ridge Branch Line. It is anticipated that the Railway will recover these costs from increased revenues generated by this project. However, the province has assured the Railway that if revenues are not sufficient to cover those costs that the Railway will be kept whole.[8]

Thus it is a plausible interpretation of current budgetary policy that welfare recipients must suffer in order to enable the government to subsidize its unsound business ventures and pay off its creditors, in an effort to maintain its credit rating.

Comparing data in the 1984 budget (pp. 29, 64) with data in the *Public Accounts*, one finds further guaranteed debt for dubious commercial ventures: $57 million for B.C. Place as of December 31, 1983, with $74 million more to be borrowed in 1984/85; and $38 million for Expo 86 with $100 million more — press reports suggest this is a seriously understated figure — to be borrowed in 1984/85. The debt of B.C. Transit rose by $165 million between March and December 1983, with $318 million to be borrowed in 1984/85, presumably for the Lower Mainland's rapid transit system. Further increases in the debt of B.C. Hydro and B.C. Rail are also indicated.

Conclusion

There is no good *fiscal* reason for the government's policy of "restraint". The policy seems to have the questionable aim of freeing up funds to guard against the possibility that the government's unsound commercial investment projects will undermine its credit rating. The provision in the 1984 budget of $470 million to reduce the debt of B.C. Rail makes sense as an attempt to partially "repair" damage to the government's reputation due to a bad investment decision.

As we have indicated before, however, the cost of any possible damage to the credit rating is trivial — one-eighth or one-quarter of a percentage point on the interest rate.[9] Concern about the credit rating cannot possibly justify the spending cuts and the unemployment and misery that the last two budgets have caused. Moreover, the damage done to the economy by the government's unsound investment decisions cannot be repaired. What the government's fiscal policy does is to transfer the resulting losses to the shoulders of those least able to bear them: welfare recipients and those deprived of employment by the "restraint" measures.

The Hidden Agenda
of "Restraint"
John Malcolmson

IN THE PAST two years "restraint" has become an
all-purpose explanation of provincial government
policy. The word has been pressed into non-stop
political service, justifying all kinds of government
action. There can be little doubt that it has borne
political fruit. While opinion polls demonstrate
widespread opposition to the government's *means*,
the supposed *ends* of restraint are widely accepted.
The Solidarity Coalition, despite its success in
mobilizing opposition, has been unable to change the
positive image of "restraint".

In identifying itself with this notion, the Bennett
government is cultivating an image of fiscal compe-
tence, far-sightedness, and determination in the face
of what it calls the near-sightedness and selfishness of
special-interest groups. For the public, "restraint"
simply involves sensible reductions in public expenditures in response to reduced government income.
The cuts are supposed to be temporary and to involve
no basic re-ordering of government priorities. It is

clear, however, that the cuts now being imposed involve not just permanent reductions in public spending but fundamental change in the character of government. This is not what most of us mean by "restraint".

The government is slashing public services in a number of areas — public schools and post-secondary education, child and family services, motor vehicle inspection, and consumer and human rights protection, to name a few. None of these measures is temporary, and they promise few substantial savings. A recent estimate suggests that the cutbacks proposed in the 1983 budget would save $100 million, a mere 1.2% of total budgeted expenditure.[1] This is modest fiscal restraint at best. The 1984 budget proposes further permanent cuts in legal services, social welfare programmes and education, but the fiscal effects are no more dramatic. The much-publicized reduction in the provincial public service — from 46,687 jobs in 1982/83 to 35,410 in 1984/85[2] — certainly *is* dramatic, but involves a permanent reduction and not a temporary restraint on public employment.

The government claims that its purpose is economic "recovery". But again we are caught in a web of misleading words. British Columbia's economy is oriented toward resource extraction and export, and it depends ultimately on forestry and mining. Mining activity depends largely on international prices and on the demand for major export commodities such as copper and molybdenum. In forestry, factors such as interest rates — with their impact on the level of construction activity — and the buoyancy of off-shore markets dictate the nature and extent of business activity. Provincial fiscal policy has little influence on these conditions, and so it is simply not the critical factor in economic recovery. Why then the pain without any obvious gain?

What is happening is something altogether different from a simple exercise in cost control. To understand what it really is, we have to go beyond the common critique of the government's means and look carefully at the ends it is pursuing.[3] These ends are connected to the interests of private business.

Resource Development and Economic Crisis

From 1975 to 1981, the Social Credit government followed an economic development strategy centred on promoting private sector resource investment. Given a generally favourable international situation, the strategy paid off in rapid economic growth. Between 1975 and 1980, B.C.'s economy expanded at an annual rate of 5.6%, a pace far exceeding the Canadian average.[4] Such expansion was reflected in a rapid growth of provincial exports: over the same five-year period lumber exports jumped 137.5%; coal, 96.2%; metal concentrates, 92.4%; and pulp, 42.8%.[5] Provincial government resource revenue also grew at a rapid rate, from $364.5 million in 1975 to $1,298.1 million in 1980.[6] Even allowing for inflation, the compounded annual rate of increase of such revenue was more than 25%. It was, in large measure, this resource-fueled boom which provided the fiscal basis for a rapid expansion of overall government expenditure and a broad extension in the range of available public services.

In mid-1981, what had been a temporarily successful economic strategy began to collapse as the world economy slipped into its most serious recession of the entire post-war period. Lumber exports tumbled under the impact of record-high interest rates and a depressed U.S. housing industry. Pulp and paper exports, while not hit as badly as lumber, were not immune to the effects of the downturn. Copper prices, which a year before had reached record highs, now plummeted in the face of collapsing international demand. Similarly, provincial coal exports began to fall in the face of heightened international competition and a depressed world steel industry. By early 1982, provincial producers found themselves under strong pressure to reduce their export prices. Exports of natural gas fell prey to a significant contraction of the American market. In short, as the province entered 1982, the entire resource-based economy was collapsing.

Obviously, the recession was not confined to B.C. In fact, while other provincial economies were beginning to contract in 1981, B.C. still had fairly high income from resources and increasing public revenues. In the corporate sector, the final phase of the resource boom produced a flurry of takeovers, as inflation produced an undervaluation of corporate assets. Because of this phenomenon several of the largest corporations found it more profitable to purchase the existing assets of competitors than to finance the development of new productive facilities. Big blocs of shares in six of the ten largest forestry corporations changed hands in 1981. MacMillan Bloedel, British Columbia Forest Products, Rayonier Canada, Tahsis and Scott Paper were all taken over in whole or in part by other companies. Many of these takeovers were financed by expensive bank loans, and as interest rates rose and resource markets fell, some of the companies concerned were pushed toward insolvency.

When the effects of the global economic downswing finally materialized in B.C., they did so in concentrated form. Between July 1981 and December 1982, the province lost close to a third of its employment in the ''goods-producing'' sectors of the economy — resource development, manufacturing, construction, etc.[7] During the same period, offical unemployment increased from 5.8% to 14.8%, the highest level recorded since the Great Depression.[8] Real gross provincial product fell during 1982 by 7%.[9]

The recession was not long in cutting into provincial government revenue. During the 1982/83 fiscal year, the resource-sensitive sectors of provincial revenue nearly collapsed. Corporate income tax, which in the previous year had provided $580 million, fell to just over $180 million. Energy revenues dropped from $357 million to $229 million, mineral revenues from $62 million to $33 million, and forest revenues from $107 million to $86 million.[10] This situation, when combined with increases in social expenditures triggered by the recession, produced B.C.'s first deficit on operating expenditures since the mid-1970s.

Phases of "Restraint"

It was in this context that the government's "restraint" programme began. It has had three phases. The first, preparatory phase ran from the beginning of 1982 to May 1983, the time of the provincial election. Early in 1982 the government foresaw a significant recession and began to plan for significant adjustments in public sector spending. February 1982 saw the introduction of the Compensation Stabilization Program, soon to emerge as a centrepiece of the entire "restraint" effort. The Compensation Stabilization Program was initially designed to cap public sector wage increases at 8% to 14%; later, toward the end of 1983, it was tightened to bring settlements within a minus-5% to plus-5% range.

Also in 1982 the government announced, with little fanfare or publicity, its plan to reduce the provincial public service by 25%. Figures released in 1983 reveal that in the preceding year 2,600 public service positions — 6% of the total — had been eliminated, mostly by attrition.[11]

In early 1982, provincial school districts were subjected to funding cutbacks — $28.3 million was chopped from district budgets in February, a further $37.5 million in July.[12] At the post-secondary level, cuts in grants pushed the province's three universities into deficit positions by fall, while colleges and institutes were forced to trim programmes and course offferings. The province also moved to place limits on hospital budgets, thus accelerating bed closures and staff layoffs. The denticare programme was cancelled, and the government entered into negotiations with doctors to reduce spending on medical services. These early moves had a stop-gap quality; there was apparently no overall plan or strategy reflected in them. Nor was the government making major structural changes to the scope and operation of the public sector. All in all, this first phase presents a picture of reactive "crisis management", lacking overall design or coherence.

The second, transitional phase ran from May 1983 to the February 1984 budget. At the outset, the Social Credit government was re-elected, shorn of certain centrist and moderating elements. It had in the meantime become apparent that initial projections about the depth and severity of the recession were seriously understated. Provincial unemployment rose dramatically, reaching a record 16.1% in January 1983, the highest level west of the Maritimes.[13] Provincial welfare rolls swelled at an unprecedented rate — from 54,770 in June 1981 to 70,660 a year later and 94,000 by December 1982.[14] The Human Resources Ministry found itself facing a $100 million cost over-run in its 1982/83 welfare budget.[15]

Faced with this situation, the provincial government brought down its now-famous July budget and legislative package. The budget itself presented an intriguing picture. Despite far-ranging cuts affecting a gamut of programmes, overall spending was to increase in 1983/84 by 12.3%.[16] This growth was mainly accounted for by expanded public works measures, higher debt servicing obligations and, most importantly, increased expenditures in social service, health and education. Higher labour costs were not the main factor: by mid-1983 public sector wage settlements were averaging only 3.3%.[17] The big cost increases were in grants for health and welfare — 8.6% for the Medical Services Plan, 6.6% for hospitals, 17.2% for welfare and related expenses.[18] These spending increases, combined with a significant fall in revenues, produced an anticipated 1983/84 deficit of more than $1.5 billion.[19]

Borrowing requirements produced by this shortfall, together with those anticipated by provincial crown corporations, created a record capital requirement of $3.8 billion.[20] Almost three-quarters of this had to be borrowed from external sources. This increased pressure for a re-evaluation of the nature and scope of public sector spending in B.C. The result was a series of initiatives to bring the "uncontrolled" costs of government — relating to social, health and education services — under a more stringent regime. The agenda was thus set for more radical efforts to streamline the public sector. Yet the government faced real problems in its attempts to contain spending. It had still to establish the institutional prerequisites for full-fledged austerity because, at this point, it lacked the control necessary to bring about overall cuts in public spending. This explains the apparent paradox of a budgetary and legislative package which slashes programmes and services and which begins a process of basic political change, while at the same time increasing spending.

The third, "downsize" phase began with the presentation of the February 1984 budget. This budget does much to bring the overall thrust and direction of the cutback initiatives into sharper focus. With its across-the-board cut in ministerial expenditure, the budget plan heralds the advent of a new period of real and major cost-cutting in the public sector, especially in education and the social services. The "Fiscal Framework" system instituted for school district budgeting will gradually reduce staffing and services to 1976 levels. In post-secondary education, cutbacks have been forced by refusing to pass on full federal education contributions. Welfare payments have been cut, and additional programmes eliminated. The only area exempt from the latest spending cutbacks is health care, an area currently the subject of intense federal-provincial debate over appropriate cost-sharing arrangements and one where, undoubtedly, the last word in fiscal "restraint" is yet to be written.

Other budgetary measures include a completion of the planned 25% reduction in public service staff, the privatization of a range of additional public functions — from licensing and forest management to child care — and a wave of new deregulation geared to economic development and resource management. In all of this, the government's efforts reflect a continuation of plans set in motion in the July 1983 budget.

Perhaps the most important newly highlighted feature of provincial public policy, and one largely ignored in the media, is the promise to lower business taxes in B.C. As Finance Minister Hugh Curtis explained,

> The main focus of revenue policy this year will be the analysis of our taxes on business. If we wish our economy to grow and develop in the future, providing employment and generating revenue for public services, we must ensure that we have a favourable environment. If we try to lower our taxes for individuals by levying higher taxes on businesses, we will succeed only in making our industries uncompetitive and in discouraging new investment. The result will be lost jobs, lost income and lost opportunities. This is the road to economic decline.
>
> . . . [C]oncerns have been expressed to me, both in recent consultations and previously, that British Columbia's taxation of business is somewhat higher than in competing jurisdictions. To ascertain whether this is the case, I have commissioned a study of the tax burden on a variety of

> types of business in several jurisdictions...In conjunction with these discussions the government will conduct a thorough review of the impact of taxation on economic development. Consideration will have to be given to innovative tax measures for stimulating new investment by large and small businesses.[21]

In short, the new tax measures will be part of a stepped-up campaign to attract more business investment to B.C.

The period of administrative restructuring to control government spending may now be over. While the process of reorganization will continue, enough of the institutional prerequisites are in place for the government to proceed in earnest with its general austerity plan. This explains the ability of the government to bring down a budget, amidst conditions of continued economic recession and inflation, embodying an unprecedented reduction in the level of overall public expenditure.

The Logic of "Restraint"

What has happened under the cover of "restraint" is a fundamental restructuring of public sector power, activity and spending. Four general strategies have been involved:

1. *The centralization of fiscal and administrative power in the cabinet or its agencies, and the corresponding suppression of alternate or decentralized arenas of decision-making.* Perhaps the most obvious example of this is the Compensation Stabilization Program which, since its inception, has imposed an increasingly strict regime of public sector wage controls. Education, both at the public school and post-secondary levels, offers another clear illustration of this trend, as the provincial government manoeuvres to undermine the power and autonomy

of elected bodies such as school and college boards in order to bring about cuts in spending levels.

2. *The undermining of institutions and processes which, until now, have provided a forum for appeal, redress or, in many cases, opposition to provincial government action.* The best examples are in the fields of human rights, consumer affairs and tenants' protection.

3. *The streamlining of government spending to make real, long-range reductions in the shares allocated to health, social services and education, and redeploying the available money to the promotion of private sector economic development.* The implementation of the 25% staffing reduction in the public service is the best example of streamlining; the cut in ministerial expenditures and the $470 million debt repayment grant to B.C. Rail in the 1984 budget best illustrate the shift in emphasis.

4. *The deregulation of private sector business activity, efforts to tilt the balance of power in industrial relations against labour, and the removal of impediments, whether legislative, procedural or social, to business activity and investment.* Provisions which reflect this strategy include the end of rent controls, the abolition of regional government planning functions, the privatization of forest management responsibilities, and the assault on trade union rights and power.

These restructuring initiatives place B.C. at the threshold of a major experiment in the field of "supply-side" socioeconomic management, an approach identified with the Reagan administration in the United States. While elements of the Reaganomic prescription — the accelerated arms buildup and high-interest monetary policies — are beyond the powers of a Canadian provincial government, other aspects of the New Right economic revolution provide an inspirational foundation for recent departures in B.C. public policy. A preoccupation with balancing the budget, emphasis upon private sector deregulation, the decision to proceed with public service reduction, the intention to overhaul the structure of business taxation in B.C. — all of these recent government initiatives bear the imprint of the "supply-side" perspective. There is much here that points to a basic redirection of public policy toward enhancing the climate for private investment and accumulation. And, as is evident from the American experience with Reagan, cuts in vital services, the erosion of basic rights and entitlements, cutbacks across wide sections of the public sector, and the promotion of record levels of unemployment are all viewed as part of the necessary price to be paid for the attainment of this objective.

It is within this general context that the government's much-publicized connection to the Fraser Institute should be noted. The Fraser Institute does not represent only the positions and interests of a far-right fringe in society.[22] During the years 1982 and 1983, Institute directors between them held more than 230 directorships with many of the largest financial, manufacturing and resource-based corporations in Canada. The Institutes's membership included the owners of 24 of B.C.'s 29 largest operating mines as well as the province's ten largest forestry corporations. In other words, the Fraser Institute speaks with some authority on behalf of the corporate elite.

The Institute has had a strong influence on Social Credit policy. Whether it concerns the cuts in social welfare and education, the abolition of rent controls, the undermining of medicare or the assault on public sector bargaining rights, government policy has, in effect, taken its lead from positions staked out by Institute economists and ideologues. The Institute has thus played the role of transmission belt for the social ideas and economic perspectives of the New Right, and as such has played an integral part in the rightward reorientation of Social Credit.

Political Departures

There can be little doubt that over the past two years much of the Social Credit government's overall strategy has revolved around efforts to send the relevant "supply-side" signals to the international corporate community. The current budget, with its emphasis on tight fiscal management, tax reform and an accelerated scaledown of government spending, reflects a continuation of these efforts. In all of this, the government is cultivating an image of tough-minded determination, whether in streamlining the public sector, trimming so-called "non-essential" services, or trying to bring the government's opposition groups to heel.

This brings up the problems of the B.C. labour movement. Current assaults on traditional trade union rights and prerogatives — as in the building trades industry — fall into place as the opening sequence in a series of planned, investor-oriented changes that together hold out dire implications for B.C. workers. Despite the partial victory of November 1983 in staving off the worst implications of Bills 2 and 3, recently-enacted Labour Code changes will make it increasingly difficult for unions to safeguard — let alone extend — past gains. In addition, government talk in its spring 1984 Throne Speech of "free trade zones" and union-free guarantees for selected sectors of the provincial economy raises the ominous possibility of a turn to Korean or Philippine development models. All of this — attacks on union rights, efforts to force wages down, barriers to future union organizing — fits well into the overall "supply-side" strategy and provides the appropriate context in which to understand government plans to attract "high tech" investment to B.C.

But the government's strategy may contain a major weakness, in that it to a large part relies on an exercise in "image management". Demystifying the prevalent "restraint" characterization and pinpointing the underlying direction and intent of the government's strategy can serve as useful elements in an attempt to revitalize the Solidarity Coalition. In addition, they can be instrumental in building the organization and protest necessary to ensure that the image of B.C. presented to the outside world is not one selected at will by a government of the far right, but one reflective of a broad current of popular determination not to acquiesce in a "downsizing" of living standards, opportunities and basic rights.

Part II
Government
and Opposition

Introduction

As was noted in Part I, the government's measures have involved a restructuring of power in favour of corporate business. This has been accompanied by a restructuring of government itself. Local authorities such as municipalities and school and hospital boards — some of which are controlled by the government's political opponents — have been stripped of much of their autonomy. At the same time, provincial agencies independent of the cabinet such as the Rentalsman's Office, the Human Rights Commission and the Agricultural Land Reserve Board have been abolished or severely curbed. The cabinet has been given more authority to act by order-in-council, without reference to the legislature. Within the cabinet itself, more power has been concentrated in the Premier's Office. Thus, the government has become highly centralized, and been freed of many of the restraints we associate with liberal democracy. It is to serve in future as an *instrument of Social Credit rather than of society as a whole.*

This political coup d'etat, *like the accompanying assault on the economy and society, occured without warning to the electorate. Milton and Rose Friedman, two of the gurus of the New Right in the United States, were impressed by Premier Bennett's wisdom in this respect, congratulating him in a recent book,* The Tyranny of the Status Quo, *for not disclosing his intentions before the election since doing so would probably have led to defeat. No doubt they were also impressed by the government's decision to ram its programme though the legislature and implement it in the face of a storm of popular opposition. For some, an abuse of the norms of parliamentary democracy is a sign of political courage.*

Social Credit seems to have been guided through-out by opinion polls which reported that the government's ends — when presented in the guise of "restraint" — were widely accepted by the electorate. It is impossible to tell whether the government anticipated the breadth and depth of the opposition to its programme. Certainly the organizers of the Solidarity Coalition were astonished by their own success. Never before had labour and non-labour groups come together in this way. Never before had so many people been mobilized for mass demonstrations. Not since 1919 had the province been so close to a general strike. Although the media were critical of strike action and carefully distanced themselves from both the NDP and Solidarity, the government faced widespread criticism for both the content of its programme and its high-handed methods.

Solidarity was initially successful in preventing measures that would have seriously eroded union rights in the province (and so weakened any future extra-parliamentary opposition). However, neither it nor the NDP could ultimately prevent the government from implementing the bulk of its programme. The

Kelowna Accord has not prevented Social Credit from moving inexorably toward its goals, including further limits on the unions. The main hope for the opposition lies in the effects of the mobilization that occured in 1983: as Bill Carroll suggests, there are signs that a broadly based extra-parliamentary opposition has emerged, and it will be a permanent force in B.C. politics.

Jeremy Wilson's analysis reminds us that a determined government, guided by sophisticated opinion polls, contemptuous of both parliamentary and extra-parliamentary opposition, and convinced of its mastery of the techniques of government-by-opinion-poll, will not easily be deterred or deflected. The long-term prospects depend on countering the ideology of neo-conservatism. As Phil Resnick suggests, this means reviving the left's critique of the centralized state and developing a programme for a more egalitarian and participatory democracy.

The Solidarity Coalition
William K. Carroll

FROM LATE JULY to mid-November 1983, British Columbia was rocked by a succession of unprecedented political protests. Thousands of people whose previous political activity had been limited to elections took to the streets in mass demonstrations, culminating in the march of 60,000 past the Social Credit convention in downtown Vancouver on October 15. Provincial government employees and teachers, most of whom had had little or no experience on the picket line, found themselves by November 8 at the centre of an economic and political struggle with the provincial government that seemed to strain the industrial relations system to its limit.

Why were so many people moved to take such drastic action, and how were they able to mobilize into a political force so rapidly? The basic answer is that their rights and welfare were at stake. In many ways, the political measures introduced on July 7, 1983 threatened the interests of various groups whose quality of life had since World War II become closely tied to a framework of basic citizenship rights and social welfare provisions.

Three distinct kinds of human rights have come into force since the emergence of market society in the 17th century.[2] Our basic *civil* rights — equality before the law, freedom of belief and association, freedom of contract — were part and parcel of the laissez-faire market societies of 19th century Europe and North America. The most important contractual relation that developed in these societies linked employers and their employees, allowing both parties individual choice in the exchange of labour for wages. The resulting mobility of capital and labour contributed to efficient employment of economic resources, but the relation between employers and workers also tended to place working people at a disadvantage, as their livelihood became tied to the caprice of profit-motivated employers and unregulated markets.

As people began to react against the effects of the market a second set of *political* citizenship rights was fought for and won.[3] It was not until 1920 that most Canadians were granted the right to vote;[4] previously, full political citizenship had been restricted to male property owners, a minority of the adult population.

Only when political citizenship rights were broadly extended did it become possible for working people to organize effectively to advance their interests within parliament.[5] The parties and unions that represented working people pressed in turn for a third set of rights: rights of *social* citizenship. These were acquired in the 1940s, 1950s and 1960s. They included the right to be represented by a union[6] and the right to basic health, education and welfare services. In post-war liberal democracies these rights have been realized in the services of the "welfare state" and in the system of free collective bargaining. Collective bargaining has brought better wages and working conditions to the 90% of British Columbians who rely on wages and salaries for their livelihood;

the welfare state has supplemented these with a *social wage*; a package of income and services — — unemployment insurance, health care, etc. — supplied not by the market but by the state.[7]

The legislative package and budget introduced in July 1983 proposed to curtail dramatically these rights of social citizenship and the social wage bound up with them. As such, the programme posed a serious threat to the vast majority of people in B.C. There was a glaring contradiction between vague principles of moderation on which the government had achieved its mandate in May[8] and the draconian measures introduced within a few weeks of the election. Many people questioned the authority of a government whose claim to power seemed based in manipulation and deception. Social Credit created its own "legitimation crisis" in its contempt for the electoral process as a forum for open political debate.

The Birth of Solidarity: July 1983

It is in this context that the rapid mobilization of unions and popular organizations must be understood. Within a week of the budget, large meetings were held in Vancouver and elsewhere to discuss the threat posed by the government's programme. The Vancouver and District Labour Council's Unemployment Action Centre quickly converted its July 11 demonstration on unemployment to an organizational meeting for a "Coalition Against the Budget". Delegates from 50-odd community organizations and unions set up a broadly representative steering committee to organize a mass demonstration later in the month. The next day, hundreds packed a Robson Square forum with members of the Human Rights Commission to protest the government's plan to abolish both the Commission and the Human Rights Branch. The following afternoon, Women Against the Budget was founded. Its second meeting drew 200 women, many of whom had no previous involvement in the feminist or trade union movements. The meeting resolved to send delegates to the next meeting of the Coalition, which in the meantime had been renamed the Lower Mainland Budget Coalition.

All these initial gatherings took advantage of existing networks and organizations in mobilizing hundreds of trade unionists, community activists and others. The emerging coalition drew upon union locals,[9] municipal organizations (such as the Committee of Progressive Electors and the Downtown Eastside Residents' Association), and various groups that had emerged from the social movements and economic distress of recent years: organizations of women, tenants, the handicapped and disabled, senior citizens, Native Indians, ethnic minorities, students and educators, gays and lesbians, the unemployed, and anti-poverty and human rights advocates.

The province's largest labour central, the B.C. Federation of Labour, also took an active part. On June 25 President Art Kube called for a coalition against what he termed the "reactionary forces of the right" and their public policy of "social and economic brutality". On July 13 the BCFed's Public Sector Committee recommended to the Executive Council that "a broad coalition be formed consisting of affiliated and non-affiliated public and private sector unions, church groups, human and civil rights organizations and other groups in our society adversely affected by current proposed legislation," and that a series of major protests and demonstrations be mounted quickly; the first would be a protest in Victoria on July 27. On July 15 a special conference of 500 unionists adopted a ten-point Programme of Action for Operation Solidarity, to be organized by a Trade Union Solidarity Committee of the BCFed executive and representatives from non-BCFed unions. The presence of the latter, including the B.C. and Yukon Building Trades Council, the Hospital Employees' Union, and the Pulp and Paper Workers of Canada, was particularly significant, as it promised an end to the disunity that had fragmented labour in the 1970s and early 1980s. Operation Solidarity also provided the means by which teachers and other workers not previously involved in the labour movement could become active participants.

By mid-July, then, two extra-parliamentary opposition groups had formed: the Lower Mainland Budget Coalition, and Operation Solidarity. Unprecedented demonstrations of 20,000 in Vancouver on July 23 and 25,000 on the lawns of the provincial legislature in Victoria on July 27 revealed the strength of both organizations. In August the two groups merged to form the Solidarity Coalition, and pledged to work province-wide to defend rights of social citizenship and to develop "a social and economic recovery alternative designed to meet the real needs of people in the 1980s." The Solidarity Coalition was to be non-partisan in its opposition to government austerity, welcoming support from all quarters of the community. Its member groups, while uniting around a common programme of action, would retain the right to act independently in opposition to particular aspects of government policy. Community group members of the Coalition would participate in it directly, while trade union members would participate through Operation Solidarity, which retained its executive along with its mission to unify the provincial labour movement. An interim advisory committee made up of Art Kube, Roman Catholic priest Father Jim Roberts and former Human Rights Commissioner Renate Shearer was mandated to assemble a Coalition steering committee representing 27 distinct areas of interest, ranging from injured workers, the unemployed, women and youth to professionals, environmentalists, small businesses and consumers.

Escalating Protest: August - October

The Coalition immediately embarked on a series of actions to pressure the government to withdraw the offensive legislation. On August 10, 40,000 rallied at Empire Stadium in Vancouver. Other demonstrations drew thousands in smaller cities and towns such as Kelowna, Nanaimo and Prince George. But Social Credit dismissed the demonstrators as "special interest groups" merely trying to fight the last election over again or to "picket their way to prosperity." When asked to comment on the massive demonstration on the lawns of the legislature in July, Premier Bennett replied that he had had larger groups to his home for his annual "tea party".

The Coalition's response was to apply more direct pressure to the government, while causing minimal disruption in the community. An August 30 assembly of 150 representatives from local communities and province-wide groups adopted an eight-week action proposal. Its objectives were to raise consciousness about the anti-democratic nature of the proposed legislation and to amass thousands of signatures on a petition to demonstrate public opposition. Local educational events in each week of the campaign were to highlight the harsh impact of the government's programme on human rights, workers, women, children, tenants, consumers, seniors, etc. The petition, worded to allow its introduction in the legislature, was to channel discontent into the parliamentary arena. In the politically charged atmosphere of September and October, however, the petition campaign's central premise — the existence of a functioning legislature able to receive such a document — soon evaporated. The campaign was never completed, and the Coalition was obliged to shift tactics.

Throughout the summer the provincial legislature had languished, as the government seemed content to

let the demonstrations and protests run their course
before proceeding to enact its legislative package.[10]
In the circumstances the Coalition and its affiliated
groups took several actions to pressure the government to withdraw or revise the proposed legislation.
These involved minimal disruption of existing institutions and practices: the focus of protest was on a
symbolic conveyance of widespread opposition.

In addition to demonstrations, there were other
forms of dissent. From July 19 to August 8 government employees of the Tranquille extended-care
facility in Kamloops occupied the facility after the
government moved its final closing date forward
from 1991 to 1984. On September 16 another
occupation took place, as 80 Solidarity Coalition
activists took over the provincial cabinet's Vancouver
offices and established a "People's Government"
there for 27 hours. Neither occupations brought
much disruption to the affected offices: the
Tranquille workers continued to provide full services
to patients while they occupied most of the facility;
the occupation of the cabinet offices lasted for a
single day. On August 27 Women Against the Budget
held a "Luncheon with Gracie", attended by 500
people in protest against social service cutbacks
brought in by Human Resources Minister Grace
McCarthy. The protest was held in front of
McCarthy's residence and featured a soup kitchen,
personal testimonials about the human costs of the
budget, and street theatre satirizing the government
and its austerity programme.

Although both the "People's Government" and
the "Luncheon with Gracie" were planned and
executed by Coalition members, neither was officially
endorsed by the Coalition. Individuals and groups in
the Coalition remained free to engage in independent
political action. Along with the demonstrations and
the petition campaign, these actions kept the issues
visible. They did not, however, have the impact of
the escalating job action that would eventually force

the government to reconsider several of its most contentious bills.

The government made little attempt to get its bills passed until September 19, when it suddenly began all-night legislative sittings and repeatedly used closure to shut off debate in face of a filibuster by the NDP. In the heat of this "legislation by exhaustion", Opposition Leader Dave Barrett was physically ejected from the House and barred from re-entry for the remainder of the session. Events like these contributed to the general unease in the province about the government's course of action. A poll published by the Vancouver *Sun* on September 24 showed that three-quarters of the respondents disagreed with the government's methods, even though most supported the idea of fiscal restraint. Only 8% of respondents were in full agreement with cuts in social welfare programmes, just 12% wanted to phase out the Human Rights Commission, and only 15% wanted increased hospital user fees. These figures were encouraging to both the NDP and Solidarity.

Nevertheless, Premier Bennett confidently told delegates to the Social Credit convention in Vancouver on October 14 that opposition to the legislation was crumbling, and that his government would never back down to a protest movement. The next day 60,000 supporters of the Solidarity Coalition marched past the convention in the largest demonstration ever against a B.C. government. Solidarity's Declaration of the Rights of the People of British Columbia (see Appendix B, page 286) affirmed the Coalition's primary commitment to defend social citizenship rights, including universal access to medical care, education and legal aid; protection from discrimination and arbitrary dismissal or eviction; and the right of workers to negotiate collectively "all the terms and conditions under which they work."

In the legislature, the NDP promised to resume its filibuster. But on October 20 Premier Bennett announced that the legislature would be adjourned for a "cooling off" period. Most of the key bills had already been passed, and royal assent was given to them the next day. Having overcome the parliamentary opposition, the premier was preparing for his showdown with Solidarity.

The November Crisis

Bringing matters to a head was the impending strike of the 35,000-member B.C. Government Employees' Union, whose collective agreement was to expire on October 31. Provincial employees were the immediate victims of much of the "restraint" legislation. Sixteen hundred of them were arbitrarily targeted for dismissal by November 1. Because the dismissals violated its collective agreement, the BCGEU vowed to block them. The union was also demanding withdrawal of the Public Service Labour Relations Amendment Act (Bill 2), which would have severely restricted collective bargaining for provincial government employees, and nullification of the already-enacted Public Sector Restraint Act (Bill 3), which abolished the principle of seniority among provincial government employees. Together with the Compensation Stabilization Amendment Act (Bill 11), which indefinitely extended wage controls in the public sector, these measures would have effectively demolished the BCGEU as a trade union.

In October, Operation Solidarity had formulated and adopted an escalating public sector strike strategy: other unions would take job action in support of the BCGEU if the government failed to withdraw Bill 2 and nullify Bill 3. The latter (like Bill 11) affected all the public sector unions, not just the BCGEU, and according to the agreement the BCGEU was obliged to remain on strike until all other unions obtained exemptions from Bill 3. In the event of government intervention during these job actions the president of the BCFed was given the authority to call for universal job action by all private and federal public sector unions in the province. This extraordinary strike plan was motivated by the widely shared analysis among trade unionists that the government's assault on its employees in the BCGEU was a first step toward broader changes in labour relations that would ultimately affect all workers. Nor would unionists have to stand alone on this matter. At its first delegated assembly on October 22 and 23, the Solidarity Coalition recorded its overwhelming support for Operation Solidarity's strike plan, up to and including a general strike.

The BCGEU struck on November 1 and was joined on November 8 by 42,000 education sector workers, including 28,000 members of the B.C. Teachers' Federation. Although only 59% of BCTF members had voted in favour of province-wide withdrawal of services by teachers, between 83% and 90% defied threats of teacher decertification, and in some cases court injunctions against striking, to support their allies in Operation Solidarity. The dual character of this job action — as a legal strike by government workers without a contract *and* as a political protest of ambiguous legality by education sector workers — raised the struggle to a new level of militancy. Demonstrations and petition campaigns are familiar and patently legitimate forms of collective action in western liberal democracies, but mass withdrawal of labour in political protest is a far less conventional tactic because it brings immediate and pervasive disruption. By November, however, the Coalition had exhausted all options short of escalating job action, and the government was showing no signs of movement.

Nonetheless, the very strength of the strike as a tactic created tensions in the Coalition. Many community groups supported their union allies by joining them on picket lines and holding demonstrations in support of the protest, such as the rally in Victoria on

November 11. However, decisions with respect to the strike were made by the Trade Union Solidarity Committee, which was dominated by the BCFed executive. The Committee was concerned mainly with the industrial relations issues at the heart of the job action. This set the stage for later recriminations from the left, as union leaders were denounced for ignoring the social issues of human rights and welfare and subverting a process that would otherwise have culminated in a general strike with mass public sympathy.[11] On the right, other Coalition members, including some church groups, were alienated by the disruptiveness of mass job action, and fell away from Solidarity in this period.

The means of resolving the strike was grasped on November 13, as the BCGEU reached what it termed a "no-concessions" collective agreement — laying the basis for the Kelowna Accord between Premier Bennett and Solidarity representative Jack Munro — just hours before the strike was to escalate to the civic and transportation sectors. The agreement entailed withdrawal by the government of Bill 2 and exemption of the BCGEU from Bill 3, with the understanding that all other unions, including the BCTF, would be similarly exempted. At a midnight press conference, BCFed secretary-treasurer Mike Kramer declared a "truce" in the war against Social Credit austerity and asked members of the Solidarity Coalition and Operation Solidarity to postpone further strike action.

The Aftermath of the Strike

Thanks to the strike, the right to collective bargaining in the public sector remained intact, but the social issues that had drawn community groups into the Coalition remained unsettled. The Kelowna Accord contained vague, unwritten provisions for the maintenance of human rights and tenant rights through ministerial consultation and an advisory commission on human rights. The government also agreed to consult with labour as it prepared a revised labour code for the province. Lastly, revenue saved by school boards during the strike was to be returned to the education system, forestalling the scheduled firings of many teachers in January.

However, these partial victories served to demobilize the Coalition and prepared the way for the government's reneging on its agreement on social issues such as human rights. Concessions on Bills 2 and 3 remedied the strikers' most immediate grievances: those pertaining to their own trade union rights. The government's move to consultation on issues less central to job action channelled people's energies into less disruptive and unfortunately less effective forms of political activity.[12] Although the forms of consultation were observed, the results were ignored. Thus the human rights legislation that had been the focus of the most vociferous protests in 1983, and had been withdrawn under pressure from Solidarity, was reintroduced and passed in virtually the same form in May 1984. The muted protest that greeted this "revised" legislation gave credence to the view that the Solidarity Coalition was no longer a force to be reckoned with.[13]

In the meantime, inter-union squabbles were resurfacing. In January the executive of the International Woodworkers of America broke ranks with other forestry unions and recommended that its members accept a three-year collective agreement that made important concessions to employers. When the Canadian Paperworkers Union and the Pulp and Paper Workers of Canada held firm in their demands they were confronted on February 1 with an industry-wide lockout. In response the unions set up legal secondary pickets at worksites owned by their employers. Although the vast majority of IWA members respected these lines, tensions ran high, and at Fort St. James and elsewhere there were ugly scenes.[14] IWA regional president Jack Munro — who had sealed the Kelowna Accord — astonished trade unionists by expressing sympathy for those who were crossing the picket lines. This was a serious break from the long tradition among unionists in B.C. of strict respect for picket lines.

In early April the provincial government took the unprecedented step of legislating the locked-out pulpworkers back to their jobs, prohibiting further work stoppages, and giving itself the power to impose a collective agreement. Although unionists quickly retaliated by replacing their "Locked Out" signs with "On Strike" placards, within a week of the legislation they had capitulated to a Labour Relations Board order to resume work. The adjournment of the legislature in May left 12,700 pulpworkers with neither a new contract nor the right to strike in bargaining for an agreement.

This back-to-work legislation was followed on May 8 by the government's long-awaited revision of the provincial Labour Code. Swiftly enacted in time for the legislature's adjournment on May 16, the Labour Code Amendment Act presents a more general threat to working people than did the anti-labour bills of July 1983. In many ways the act resembles the leaked draft of proposed Labour Code amendments exposed by Operation Solidarity in August 1983 and disavowed by the government at that time. It virtually outlaws picketing the employer at other sites; it makes it easier to decertify, and harder to certify, a bargaining unit; it prohibits unions from disciplining delinquent members except when the Labour Relations Board decides that the cause is "fair and reasonable"; and it empowers cabinet to designate any construction site an "Economic Development Project", opening it to non-union labour and forbidding unions from striking.[15]

Most ironically of all, this blow for "workplace democracy", as Labour Minister Bob McClelland described it, abolishes the right of workers to protest government actions by withdrawing their labour. In the "new reality" of 1984 the thousands of protestors who took job action a year earlier to halt the government's reactionary course would be subject to fines of $1,000 each and $10,000 per day per union. The irony of this should not be lost: "ministerial consultation", which came as a result of Operation Solidarity's job action in 1983, seems to have led to a Labour Code that outlaws the very action that forced the government to "consult".

As with the new Human Rights Act, Solidarity's response to this assault was muted. So was the reaction of the NDP caucus, which allowed the bill to pass after only five days of debate.[16] Although BCFed President Art Kube vowed to "reactivate" Operation Solidarity, the federation's strategy for opposing the new legislation made no mention of mass mobilization, while Jack Munro of the IWA dismissed talk of a general strike as "nonsense".[17] However, other labour leaders — including George Hewison, the Coalition's first chairperson, and Jack Gerow, an active member of Operation Solidarity's steering committee — called for a remobilization through escalating mass actions.[18]

Prospects for the Coalition

It is unclear whether the labour movement will ultimately opt for a renewal of Operation Solidarity's extra-parliamentary struggle or resign itself to a period of recuperation, anaesthetized by the hope of electing a New Democratic government several years down the line. In the short term at least, the fate of the Solidarity Coalition rests largely on this decision, because trade unions are the organizations through which working people collectively control their most strategically important resource: their own labour.

The recent events furnish scant grounds for optimism about the Coalition's future. The Bennett government has managed to renege on all the social provisions of the Kelowna Accord while introducing a new budget and Labour Code that take the right-wing measures of 1983 even further. Social Credit has faced only token opposition, both in the legislature and outside it. "Divide and conquer" seems to have been the lesson of 1983. Instead of giving progressive groups a ready target around which to coalesce, the government has introduced its measures in staggered, piecemeal fashion, while attempting to stir anti-union sentiment by blaming labour for industrial conflicts in the construction and forestry sectors. However important was the successful defence of trade union rights in 1983, more significant still was the militant unity of labour and popular organizations that was forged then. That unity may prove to be no more than an ephemeral alliance in response to an immediate threat from the right.

On the other hand, there are some indications that the mass mobilization of July to November laid the basis for a durable extra-parliamentary movement. Shortly after the November strike, the BCFed set a precedent by opening its annual convention to community groups and non-affiliated unions. The convention renewed support for the Solidarity Coalition and extended Operation Solidarity's mandate and funding for three years. At the BCTF's annual general meeting several months later a similar renewal took place, as the teachers voted overwhelmingly to continue the activist path they had chosen in November. They agreed to remain in Operation Solidarity, to establish a defence fund, to challenge the newly-amended School Act as a violation of the Charter of Rights, and — most revealingly — to support unionized construction workers picketing the Penny-farthing site in False Creek, near the Expo 86 grounds.[19]

In the new year the Coalition underwent restructuring and reorientation. Eleven regional delegates selected by local coalitions were added to the representatives of 25 social and two union sectors on the Coalition's steering committee, allaying the grievances of some smaller communities. The reconstituted steering committee was to hold regular monthly meetings, supplemented by quarterly assemblies at which all local Coalitions would be directly represented. A permanent office in Vancouver with a full-time staff of four and a biweekly Coalition Bulletin were also established in January, providing the basis for a stable, province-wide organization. Operation Solidarity was similarly consolidated in January with the adoption of a formal executive structure more representative of the labour movement in B.C. and with the addition of full-time organizers to establish regional Operation Solidarity committees.

As of May 1984 there were 58 local Coalitions throughout the province, from Fort St. John in the north to Victoria in the south and from the Queen Charlotte Islands in the west to Sparwood, Elkford and Fernie in the east. Forty-one organizations with province-wide memberships were active members of the Coalition, among them seven women's organizations, six groups advocating social welfare services, six Native and ethnic minority rights organizations, five groups defending the quality and accessibility of education, three organizations for the disabled or handicapped, and three human rights groups.

The Coalition's programme theoretically continued its commitment to large-scale collective action when warranted by the situation, but the emphasis in the six-month plan was on developing long-range social and economic alternatives to the government's agenda. The progressive alternatives to austerity were to be worked out (1) within local communities through a programme of dialogue and popular education designed to raise public consciousness about the nature and sources of contemporary social and economic problems, and (2) in a series of position papers commissioned by the Coalition from sympathetic intellectuals in the province. By May 1984 community conferences had been organized in several centres, and 50-odd position papers were completed or in preparation. The Coalition was also planning a "people's commission" to tour the province in the fall of 1984, and a national conference on progressive grassroots coalitions, at which trade unionists and community activists from across Canada would formulate strategies of resistance to the New Right. It remains to be seen whether these initiatives, together with the restructuring of the Coalition, will translate themselves into a strong, continuing extra-parliamentary opposition to neo-conservatism in B.C.

The Coalition in Perspective

What are the lessons to be drawn from this period in B.C. politics? It is undeniable that the Coalition's actions in the fall of 1983 had an impact on government policy unattainable within the realm of parliamentary politics. A basic right of social citizenship — the right of public-sector workers to be represented effectively by a union — was defended against a regime bent on its curtailment. If efforts to solidify and broaden the Coalition can be sustained, there will be more open and critical discussion of political issues, and more effective extra-parliamentary pressure on the government from working people and the community.

In the summer of 1983 British Columbia provided fertile soil for the growth of a labour-community united front. On the one hand, the strength of trade unionism in the province, both in terms of the high percentage of organized workers and their long history of political activism,[20] provided a large, disciplined, committed core around which a variety of community groups could coalesce. On the other hand, the reactionary political programme introduced by the government — incorporating in a single package many of the most blatant anti-welfare and anti-labour policies of likeminded regimes in Britain and the United States — galvanized popular resistance as it pushed labour and the community into a position of common cause.

These conditions are to some extent unique to British Columbia, but similar though less spectacular labour-community alliances have developed amid present conditions of economic depression and state austerity in the U.S. and elsewhere.[21] In Quebec there has been a burgeoning of grassroots movements uniting around labour, women's, environmental and minority-rights issues.[22] In Alberta, a province not known for its labour militancy but facing legislative challenges similar to those posed by the B.C. government in 1983, delegates to the Alberta Federation of Labour's annual convention in February 1984 unanimously approved the formation of Solidarity Alberta, a coalition of unions and community groups inspired by the accomplishments of the Solidarity Coalition in British Columbia.[23]

Although these popular movements are often denounced by governments as "anti-democratic", they actually deepen democracy. Liberal democratic institutions are often described as the bridge between individual citizens and the state, but elections, parties and parliaments seem increasingly ineffective for this purpose. This is especially so whenever corporate profits sag. Indeed, "the more serious these problems become the less can governments afford to allow the type and exact timing of their policy to be determined by whatever consensus does — or does not — emerge from the process of democratic politics."[24] Governments become desperate for private investment and try to by-pass normal democratic procedures. In the circumstances, people have to resort to unconventional means to make their influence felt. This is what extra-parliamentary politics is all about.

The brief history of the Solidarity Coalition presents a compelling example of these processes at work. From May to October 1983 the provincial government showed contempt for the electorate and for parliament, relying instead on the ultra-conservative Fraser Institute in formulating its severely reactionary legislation.[25] Unyielding government efforts to pass that legislation made a mockery of the legislature and led ultimately to a political crisis that could not be resolved within parliament. The extra-parliamentary actions of the Coalition were simply the local response of aggrieved people who had seen their bridge to the state closed by Social Credit. The apparent reopening of that bridge for ministerial consultation in the wake of the strike proved to be a manipulative detour, as the government proceeded to disregard the results of consultation and to enact by May 1984 much of the reactionary legislation that had stirred such broad opposition in 1983.

The real threat to democracy in the West stems not from grassroots organizations such as the Solidarity Coalition but from the characteristic responses of neo-conservative governments to the economic crisis of capitalism. Increasingly, the state is directed less by elections and parliamentary debate than by the perceived imperative to attract larger shares of diminishing world capitalist investment by improving the local climate for private investors. In essence, this ''new reality'' requires wholesale withdrawal of social citizenship rights and slashing of wage rates in both their social and individual forms. As such, neo-conservatism comprises a profoundly anti-democratic challenge to the majority of working people, whose rights and welfare it would sacrifice in deference to a small minority of employers and investors. Far from *negating* democracy, labour-community alliances committed to extra-parliamentary action are a means of *extending* democracy by breaking beyond the narrow bounds of electoral politics, to involve people directly in the debates and decisions that will significantly affect the course and quality of their lives.

The Legislature Under Siege
Jeremy Wilson

FOR MANY British Columbians, outrage over the government's July measures was heightened by indignation over its legislative tactics. Events in the legislature provided a graphic reminder of the crude simplicity of the British system on which ours is modelled. In Bernard Crick's words, government in that system

> can act, for good and ill, with an unparalleled concentration of power;...it will be restrained only by its own morality and good sense and by the broad, crude, drastic test of a general election. Abuses which are not likely to affect which way people vote are not likely to worry governments.[1]

The sobering message of the 1983 legislative session was that many actions that might be considered "out of bounds" in other countries or provinces were *not* perceived by Social Credit as likely to offend the electorate. What was disturbing was not just the reminder that, in the short term at least, majority governments can get away with whatever they think they can. It was that our government believed it could get away with so much.

Most importantly, Social Credit felt it could get away with implementing a stretched version of the "mandate" it received on May 5. Not only did Bennett's campaign fail to indicate what his government would do a few months later; it actually disavowed some of the measures that would show up in the July 7 package. It is true that the election had been about "restraint". But the clear message had been that the government would continue, without radically escalating, the measures it had taken earlier. Although it was obvious that, if re-elected, it would hold the line on both wages and employment in the public sector, a New Right revolution was never intimated. The *Sun* was reflecting a common perception when, in its pre-election editorial, it urged voters to support Social Credit because it was "not likely to start taking reactionary measures."

One interpretation of Social Credit's legislative methods was that they reflected a kamikaze bravado fostered by the "second life" euphoria that followed Social Credit's victory in an election it did not expect to win. It seems more reasonable, however, to surmise that Social Credit's approach reflected the evidence it was receiving from its public opinion polls and its faith in its ability to repair any political damage before the next election. Social Credit's depiction of its opponents as losers who were refighting the last election was more than a taunt. It summarized the government's belief that the opposition was coming mainly from those who had not supported it in 1983, and would not, in any event, support it in 1986. This perception may prove to be ill-founded, but while we wait to find out we should consider why neither the parliamentary nor the extra-parliamentary opposition was able to convince the government that the political costs of its programme and methods were too high.

The Legislature: 1983

> When you are out in the real world, away from this never-never land over here, you know what goes on over here is so insignificant, the people don't give a damn. They elected us to run the government and it's time we got doing it.[2]

These remarks, by Social Credit cabinet minister Don Phillips, illustrate the government's attitude. Political scientists might lecture about the importance of unwritten and written parliamentary rules, citing instances such as the great pipeline debate and its aftermath to illustrate how public opinion can punish a government that dares to violate those rules. But Social Credit did not over-estimate the public's capacity for outrage.

The key written rules governing use of the B.C. legislature are those prescribing the length of speeches. Under provisions adopted in 1974, the leader or "designated speaker" from each party is allowed unlimited time in the budget and Throne Speech debates, in second reading debate on bills, and on "all other proceedings...not otherwise specifically provided for." All other members are limited to 40 minutes. The standing orders also provide a "closure" procedure. It allows the majority to end debate simply by moving "that the question be now put." The Speaker may block such a move if he judges the motion "an abuse of the Rules of the House, or an infringement on the rights of the minority." In Britain, where the Speaker's impartiality is unquestioned, closure is applied frequently with minimal protest. In B.C., impartiality of the Speaker is not so well established, and any application of closure is controversial.

A significant unwritten rule bearing on conduct in the House pertains to what has come to be known as legislation by exhaustion. Frequent, though by no means unrestrained, use of legislation by exhaustion tactics to pass both spending estimates and bills was a hallmark of W.A.C. Bennett's treatment of the legislature. But after the NDP government made a commitment to observe the 11 p.m. adjournment time, late or all-night sittings became very rare. By the beginning of the 1980s it seemed that such tactics had been rendered taboo by the practice of governments after 1972.

The 1983 session marked a return to the worst of the past. Indeed, legislation by exhaustion was used on a scale that made W.A.C. Bennett's practices look tame. And closure, which had not been used since 1957, was invoked twenty times. The elder Bennett had seldom forced more than two or three all-night sittings in any session, and back-to-back all-night sittings were rare. By comparison, in the first four days after the government's declaration of legislative war measures on September 19, 1983, the House sat almost continuously, with successive all-night debates adjourning at 9:10 a.m., 1:46 p.m., 5:16 a.m., and 9:20 a.m. respectively. The House sat for more than 76 hours in the first week after September 19, for more than 60 in the second, and for nearly 50 in the third. All told, it sat past midnight on eleven of 22 days in the "siege" part of the session, with seven of those sittings extending into the dawn hours or beyond.

It is not clear whether the government's legislative strategy was planned from the outset. In mid-August, *Sun* columnist Marjorie Nichols described a House "bogged down in confusion and disarray," being led helter-skelter from one bill to the next by a government incapable of deciding what bills it wanted to debate on any given day.[3] The session's first ten weeks certainly did leave that impression. The government made some attempt in July and August to bring debate on three of its more contentious pieces of legislation, but when these bills met determined opposition, it turned to an assortment of minor matters. When it became apparent that the opposition was determined to delay even minor bills as long as possible, the government returned to the budget debate it had adjourned five weeks earlier. These events may indicate that in throwing together its New Right revolution the government and its advisors either forgot that legislative approval was necessary, or neglected to consider the difficulties involved. It is possible, though, that the government recognized from the beginning that extraordinary measures would be required, and viewed the summer months as a time in which to prepare for the inevitable state of siege.

By mid-September the stage was set. Although the opposition had allowed some minor bills to pass, it signalled clearly that in the case of what it called the "dirty dozen" it would be exercising the opposition's time-honoured right to use every means at its disposal to stop or delay passage of legislation judged to be ill-conceived. The government, meanwhile, was growing concerned about the imminent showdown with its employees. It was also feeling pressure from backbenchers impatient to "implement the mandate." In August, Marjorie Nichols had wondered:

> Are the Socreds really willing, or able, to ride out the storm that will accompany the use of crude majority force in the form of closure at least a dozen times? Somehow I doubt it...I doubt very much that even the defiant Mr. Bennett would want to go down in the history books as the man who used closure more times in a single legislative session than had all his predecessors in the previous hundred years.[4]

By mid-September Mr. Bennett was ready to say "just watch me."

The government's new strategy involved not only legislation by exhaustion and closure on an unprecedented scale, but also an attempt to undercut the opposition's delaying tactics. When Dave Barrett, the opposition's designated speaker on the Public Sector Restraint Act, rose on September 19 to continue debate on an NDP amendment, his status was challenged by cabinet minister Harvey Schroeder. House Speaker Walter Davidson, who had obviously anticipated this challenge, rose immediately to deliver a prepared ruling on whether designated speakers could talk for an unlimited time on amendments. Although the relevant rule does not address the matter directly, Davidson ruled that the unlimited time provision did not apply to debate on amendments. Although he failed to specify the new time limit, it was assumed that the new limit was 40 minutes. Thus Barrett was forced to relinquish the floor. When he protested he was ejected from the chamber.

Marjorie Nichols expressed many people's outrage:

> Minutes after he had evicted Opposition leader Dave Barrett from the legislature yesterday afternoon, Speaker Walter Davidson received a big grin and a hearty slap on the back from Premier Bill Bennett. It was a well-deserved backslap. As long as the Social Credit government has Speaker Davidson in the chair, it doesn't need to worry about either its enemies or the proprieties of the British parliamentary system. Yesterday's events simply demonstrate anew the fragile nature of our democracy, given a majority government willing to sacrifice honor and decency and tradition to the achievement of its goals... There was nothing complicated about the game plan that was put into effect yesterday that resulted in Mr. Barrett's eviction. The only potential risk was that Speaker Davidson would take a strong indepen-

dent and non-partisan position. Fortunately for the government, the Speaker was easy...Mr. Davidson was unable to cite a single precedent for his decision. Never before in B.C. has a designated speaker been stopped from speaking. What the Speaker did is quite simple. He re-wrote the rules of the legislature, thus giving the government a new form of closure that has previously been unavailable to any government. I guess it should come as no surprise that there was no embarrassment in government ranks at the knowledge that the unlimited debate rule was demanded by the Socreds when they were in opposition and filibustering the former NDP government's controversial legislation. This government does not believe in playing by the same rules that it demanded of the Dave Barrett government.[5]

Barrett's second ejection came in the early hours of October 6 and led to his suspension for the rest of the session. Again events began with a government attempt to disarm the opposition. In the early part of the siege, the NDP had pestered the government by proposing periodic adjournment motions throughout the night. When these motions were disallowed by the chair, the NDP would appeal the ruling, thus necessitating a division and forcing government members to rouse themselves from the makeshift bunks that had been set up around the buildings. Starting on September 22, the government put into effect a plan to blunt this tactic. House Speaker Davidson stated his view that in disallowing adjournment motions, the chair was not making a ruling, but simply applying a rule, thus the decision could not be challenged. The government subsequently used this gambit without much protest on a couple of occasions but on October 6 Barrett decided to challenge a 4 a.m. application of it by John Parks, one of the team of government backbenchers who filled in for

Davidson as Speaker during the extended sittings. In the ensuing imbroglio Parks ordered Barrett to withdraw from the chamber. When he refused, Parks ordered his removal by the sergeant-at-arms. Barrett, in full passive resistance stance, was tipped out of his chair, dragged from the chamber and dumped on the corridor floor.

The Speaker, who had chosen to leave the crisis in the House in the hands of the rookie backbencher so he could police his recent ban on media photography in the corridor, returned less than two hours later to deliver a judgement suspending Barrett for the remainder of the session.

The government's attitude toward the whole affair was nicely illustrated at the Social Credit annual convention held on October 14 to 16. One of the weekend's highlights was a party fund-raising auction that included the "boot" used by John Parks to eject Barrett from the house. It fetched $1,195. It is not known whether Davidson or anyone else sought to stop this tawdry affront to good taste and the impartiality of the Chair.

The first week after the September 19 declaration of the siege brought second reading approval of three major pieces of government legislation. The Education (Interim) Finance Amendment Act passed at 3 a.m. on September 20 (sitting day) after nearly 36 continuous hours of debate. The House then returned to the Public Sector Restraint Act and debated it practically non-stop until 5:16 a.m. the following morning. Both of these bills passed without closure, but the Municipal Amendment Act — sardonically dubbed the Spetifore Bill because of the perception that it was at least in part designed to facilitate Dawn Development's attempt to rezone a parcel of Delta farm land previously owned by Social Credit supporter George Spetifore — passed only after a 6 a.m. closure ended nearly ten hours of debate. Closure was subsequently used to force second reading of the Compensation Stabilization Amendment Act, the

Income Tax Amendment Act, the Public Service
Labour Relations Amendment Act, and the Social
Service Tax Amendment Act. By the third week of
the siege any reluctance to use closure had vanished,
and backbenchers were finding it difficult to resist. It
was used three more times in committee stage for the
Municipal Amendment Act and ten more times as the
government pushed to get the Public Sector Restraint
Act through committee and third reading in advance
of the Social Credit convention.

The House finally recessed on October 21 after
Premier Bennett went on television to announce a
cooling-off period. Before the House adjourned,
Royal Assent was given to seventeen bills. The
government had succeeded in its goals of defining the
rules of the game and the stakes for the upcoming
bargaining showdown with the BCGEU. Hanging
over the union's head as it entered negotiations were
Bill 3, which even after amendments still gave public
sector employers wide powers to dismiss employees,
and Bill 11, which extended public sector wage
controls. Bill 2, which the government had not
proceeded with after second reading, had been cast in
some doubt by an Ontario court ruling, but it too
represented a cudgel that might fall on BCGEU
heads unless the union made concessions. Thus, the
government had ensured that negotiations would be
conducted on its terms, and that even if public sector
unions won "concessions" they would still lose much
of the position they had enjoyed a few months
earlier. To a considerable extent, the legislative
session had been designed to give the government
these bargaining clubs.

Eight bills were left in limbo when the session
recessed. These included the Residential Tenancy
Act, the Human Rights Act and the Medical Services
Act. The government had clearly decided that there
was no point in fanning the fires further as it moved
toward the BCGEU bargaining showdown and the
possibility of massive work stoppages. The Resi-

dential Tenancy Act and the Human Rights Act were both passed in somewhat altered form early in the 1984 session.

As the table on the next page shows, the first major bills passed after September 19 received some second reading debate (including a few speeches in defence from the government) prior to the escalation of legislative warfare. For the government, this justified extraordinary measures to cut down the opposition's attempts to delay. This defence could not, however, be made for pushing through a second set of major bills after September 26. These bills, including the Compensation Stabilization Amendment Act and the Public Service Labour Relations Act, were not introduced for second reading until the second or third week of the siege. They had, that is, received no consideration during the long weeks when calmer, more reasoned debate was possible.

Contempt of Parliament?

Closure has long been an accepted and regularly used part of the government arsenal in the British house. In most mature parliamentary systems, governments make some use of closure and other mechanisms to end debate. Thus, while no previous B.C. government has found it necessary to resort to extensive use of closure, it is difficult to sustain a blanket condemnation of its use. This is particularly so where, again to use Bernard Crick's words, bills have been thoroughly canvassed "in circumstances designed to make criticism as authoritative, informed and as public as possible."[6] What is questionable is the use of closure and of legislation by exhaustion before there has been a chance for extensive debate. In a political system such as ours, where governments already depend much too heavily on ignorance and apathy to obtain consent, it is difficult to justify

Table 1. Major Bills, 1983 Session – Order of Passage and Debating Times (in hours:minutes)

Bill #	Title	Date of Second Reading Approval	Total Time in Debate at:		Portion of Second Reading Debate Used by:		Portion of Second Reading Debate Occurring:	
			Second Reading Stage	Committee Stage	Govt. Speakers	Opp. Speakers	Pre-Sept. 19	Post Sept. 19
13	Tobacco Tax Amendment Act	Sept. 13	9:16	:07	:49	8:27	9:16	0
6	Education (Interim) Finance Amendment Act	20	34:41	1:10	2:23	32:18	11:15	23:26
3	Public Sector Restraint Act	21	53:33	19:47	4:38	48:55	30:57	22:36

7 Property Tax Reform Act (no. 1)	22	16:45	2:03	:26	16:19	15:09	1:36
9 Municipal Amendment Act	22	26:12	4:36	2:40	23:32	16:00	10:12
6 Compensation Stabilization Amendment Act	28	20:29	5:22	3:36	16:53	0	20:29
4 Income Tax Amendment Act	29	18:59	1:21	:41	18:18	4:04	14:55
26 Employment Standards Amendment Act	29	13:52	1:40	:26	13:26	0	13:52
15 Social Services Tax Amendment Act	Oct. 4	10:58	1:28	:40	10:18	0	10:58
2 Public Services Labour Relations Amendment Act	6	17:47		:59	16:48	0	17:47

measures which limit the public's right to be informed
by parliament.

In the case of the second set of bills it pushed
through the house, Social Credit showed little regard
for that right. Although it would be naive to
exaggerate the quality or educational impact of
normal debate in the B.C. House, there are often
careful, thoughtful exchanges. But bills dumped on
the House in the midst of its second or third week of
late- or all-night sittings have little chance of receiving such consideration.

At the root of the government's disdain for the
parliamentary process was the decision to overload
the legislature's agenda. It was not just legislation by
exhaustion, it was legislation by inundation. This
decision, and the subsidiary decision not to establish
(either by negotiation or decree) a reasonable timetable for full and careful debate, guaranteed that the
government's package would not receive the careful
consideration its significance demanded. A government with more respect for the public's rights would
have been content with less; a patient one would have
made sure that all of its legislation received substantial, even exhaustive consideration before the legislature was pushed over the brink. But the Social
Credit government failed to propose, let alone
negotiate, a timetable for debate. And it insisted on
throwing into the "restraint" pot a number of
controversial bills whose aims were tangential to the
professed aims of the restraint package.

The government seems to have decided to push
through controversial bills such as the Employment
Standards Amendment Act and the Municipal
Amendment Act under the cover of restraint symbol-
ism, because it recognized that the political costs of
adding such bills to an already overloaded agenda
would be lower than the cost of bringing them back
later as part of a shorter agenda. It is difficult to
interpret these tactics as anything but cynical. The
inclusion of the Municipal Amendment Act was

particularly questionable. Despite talk of streamlining and deregulating planning processes, it seemed
to be peripherally connected to the main thrust of the
restraint programme. The opposition, nauseated by
the bill's political stench and galled by the possibility
that at least one member on the government side
stood to gain financially from its passage, felt
compelled to fight it.[7] Thus an already overloaded
house was further burdened, an already sour atmosphere further poisoned.

The government's determination to overload the
agenda is particularly disturbing in light of the
suspicion that it intentionally wrote some of the
legislation in extreme terms so that it would have a
"big stick" at the bargaining table and more
"capital" to bargain away. It is not clear whether the
subsequent moves to abandon Bill 2 and negotiate
exemptions to Bill 3 were part of the plan from the
beginning. But there is certainly something unseemly
about a government using the legislature — and
bringing the legislative process into disrepute — in
order to pass laws it had no intention of
implementing.

In essence the legislature was assigned a limited
and demeaning role in the Social Credit plan. The
legislature was a forum, complete with a very
predictable sparring partner, in which the government
could demonstrate its resolve to public sector
workers, to Milton Friedman and its other fans, and
to the international investment community. Once the
legislature had fulfilled that role and given the
government the bargaining clubs it needed, the action
moved to another stage. It was fitting testimony to
the decline of the legislature that it was the Jack
Webster show, not the House, that served as a forum
for questions to the premier once the Kelowna
Accord was achieved.

Government by Opinion Poll

While some commentators predicted big political fallout from its tactics, Social Credit seems to have forecast public opinion more accurately. It recognized that in a province as polarized as B.C., most of its supporters would accept that the ends justify the means. It knew that those with the power to deflect it from its course — the business community — would not be concerned with its tactics. It saw that many uncommitted voters would ignore events or adopt a "plague on both their houses" attitude. And it gambled that the political costs of devices like closure would decline as each usage inured the public to the next. In short, Social Credit made a calculated decision not to over-estimate the public's threshold for outrage. This judgement seems to have been proven correct. Although its legislative tactics intensified the anger of those opposed to the substance of its programme, the government found that the "silent" portion of the electorate greeted events with equanimity.

To some extent, the public's reaction was conditioned by the media's. While far from favourable, the media's response to events in the House was hardly one of sustained outrage. The *Sun*'s treatment of Barrett's first expulsion and the first all-night sitting nicely illustrates the response. On the editorial pages, Marjorie Nichols railed against the Socred's "calculated and cynical gamble that the populace is too stupid and/or lethargic to care about the parliamentary tactics that are employed to gain passage for the...legislative package."[8] But the front page of the same day's edition of the *Sun* provided a graphic illustration of why the government might be excused for concluding that the "gamble" held few risks. Coverage of the events in the legislature was given second billing to the murder of strip club operator Joe Philliponi.

Generally the media resorted to the safe "plague on both their houses" stance. Those commentators who did maintain a high level of indignation were soon left fulminating repetitiously, superlatives exhausted, their impact submerged by coverage and commentary issuing from more blase colleagues. The media made little attempt to explain why, apart from the substantive issues at stake, there was cause for concern about the procedural precedents being established. And once extraordinary tactics become routine, the media generally treated them as such. Its coverage proved the adage that what is new is news. As a consequence, it contributed to the desensitization of the public.

We may be inclined to attribute Social Credit's dogmatic refusal of compromise to its ideological zeal, or we may even be tempted to resort to some amateur Freudianism. However, Social Credit's insensitivity to liberal-democratic niceties may owe as much to its reliance on polling as it does to its ideological fervour. In particular, the incentive to accommodate may decline as the reliance on polling increases. When a government is not certain what wider currents of public opinion are reflected by protesting groups, it is prudent to be accommodative toward those groups. Where polling allows that uncertainty to be removed, the need to accommodate evaporates. Thus Bill Bennett's attitudes to the political process have somewhat different roots from his father's. W.A.C. Bennett's thinking was based on his scorn for accommodative politics and his skepticism about the ability of leaders of groups such as unions to deliver the votes of their members. In his son's time those sentiments are, if anything, held with greater conviction. With polling data at its fingertips, the government's disdain for those it perceives to be in the minority has increased.

It is still possible that Social Credit's actions since the 1983 election owe more to overzealousness than to an accurate political assessment. The next election may reveal a higher political toll than the government expects. But it seems unlikely that Social Credit would have stayed so close to its chosen course had its polls not told it that the political costs could be borne. If so, the opposition's failure to deflect the government from its course and the government's disdain for accommodative politics have the same roots. Quite simply, the government proceeded as it did because it doubted the NDP's ability to reach and win over the portion of the electorate that gave Social Credit its majority. Thus, the lesson here is a simple one: in our political system, "close" does not count. Nor do tens of thousands of people in the streets. What counts are majority governments. And to win a majority against the New Right revolution means facing some hard realities. One of these is that a commitment to the niceties of parliamentary democracy counts for little electorally.

The Ideology
of Neo-Conservatism
Philip Resnick

THE ELECTION OF Margaret Thatcher in Great Britain
and Ronald Reagan in the United States symbolized
more than a passing moment in the evolution of
western societies. It unleashed a frontal attack on
government spending and social priorities. It placed
some of the familiar values of western society, such
as equality and social justice, into jeopardy. It
entailed a re-definition of the relationship between
private and public goods. And it forced the left — in
both its social democratic and socialist versions —
onto the defensive.

For almost 30 years after 1945 the western world
experienced a long wave of prosperity and economic
growth, coinciding with the adoption by governments
of Keynesian-type economic policies and vastly
expanded social programmes. Large-scale unemployment became a distant memory, associated with the
Depression of the 1930s. Steadily increasing productivity had resulted in higher real per capita incomes
and provided the means to increase government

services, from health and hospital insurance to public housing. Such measures alleviated the old class differences and gave a reformed capitalist system a new lease on life.

Liberals, social democrats and moderate conservatives all seemed to agree on the basic premises of the new order. The role of the state — as entrepreneur and regulator of the economy — was significantly enlarged. Trade unions were recognized as legitimate economic actors with whom governments and corporations had to deal. The large (and sometimes smaller) corporations continued to dominate the process of production and distribution, but with a greater acceptance of their social responsibilities in a modern economy. Taxation was used, not to *radically* redistribute wealth, but to allow for a modest reallocation of the fruits of increased prosperity. In other words, an expanding economic pie helped pay for the welfare state.

The economic crisis of the 1970s — the balance of payments problems experienced by the United States largely as a result of the Vietnam War, the quadrupling in the price of oil, increased industrial competition from south European and third world countries — led to a profound change in the equation which had formed the foundation of economic policy-making until then. The rates of growth of western economies were severely pruned, to half or less of what they had been a decade or two earlier. Western economies began to experience high rates of inflation while unemployment rates edged stubbornly upward. Governments incurred ever-larger deficits, having failed to accumulate surpluses during the long years of post-war prosperity with which to balance these out. The increase in government spending exceeded the increase in economic growth.

While some on the left talked about a "fiscal crisis of the state" and a potential "legitimacy crisis" in the capitalist system, a quite different attack was about to be mounted from the right. For spokesmen from this camp, it was the legitimacy of Keynesianism and of the welfare state that was in question, and the post-war consensus that needed to be rejected.

There are different versions of this onslaught from the right. One, associated with the Trilateral Commission,¹ says the "excessive" expectations and demands of people posed a threat to representative governments. The language of participation and of rights, so typical of the 1960s, had drowned out reverence for more traditional values such as authority and obedience. In this view, what is needed is a return to the old pattern of relations between governors and governed, coupled with reduced expectations of what economic and other goods governments should provide.

A second version of the neo-conservative view is derived from the writings of old-fashioned "liberal" economists like Hayek and Friedman, who for decades have defended market principles against state intervention. These men oppose the Keynesian policies practiced by Western governments as inherently inflationary. They reject the "redistributionist" logic of social democracy and the more progressive versions of liberalism, calling for a roll-back in the functions of the state to those specified by 18th or 19th century laissez-faire doctrine (i.e., defence, the administration of justice, certain public works). Not all go quite so far in their proclaimed intentions, but the adherents of Friedmanite or "public choice" economics agree strongly on the need to deregulate large sectors of economic life, privatize public corporations and activities, and impose strict limitations on government spending. For them, "the Keynesian paradigm is afloat without a rudder, and its own internal forces, if left to themselves, are likely to ground the system on the rocks of deep depression."² The pursuit of balanced budgets becomes an overriding obsession, at the expense of all other ends.

The third element to enter into neo-conservative

thinking is a throwback to time-honoured conservative conceptions of morality, religion, etc. The "Moral Majority" in the United States, for example, talks of permissiveness in the schools, promiscuous sexual behaviour, and the decline in religious observance as the supposed consequences of excessively liberal attitudes. It associates the latter with "dissident" elements in American society — middle class intellectuals, unpatriotic film stars, male-hating feminists, environmentalists, gays. Neo-conservatives of this stripe support school prayers, the sacredness of pregnancy, law and order, and anti-communism in their invocation of the good society. This argument often has a strongly populist underpinning, attacking the liberal members of the "new class" who supposedly dominate big government, the media and the bureaucracy, for having instigated undesirable change.

The confused melange of New Right thinking becomes apparent from the following quotations:

The Conservative knows that to regard man as part of an undifferentiated mass is to consign him to ultimate slavery.

●

The program of the welfare staters (is)... an assault upon the dignity of the individual... The collectivists... have learned that Socialism can be achieved through Welfarism quite as well as through Nationalization.

●

By any absolute standard there is little poverty in Britain today... It is not right to turn the discussion of real needs into a discussion of something else by so defining poverty as to introduce into it a very different conception of inequality.

●

Liberal democracy can yet be saved if contemporary egalitarianism were to lose its hold over the intelligentsia. But this will happen only if those who recognize it for the disease it has become are prepared to come out in the open and have uncongenial labels placed upon them.

•

The Old Right is as elitist as the liberal intellectuals.

•

I advise intelligent, ambitious, and morally serious young Christians and Jews to awaken to the growing dangers of statism. They will better save their souls and serve the cause of the Kingdom of God all around the world by restoring the liberty and power of the private sector than by working for the state.

The first two quotations are from U.S. senator and former Republican presidential candidate Barry Goldwater.[3] They hark back to a traditionally liberal rather than conservative conception of society. Individualism, after all, was historically a core value of market society and its liberal defenders. Conservatism, by contrast, had an organicist, even collectivist view of society, in which persons were not simply maximizers of individual liberty, hustling and colliding with one another and shorn of social obligations. But in an interesting ideological reverse, neo-conservatism in the English-speaking world has come to identify itself with the values of individualism and liberty which are *anything but* conservative in origin.

The attack upon the welfare state which Goldwater inaugurated in the early 1960s is another example of a major shift from traditional conservative tenets. After all, the pioneers of the modern welfare state, with its pension and health legislation, were 19th century authoritarian conservatives such as Bismarck. The purpose of the legislation was to undercut the appeal of a rising socialist party and to ensure the integration of the working class into the state on conservative terms. Intelligent 20th century conservatives from Churchill to de Gaulle followed Bismarck's lead.

In the 1970s a reversal of historical attitudes became possible. Western economies encountered high rates of inflation and low rates of economic growth, a combination that made it possible to blame social spending for the fiscal crisis. "Too few producers" is the refrain of conservative economists in Britain, according to whom the welfare state undermines that very "productionist" ethic which was the glory of a once-prosperous British economy. "The government itself has gone into the business of manufacturing poor people," asserted Howard Jarvis during his successful campaign for his tax-cutting Proposition 13 in California in 1978.[4]

Attacks on social expenditure are the central theme for politicians of the New Right. They point to the increased percentage of gross national product being appropriated by the state, wrap themselves in the flag of individual liberty and private initiative, and find themselves on the same wavelength as members of the "me generation". The old social solidarities born of the Depression and the Second World War have dissolved. Among the ranks of the home-owning working class and middle class of Britain, in the sunbelt states of the United States, in the Canadian New West of oil and gas and real estate bonanzas, the new conservatism has taken root.

The third and fourth quotations come from British Conservative politician Sir Keith Joseph and financial journalist Samuel Brittan.[5] Both adopt an open defence of inequality, after decades when equality and liberty had been closely linked in the public philosophies of western societies. Had freedom from want not figured prominently in Roosevelt's grand proclamations of the war period? Was equality of opportunity not a central premise in the liberal defence against Communism during the Cold War years? Had the American civil rights movement of the 1970s and the "war against poverty" not set out to rectify the fundamental inequality remaining twenty years *after* the coming of the welfare state?

All this matters little to neo-conservatives who are persuaded that equality is part of the problem, not of the solution.

Here, they are consistent with the premises of an earlier conservatism. Conservatives from the late 18th century on never accepted the abstract ideal of equality. They believed in the natural inequality of persons, justifying class divisions on traditionalist grounds. Egalitarianism, along with an excessive concern for rights at the expense of obligations, was blamed for destroying society.

Such claims were muted during the Second World War and the immediate post-war years, but the situation changed 30 years later. Keith Joseph and others argue that Britain and other western countries have had all the egalitarian reforms they can afford. Starvation has been eliminated, minimal social nets are in place, a generous infrastructure of public services exists. The time has come to downplay egalitarianism and remember that the basis of economic prosperity lies in nurturing the inequality that, it is argued, contributes to productive initiatives. If British productivity is lagging, if even American growth has sagged, it is because both societies have gotten too egalitarian, too far ahead of themselves in their public generosity.

It matters little to these new conservatives that British and American rates of public spending are below those of many booming industrial countries. Ideologically, they are on to a good thing and are prepared to milk it for all it is worth. As Thatcher and then Reagan came storming into power with a pledge to put the "private" back into "private enterprise" and get their respective economies moving again, "equality" became a dirty word. Joseph, Brittan and their associates have succeeded beyond their wildest dreams in altering the social agenda.

The fifth quotation is from Paul Weyrich, one of the ideologues of the American New Right.[6] It points to one major difference between the older version of conservatism and neo-conservatism — the overtly populist tone the latter adopts. Liberals and social democrats, especially in the bureaucracy, media or academic world, are castigated as elitist, while the neo-conservatives pretend to identify with the ordinary Joe. Weyrich and others claim to have roots solidly in the middle-American tradition, to be truer believers in democracy and more compassionate in their social vision than the liberal establishment they attack. The "new class" in the United States, they argue, advocates busing while they send their own children to private schools. It is the bureaucrats in Washington (or Ottawa or London) who thumb their noses at the remainder of the population which must somehow support and finance their every whim. (The role of the corporate elite or multinational enterprises, needless to say, merits no attention from such critics.)

The sixth quotation, from Michael Novak of the American Enterprise Institute,[7] underlines the link between the theology of the New Right and its anti-statism. Indeed, it makes reduction of the state a moral imperative, of about the same intensity as school prayers or the "right to life." Anti-statism has here become an article of faith, with private enterprise harnessed to the theology of both Old and New Testaments. History seems to have come full circle, with traditional piety now legitimizing that most untraditional and secular of economic credos, capitalism.

Neo-conservatism thus encompasses a number of elements. It invokes individualism against collectivism, and repudiates the principle of equality (both of opportunity and condition). It rejects the redistributionist ethic of the welfare state and the interventionist role of government. It evokes populism and traditional morality in defending the social order of capitalism. It claims to be more democratic than its liberal or social democratic rivals. In various combinations, these ideas have contributed to the electoral victories of the New Right in the U.S., Britain and Canada.

It is tempting to think of the New Right as a passing aberration, or to convince ourselves that the welfare state is really the best of all possible worlds. If we can somehow survive these few years of low economic growth, the argument goes, we will be able to return to the expansionist policies of the Keynesian past. If the left could only remind the electorate of all the good things that had come its way from the state, public opinion would pay less heed to the barrage of New Right propaganda; if we could only reiterate the virtues of crown corporations such as the CNR, the CBC and Petro-Canada, all would be well. It would be nice to think that if we could stick to the prescribed agenda of large-scale expenditures for health or education or social services, the electorate would once again come to see where its true interests lie.

But we need a different model of socialism for the 1980s. As David Held and John Keane recently remarked:

> Socialists who call for less bureaucracy have failed, with few exceptions, to recognize that some positive things can be learned by engaging the new right, which has taken the lead in popularizing the demand for less state action.[8]

This does not accept the agenda of neo-conservatism, but recognizes that the theme of anti-statism is important. It is the left that should be putting forth an anti-statist position. The crisis of capitalism and the corresponding crisis in both Keynesianism and social democracy should be an occasion for re-thinking our position on major questions — parliamentary vs. participatory democracy, community control vs. state control, industrial democracy vs. state ownership, social security as we know it today

vs. a new social contract for an increasingly automated society.

This does not mean that we must jettison the
welfare state or follow the New Right into an orgy of
privatization and slashing necessary services, but we
must recognize that the welfare state has come to be
associated with the bureaucratic state. Here the New
Right (including its nasty, local variant) has been able
to make much hay. What is required is "a long-term
socialist public philosophy which emphasizes decen-
tralization, less bureaucracy and more democracy."
More concretely, we must start developing the basis
for a non-statist (or at least less-statist) version of
socialism, which does not simply equate collective
ownership with a more powerful state machine. One
derives no particular joy from knowing that B.C.
Hydro is a publicly-owned enterprise, for example; in
their disregard for community concerns, or environmental factors, or the long-term public interests,
crown corporations such as B.C. Hydro are hardly
distinguishable from MacMillan-Bloedel.

Back in the 19th century the left, in both its
anarchist and Marxist variants, was a committed
critic of the state. The state was seen as an instrument
of class domination, of aristocratic privilege and
capitalist power. "The emancipation of the working
class will be carried out by the working class itself,"
proclaimed the Statutes of the First International in
1864. The alternatives they envisaged lay beyond the
parameters of the existing state machinery, in a world
where the state would "wither away".

In practice, the state has done anything but wither.
As an institution, it has emerged enormously
strengthened out of economic depression and two
world wars. It has been strengthened even more
through Marxist-Leninist revolutions. Much of the
dissatisfaction in the West with socialism comes from
the negative features of the Soviet Union and other
self-professedly socialist states. But it also arises
from a perception that social democracy has only a

somewhat more chastened version of state bureaucracy to offer in its place.

When Kafka in the early 1900s wrote, "The chains of the world are made of office paper," he could not anticipate the microfiche and the computer, but he was not wrong. We need something better than a model of undiluted state and bureaucratic power to propose to the electorate today. The neo-conservatives have their version on the agenda — the left will not become relevant again until it develops its own.

The key components would include:

1. a clear distinction between civil society and the state, and an attempt to maximize the role of autonomous citizen-controlled institutions;

2. some form of base-level democracy, to allow direct and ongoing citizen participation between elections in political affairs;

3. an economy based on worker-controlled industries and community-controlled activities rather than on the large corporation or the bureaucratically administered state;

4. a fairer sharing of work, a general reduction in working hours, and better protection for the environment;

5. a recognition of our place in a larger international order that imposes obligations as well as opportunities.

The *economics* of this model can be called market socialism. It entails the continued existence of private property and small-scale private ownership (shops, land). But it also entails a form of workers' control in all larger enterprises as an alternative to both the large corporation and the centrally planned (and coercive) system of the socialist states.[10]

The *politics* of such a model would be distinctly participatory. We would not have to galvanize a Solidarity Coalition into existence every time we want to react against unpopular measures taken by governments. If a mechanism for fostering ongoing citizen involvement — at the base level — existed, the nature of politics would be radically transformed.

The *social arrangements* of such a model would address more closely the problems of the two-class society we are entering. This is a society divided between those who have jobs and those who do not, in which work-sharing and similar schemes constitute the only fair response, in which we may finally begin to move away from the work ethic of the capitalist system to a different definition of socially valuable activities.

I do not hold out much prospect for any immediate move toward a market socialist economy, toward a more participatory type of political structure, or toward a reorientation in our international relations with the third world. These, however, are the sorts of ideas the left should be putting on the agenda.

We fool ourselves if we underestimate the ideological appeal of neo-conservatism and the intellectual activity that has gone into it. The failures of Keynesianism and the deficiencies of the welfare state are the starting points for the selfish market and free enterprise solutions now being proposed. Not all of this political and economic thinking is trite or silly — some is as sophisticated as anything proposed on the centre or on the left. If we are to win back ground from the New Right, it will have to be through the vigour of our arguments in making socialism once more a *morally* and *practically* attractive proposition, one whose economics and politics differ significantly from the heavy-handed politics that, rightly or wrongly, many have come to associate with both Marxism-Leninism *and* social democracy. In trying to win back the 20- and 30-year-olds in our society, the organized and unorganized working class, white collar workers and professionals, to a collectivist — as opposed to individualist — solution to our problems, we will need generosity, imagination, honesty, a willingness to think things through *radically*, and to drop those elements of earlier arguments that stand in the way of rejuvenation.

In this period of structural change and high unemployment, there is a very important place for a left alternative. But it can no longer espouse the political philosophy of the classical welfare state, the Regina Manifesto, or the Communist Manifesto. It will have to be a philosophy that combines the best movement groups — environmental, women's and other citizen groups — with the egalitarianism of the socialist tradition and the emancipatory objectives of democratic theory. It is only such a perspective that can attempt with any conviction to slay the dragon of neo-conservatism.

Part III
Rights Under Attack

Introduction

EQUALITY OF RIGHTS, *opportunity and treatment are part of the very meaning of democracy. Democracy depends on their assurance and is designed to protect them. Human rights encompass a broad range of civil rights, political citizenship rights and social citizenship rights — for most of us, human rights have come to mean those basic rights which accrue to us simply because we are human beings. Besides the freedom of thought and expression, these include the right to adequate housing, food and clothing; the right to a job, and to work under terms and conditions which have been negotiated freely and collectively and which ensure employees' health and safety; the right to basic social services and income assistance; and the right to protection from unreasonable discrimination.* The Bennett government's*

* These rights and others were given international recog-

147

recent attack on virtually all of these human rights was an attack on democracy itself, and aroused an unprecedented protest.

Over the past decades, successive governments have taken certain steps to secure these fundamental rights for all British Columbians: legislating fair accommodation practices, establishing rent controls and a Rentalsman's Office; legislating fair employment practices, moving from patronage to a merit-career orientation with employment security for provincial civil servants, replacing paternalistic unilateralism with the recognition of full collective bargaining rights in the public sector, and guaranteeing minimum health and safety standards for all those working under collective agreements; establishing and funding a number of social service and income assistance programmes; passing legislation prohibiting discrimination "without reasonable cause"; and assuming an educative and advocacy role to combat unreasonable discrimination through the creation of a Human Rights Branch and Commission.

In a dishearteningly short time, the B.C. government with its "restraint" programme has managed to reverse this progress in securing human rights. Social Credit's attack has included abolishing rent controls and the Rentalsman's Office; unilaterally imposing personnel policies in the public sector and taking back employee rights won in collective bargaining, extending indefinitely public sector wage controls

---

nition in the United Nations Universial Declaration of Human Rights (1948), and reaffirmed in 1975 by Canada and other signatories to the Final Act of the Conference on Security and Co-operation in Europe, at Helsinki. They entered into force as international law in 1976 with ratification of the International Covenant on Economic, Social and Cultural Rights and the International Covenant on Civil and Political Rights. See Ian Brownlie, ed., *Basic Documents on Human Rights*, 2nd ed. (New York: Oxford University Press, 1981).

and imposing more restrictive wage guidelines, eliminating hundreds of jobs in the provincial government public service and laying off employees, revising the B.C. Labour Code to make union organizing more difficult and to centralize decision-making, removing the automatic coverage by minimum health and safety standards for those working under collective agreements; reducing or eliminating funding for a broad range of social service and income assistance programmes; drastically restricting the definition of discrimination by removing the "reasonable cause" clause, and abolishing the Human Rights Branch and Commission. The following chapters discuss these "restraint" measures in their historical context and consider their implications for British Columbians.

Even those who believe that there is a fiscal crisis which requires restraints can find little justification for the bulk of these repressive measures. The rhetoric in which the government's attack on rights is couched might lead us to believe that these changes improve the economy. Yet as Stan Persky and Lanny Beckman point out, public sector wage restraint and disemployment lead to depressed consumer purchasing power, bankruptcies, worsened unemployment, and an erosion of investor confidence. Moreover, the alleged saving achieved by the 25% cut in the civil service payroll is misleading because many of the jobs have been shifted to other workers. The cost of the Rentalsman's Office was negligible, and as Murray Rankin notes, replacing the Human Rights Branch and Commission by the B.C. Council of Human Rights results in insignificant savings. In addition, removing individuals' protection against discrimination "without reasonable cause" may well increase costs in the long run. The same is true of the cutbacks in social service and income assistance programmes. As far as the undermining of collective bargaining is concerned, Norman Ruff concludes that the result is likely to be reduced efficiency and lower productivity — *a conclusion echoed by Persky and Beckman.*

Why, then, has the Social Credit government undertaken this attack on fundamental rights? Who do the changes harm and who do they benefit? Stella Lord and Murray Rankin argue that the effects on already-disadvantaged groups are likely to be devastating. Moreover, those who have been politically outspoken fare badly under the "restraint" measures, as Lord, Persky and Beckman note. By contrast the removal of rent controls benefits landlords, while the relaxation of health and safety standards enables employers to lower their costs and increase their profits. Taken as a whole, the government's attack on rights is part of its policy of restructuring economic, social and political life with a view to enhancing private investment and maximizing corporate profits. As in other areas of its "restraint" programme, this restructuring involves a move to privatization, centralization of decision-making, a weakening of labour, and the undermining of those most likely to challenge the status quo. The most blatant examples, respectively, are the privatization of human rights enforcement via the new Human Rights Act, the reversion to unilateralism in public sector personnel policies, the undermining of unions' power via the revisions to the B.C. Labour Code, and the cutbacks for groups — such as Vancouver Status of Women — which advocate change. The government's attack on rights feeds a pervasive sense of individual powerlessness which weakens resistance and reinforces the status quo. The ideology of "restraint" further deflects attention from the real problems of unemployment and discrimination.

As part of the justification for its restraints on fundamental rights, the government has argued that its present policy increases the autonomy of the individual by removing restrictions and encouraging self-reliance. This in turn supposedly improves the economy, increases prosperity, and makes for gen-

eral happiness. Precisely the opposite is in fact the case — for all but a privileged minority. For the majority of British Columbians, the current policy means a drastic restriction in those basic rights which belong to them as human beings. Far from increasing their freedom to develop their full human potentialities, the "restraint" measures curtail even the minimal conditions requisite for any such development — affordable housing, jobs and decent working conditions, basic social services and income assistance, and protection from unreasonable discrimination. By attacking these conditions Social Credit undermines people's participation in the decisions affecting their lives. Behind the government's rhetoric is the reality of a severely curtailed democracy.

Social Credit as Employer
Norman Ruff

"RESTRAINT ON PUBLIC sector wages is the only way to protect jobs," claimed a Social Credit advertisement that appeared during the 1983 provincial election. "In his scramble to make promises that sound good," the ad continued, "Dave Barrett has put several thousand public sector jobs on the line in British Columbia."[1] Three months later the re-elected Social Credit government announced that it would eliminate 1,600 jobs in the government public service — in addition to the many lost due to budget cutbacks in the school and hospital systems.

A government is the only employer that can change the rules of the game it plays with its employees. The Bennett government embarked on this course in 1982 and, with its 1983 escalation of "restraint", radically changed the rules of labour relations in the provincial public sector.

Premier Bennett asserts that a balanced budget is

the way to economic recovery. Controls on public sector wages, a cut in the number of public employees, and a reduction in the scope of government activity are the Social Credit solution to the fiscal problems produced by the decline of the British Columbia economy. It seems that only the high economic growth rates of the kind that we enjoyed in the 1960s and 1970s allow the government to be a good employer. In the current depression, public sector workers are to be disciplined by their employer as an example to the private sector. Charles Levine, a leading American expert on cutbacks in government, has argued that in today's environment of resource scarcity "the dominant management imperatives will likely involve a search for new ways of maintaining credibility, civility, and consensus."[2] This search has been strikingly absent in British Columbia, and as a result the province has been plunged into an unprecedented state of political turmoil.

The attempted subversion of collective bargaining is only one aspect of the costly burden of "restraint". Equally significant has been the undermining of the concept of a merit-based, career-oriented provincial public service and of the level of morale required to sustain an effective working environment. The continued relevance of collective bargaining and of responsible government are called into question by the prospect of permanent wage controls administered by an appointed commissioner with considerable powers to determine wage levels — based in part on his assessment of government's "ability to pay".

Provincial Government Employment

Over the past 30 years Social Credit and New Democratic governments built an efficient, professional career-oriented public service in British Columbia. But in the last two years the current Social

Credit government has begun to dismantle much of what it and its predecessors have built.

In the 1950s and 1960s, W.A.C. Bennett converted what was still largely a patronage-ridden civil service into a merit-based, modern administrative machine. The Barrett government advanced personnel practices from a paternalistic unilateralism into a fully fledged system of free collective bargaining. By 1982 the number of provincial public sector employees had grown to 213,833 — 43,458 directly hired by the government, 77,500 in the education system, 69,354 in health, and 23,521 in government corporations, etc.[3] The growth in numbers was the product not only of the short-lived New Democratic government but also of Social Credit.

The first seven years of Bill Bennett's premiership saw some fine tuning in employment policy. In 1977 the right to strike by public employees was restricted under the Essential Services Disputes Act, and after 1979 the image of the government as a good employer began to fade. Nevertheless, the system of public personnel management remained based on the democratic values of employee participation in the determination of working conditions.

In order to ensure an efficient, patronage-free public service, recruitment and advancement of ministry employees followed the basic principle of appointment by merit. The merit system carried with it the presumption that in exchange for an individual's career commitment the provincial government would offer employment security. The screening of prospective public sector employees and use of probationary periods is generally more demanding than within the private sector. By holding out the prospect of career advancement within the public sector, government hoped to motivate employees to develop their skills and retain a strong sense of ethical commitment to the public service.[4]

Just as the merit-career system contributes to the efficiency and morale of the B.C. public service, so too did the recognition in 1973 of full collective bargaining rights for direct government employees. In the contracts negotiated between 1973 and 1979 there were significant improvements in working conditions, including the curbing of arbitrary management decisions and an attempt to reach a joint accommodation of interests.

Restraint on Government: From Controls to Cutbacks

The attack on public sector employees began not with the July 7, 1983 budget but on February 18, 1982. In a television address given two weeks after a first ministers' meeting on the economy, Premier Bennett announced a hurriedly-assembled "restraint on government" programme[5] to help fight the battle against "the twin evils of high inflation and high interest rates." Bennett said that he rejected the advice of experts who recommended maximum pay increases of 6% or even a freeze; this, he said, would be "unfair, unworkable, and unequitable". But he was soon to reverse this position and accept the advice of those unidentified experts.

The first version of this programme had three main components:

• a 12% ceiling on 1982 and 1983 spending increases on the entire provincial public sector;

• a two-year "Compensation Stabilization Program" which imposed a ceiling on all public sector pay increases of between 8% and 14% in the first year and a cost-of-living increase ceiling in the second;[6] and

• an immediate salary freeze, pending a review, for all 700 senior public sector managers.

It soon became apparent how hasty and inadequate were the preparations for the entire programme. Bill 28, the Compensation Stabilization Act, was introduced to the legislature on April 13, 1982. Within

three weeks Premier Bennett indicated that some
employees might be asked to take a wage freeze or
even a cut to avoid public service layoffs. New
guidelines defined the programme as not only to
restrain and stabilize wages but also to enhance job
security and to preserve services within the employer's
"ability to pay".[7] By July 1982 the wage controls
became more severe. On June 28 the federal government had announced a two-year Public Sector
Compensation Restraint Program with wage limits of
6% and 5% for federal employees. Four weeks later
British Columbia lowered the ceilings on its own
programme to between 0% and 10% in the first year
and between 0% and 9% in the second.[8] If collective
bargaining failed to produce an agreement within
these "voluntary" guidelines, the Compensation
Stabilization Commissioner could impose a set of
still more stringent regulations.

Prior to the imposition of the wage control
programme, the British Columbia Government
Employees' Union (BCGEU) had been preparing for
a "catch up — keep up" settlement. Their 1979 wage
settlement of 8% in each of its three years had seen
their real wages fall, and now they sought a one-year
contract with a $1 an hour across-the-board wage
increase plus a 5% general increase and a cost-of-
living allowance. When talks began with the Government Employee Relations Bureau (GERB) on May 3,
1982 the government negotiating team made no wage
offer, but asked for a 4% increase in productivity
and for 98 "givebacks" from the contract due to
expire July 31.

After thirteen weeks of desultory bargaining,
mediation and a meeting with the premier, there was
no progress. GERB's final offer was 6.5% and 5%
over two years. On August 6, 1982 the BCGEU
embarked on its first-ever strike. A new brand of
public, politicized bargaining followed. Bennett
charged that BCGEU members would accept his final
offer if they had a chance to vote on it. BCGEU

leaders responded by indeed putting it to a vote — in which it was rejected by 93.4%. But as a token of good faith they returned to work after five days off the job.

When further negotiations dragged, the BCGEU began rotating strikes and held talks with the B.C. Federation of Labour to plan further province-wide action. Only an offer by John Fryer, the BCGEU general secretary, to reconsider wage demands if the savings were used for job creation led to a resumption of negotiations. The parties were finally able to conclude an eighteen-month contract with a 7.8% wage increase.

Both sides made important concessions in order to achieve an agreement. Within the limitations of wage controls, it appeared to be a triumph for the bargaining process. The Social Credit government seemed prepared to live up to its commitment to respect free collective bargaining, under the terms of the Compensation Stabilization Program. But within four months it was apparent that the new master agreement was only an uneasy truce, not a resolution of the fundamental differences. Despite Premier Bennett's assurances that his government was the best guarantor of job security, Finance Minister Hugh Curtis warned that revenue would trail expenditures unless programmes were eliminated and the size of government was reduced. Curtis promised that these problems would be addressed in the budget for the coming year.[9] Some of the terms of the agreement with the BCGEU also proved to be empty promises. A new joint productivity committee, for example, failed to function effectively and the BCGEU's claim for an April 1983 wage increase (based on an economic recovery formula provision of the agreement) was denied.[10]

After the May 5, 1983 provincial general election, the government became more coercive in its efforts to control the wages of its employees and to force other concessions. The entire structure of public sector

employment and its personnel practices become the
target of a legislated "restraint on government"
program. Ignoring previous commitments, Bennett
called for the layoff of government employees and
radical modifications in their terms and conditions of
employment. Formerly recognized employee rights
were redefined as "privileges" in the face of an
overriding priority given to a balanced budget and
curbing the growth of government. Public sector
wage controls were extended indefinitely.

Permanent Controls, Bargaining Rights and Layoffs

The Social Credit "restraint on government"
programme is identified today with the 26 bills that
were tabled with the July 7, 1983 budget speech. The
12.3% increase in estimated operating expenditures
and increases in sales tax, health and other charges
plus the estimated borrowing requirement of $1,550
million showed little evidence of restraint in the sense
of curbs on total spending and government revenue
raising. But a commitment to reduce government
employment by 25% for September 1984, and the
absence of any wage increase provisions, did form
the core of a package designed to attach lower
priorities to certain government services. Together
with such measures as the reduction of human rights
and tenant protection, which withdrew services for
all British Columbians, Bills 2, 3 and 11 asked public
sector workers to bear still greater burdens of
"restraint".

Bill 11, the Compensation Stabilization Amendment Act, removed the 24-month limit on wage
controls and applied the guidelines to arbitrated
awards in the public sector. All provincial public
sector employers and arbitrators were now instructed
to make the principle of "ability to pay" the
paramount consideration in their wage settlements.[11]

In keeping with the new thrust of the "restraint" programme, the new guidelines made no mention of job security or the preservation of public services. On the surface they allowed more flexibility than their earlier versions. However, the discretion given the Compensation Stabilization Commissioner to rule on ability to pay, plus the lowering of the allowable range of settlements to between minus-5% and plus-5% tightened the grip of wage control.[12] Not only is the new range far removed from the original February 1982 ceilings, the assertion of the "ability to pay" principle enables the provincial government to cut back on wage and salary expenditure budget allocations and plead inability to pay. Ed Peck, the Compensation Stabilization Commissioner, has supported the political right of the government to adopt such tactics. He argues that "to focus upon the taxation power of the Government in determining the resources available to provide wage increases ignores the Government's right to make political judgements, which are redressable at the ballot box, concerning the level of services it will fund and maintain."[13] This criterion ensures that provincial public wage levels are no longer determined primarily by bargaining or independent arbitration, but by the unilateral budgetary priorities of the Social Credit government, as interpreted by its own appointee.

Section 13 of the existing Public Service Labour Relations Act had affirmed a broad definition of what could be included in a collective agreement. Nevertheless, it recognized that the merit principle and certain organizational matters would be excluded from the scope of bargaining. Bill 2, the Public Service Labour Relations Amendment Act, proposed a dramatic expansion of managerial rights. Questions related to the establishment and elimination of positions, the assignment of duties, work scheduling, and the effect of staff reductions would no longer be bargainable. Bill 2 was an attempt by the employer — government — to gain through legislative power what it had been unable to achieve at the bargaining table in the summer of 1982.

Bill 3, the Public Sector Restraint Act, would have ended employment security for *all* public sector employees. The number of positions eliminated from the payroll was to be the chief indicator of its success. Full-time equivalent (FTE) positions for employees of government ministries would be reduced from 46,806 to 39,965 in 1983/84 and further reduced to 35,410 in 1984/85.[14] The day after the provincial budget was presented, the first 400 of 1,600 employees to be terminated by October 31, 1983, received their pink slips. Earlier reductions in school financing had already eliminated 1,000 teaching positions and a further 3,000 were threatened.

Bill 3 would have given the government the power to "terminate the employment of an employee without cause." The cabinet could unilaterally impose whatever regulations were considered necessary to implement its planned firings and set the terms of any severance payments. When the government met with concerted protests against the arbitrary nature of these powers, Provincial Secretary Jim Chabot presented a series of amendments to the bill which defined the conditions for termination and removed the "without cause" provisions. The new conditions were to be insufficient work; insufficient funds budgeted; change in organizational structure; discontinuation of a programme, activity or service; or reduction of the level of an activity or service. These changes did little to reduce the scope of the Social Credit government's termination powers, which were also broadened to include layoffs. A more important concession allowed the Compensation Stabilization Commissioner to approve exemptions from Bill 3 if a collective agreement contained provisions for employee termination and severance pay which were equivalent to those in the bill. All terminations were also made subject to review by a panel with further right of appeal to the courts.

Fired employees were given the choice between two weeks severance pay for each year of service *or* placement on a recall list. This ran counter to the severance pay and recall clauses of the existing BCGEU master agreement. It also posed a difficult dilemma for the employee faced with a choice between immediate compensation for losing a public service career or the uncertainty of job vacancies and recall at the discretion of the employer.

Solidarity and the Kelowna Agreement

The BCGEU, the B.C. Teachers' Federation and the Hospital Employees' Union — all of them threatened by the new bills — combined with other elements of the labour movement and a number of diverse community and citizens' rights organizations in the Solidarity Coalition against the entire July 1983 package.[15] Public sector unions formed the core of the Coalition and protests that escalated toward the threat of a provincial general strike. The dismantling of the Human Rights Branch and Commission, the abolition of the Rentalsman's Office, the centralization of control over school and hospital boards, and other aspects of the "restraint" bills brought people from all walks of life into common cause against the Social Credit cutbacks.

Negotiations between the BCGEU and GERB for a new master agreement began on October 3, 1983. They soon reached an impasse over the application of Bill 2 and the firing, outside the terms of the expiring contract, of 1,200 employees. By the middle of the month, 87% of the BCGEU membership voted in favour of a strike. Their strike, scheduled for November 1, was to be the first stage in Solidarity's planned timetable of walkouts culminating in a province-wide general strike.

Premier Bennett again turned to television on October 20 to announce that the provincial legislature would be adjourned to provide a cooling-off period and an opportunity for consultation on the remaining items in his legislative package. Before the House adjourned on the following day, royal assent was given to Bills 3 and 11 — but not to Bill 2.

As in 1982, the resumption of talks with the BCGEU saw the government's GERB negotiators pushed to the sidelines. This was a second tacit admission of the inadequacies in GERB's bargaining tactics.[16] But the move was too late to avert the strike by the BCGEU membership. Teachers and school staff followed seven days later and British Columbia appeared headed for a general strike. By November 10, however, with agreement close at hand between Norman Spector, deputy to the premier, and Cliff Andstein, chief negotiator for the BCGEU, Solidarity leaders also agreed that the strike could be averted. The Social Credit government would have to allow seniority exemptions from Bill 3 for other public sector workers and consult with interested groups before proceeding with its amendments to the human rights and landlord-tenant legislation. This understanding formed the basis for the November 13 Kelowna agreement.

Despite the inauspicious beginnings to its negotiation and the crisis precipitated by the Social Credit government's legislative package, the final settlement reached with the BCGEU was one in which both the premier's personal representatives and the union's bargaining committee could point to gains. The government would allow Bill 2 to die on the order paper of the legislative assembly. It also agreed to be bound by the decisions of hours-of-work umpires on government work scheduling and to give continuously employed auxiliary employees regular appointment status. The union conceded to a two-year agreement with a wage freeze in the first year, a 3% increase at the beginning of the second, and a further 1% in April 1985. The two parties also negotiated layoff provisions and a complex system of bumping rights which exempted the BCGEU membership from Bill 3.

In the short run the Social Credit cabinet appears to have achieved many of its objectives. Stringent wage controls and new mechanisms for employee layoffs are in place. The social costs of attaining these, however, have been far too high.

Impacts

The link between the stated objective of the Bennett government — economic recovery — and its radical changes in provincial public policy remains at best tenuous. It is claimed that a leaner public service and a reversion to unilaterally-imposed personnel policies will make government employees more efficient and productive. In fact, the threats of layoffs, lower real wages and the takeback of employee rights are more likely to reduce efficiency. In an atmosphere of fear it is sick leave, not labour productivity, that will increase.

For the private sector, stricter controls may lead to higher productivity where individual workers see a direct connection between their own increased effort and an improvement of the ability of the company to compete. But layoffs in the government reflect less an individual worker's productivity than the ideological priorities of the political zealots who currently advise our provincial government.

It is never easy in the formulation of any policy to distinguish clearly between ends and means.[17] If there is little apparent connection between them, there is good reason to suspect that the means are badly chosen or are also ends in themselves. In British Columbia, the body count of eliminated public sector jobs has become an end in itself. The means chosen to attain it come at the expense of the more substantive long-term objectives of increased efficiency and productivity. It is difficult to escape the conclusion that for Bennett's administration the discipline of government employees is a more important consideration than the long-term managerial needs of the public sector.

Many believe that only a return to economic prosperity will help ease the tensions of the past two years and secure a complete return to free collective bargaining. A more buoyant economy and government revenue fund will not, however, guarantee a return to a sane political strategy or more appropriate negotiating tactics. This will only be attained by a change within, or of, government.

Human Rights
Under Restraint
Murray Rankin

IN THE 1984 SPEECH from the Throne, the government announced that human rights were to be made a matter of individual initiative. Bill 27 and its recent replacement, Bill 11, "privatize" the enforcement of human rights in British Columbia. Complaints from groups will no longer be accepted. There is no longer a Human Rights Branch which can hire staff to assist complainants in advancing their allegations of discrimination. The new legislation eliminates the flexibility boards of inquiry had to determine whether there was "reasonable cause" for certain kinds of discrimination.

The public interest in human rights has been downplayed in making adjudication the responsibility of the complainant, a responsibility which is not shared by the Branch on behalf of the public. In the past, the Human Rights Branch tried to bring about settlements; if unsuccessful, it provided a lawyer at the hearing stage, at no expense to the complainant. No similar provisions exist in the new legislation.

Unintentional discrimination is also not covered. Proving that the landlord or employer specifically *intended* to deny *you* as an individual accommodation or employment will be an uphill battle which few complainants will pursue. Quasi-criminal or civil proceedings based on discrimination are also unavailable. Unlike the old Code, the new legislation contains no provision creating an "offence" of discrimination. Likewise, no civil law tort of discrimination is created by the new Act.

The new human rights legislation means that more people will be unemployed, on welfare or in need of public housing because of discrimination by employers and landlords. By making the enforcement of human rights legislation a more adversarial process and a responsibility falling upon the shoulders of the individual, Bill 27 and its successor, Bill 11, are consistent with Social Credit ideology. However, individual initiative is not the complete answer to human rights. There is a public interest which cannot be ignored. On balance, Bill 11 represents a regressive step. It has little to do with financial restraint, but much to do with squandered human opportunities.

Human Rights and the "Restraint" Budget

Bill 27, introduced July 7, 1983 as part of the government's "restraint" package, resulted in the immediate lay-off of twenty investigative officers in the Human Rights Branch. What remained was a skeleton staff of one administrator and seven clerks to handle the 700 cases which were pending.[1] On July 15, Hanne Jensen, director of the Human Rights Branch, was fired by Labour Minister Bob McClelland for refusing to dismantle the Branch. She argued that she was merely attempting to enforce the Human Rights Code (which was still in force).[2]

Bill 27 became a focal point for the Solidarity Coalition in its campaign against the Social Credit legislative package. The abolition of the Human Rights Commission and the Human Rights Branch and their replacement by a council was seen as difficult to justify in terms of fiscal "restraint". A wide range of community groups, handicapped groups, women's groups and other organizations joined the Solidarity Coalition in large measure because of Bill 27.

Opposition to the legislation came from other quarters as well. Gordon Fairweather, chairman of the Canadian Human Rights Commission, said the new bill did not live up to the obligations which Canada assumed as a signatory of the International Covenant on Economic and Social Rights and the Covenant on Civil and Political Rights,[3] and called Bill 27 "emblematic of a police state."[4] Federal Secretary of State Serge Joyal provided a $19,050 grant to the Vancouver Island Human Rights Coalition, an organization dedicated to fighting Bill 27. When Bob McClelland complained that this federally-funded organization was designed to support the overthrow of the Social Credit government,[5] Joyal responded by suggesting that Bill 27 be amended or withdrawn and repeated his support for the Human Rights Coalition.

Finally, after considerable public outcry, McClelland announced in December 1983 that the controversial bill would be permitted to die.[6] He indicated, however, that new legislation would be introduced during the next session of the legislative assembly to replace Bill 27. The government promised to consult with an advisory committee before enacting further human rights legislation. But Bill 11, introduced just two working days after that committee reported, was substantially the same as Bill 27.

The government's lack of commitment to human rights was underscored in the 1984/85 Ministry of Labour budget. Human rights programmes, which had received $1,253,284 in the 1983/84 fiscal year, would get $692,795 in 1984/85 — a 44.7% reduction. The budget for salaries was reduced 72%, from $832,868 to $231,478. Individuals with complaints of discrimination were told that they were, in effect, to fend for themselves, that no group could take up the case on their behalf.

History

In order to appreciate the full significance of the government's present position on human rights, it is necessary to situate Bills 27 and 11 in their historical context.

Every province of Canada has some legislation on human rights. Canada has a Charter of Rights and Freedoms, binding upon both the federal government and provincial governments, which guarantees certain fundamental freedoms, democratic rights, legal rights, equality rights and linguistic rights. The Charter constitutes the supreme law of Canada, overriding any law inconsistent with its provisions. However, the various human rights laws of the federal and provincial governments are not really "human rights" legislation in the same sense the Charter is.

Bills of rights traditionally are concerned with freedom of speech, religion, association and other traditional political rights; human rights acts are generally concerned with discrimination (for example, prohibiting discrimination with respect to employment or accommodation). Women, racial minorities, the disabled, homosexuals, the elderly and the young are all disadvantaged groups in our society who benefit from such legislation. More appropriately, legislation such as the B.C. Human Rights Code, Bill 27 and Bill 11 should be termed anti-discrimination legislation. No one of these is an all-encompassing bill of rights, but rather a statement of principles concerning certain types of prohibited discrimination and an enforcement mechanism.

British Columbia's first human rights legislation was the Fair Employment Practices Act, enacted in 1956. It was followed by the Fair Accommodation Act in 1961. British Columbia has a rather unenviable record in human rights. For example, it was not until 1949 that the Japanese and Native Indians could vote in provincial elections. Certain rights, however, did receive early recognition. After 1932 B.C.'s Unemployment Relief Act prohibited discrimination in employment on the basis of political affiliation, race or religion. There was no enforcement mechanism and there do not appear to have been any prosecutions under the act, but at least the law expressed what "respectable" people thought right.

By way of contrast, Ontario's legislation in the 1950s respecting employment and accommodation practices became the model for contemporary human rights codes. Once a complaint of discrimination was received, a conciliation officer was empowered to make enquiries and try to reach a settlement. If such attempts failed, the minister of labour could appoint a commission to conduct a formal inquiry and make recommendations to the minister. If an order by the minister implementing the recommendations of the inquiry was ignored, the act provided for a summary conviction offence. With important variations, this framework of human rights legislation has remained the norm in Canada ever since.

British Columbia passed its own Human Rights Act in 1969. It was basically a consolidation of the Fair Employment Practices Act and the Fair Accommodation Act, with sex added as a prohibited ground of discrimination. In its last full year of operation, 98 complaints of discrimination were investigated.[7] But the Human Rights Act did not provide the Director with staff. The Human Rights Code, which replaced the Act in 1973, rectified this deficiency, and in the first year of the Code's operation more than 700 complaints of discrimination were filed and investigated — the public was starting to use the legislation. B.C.'s original Human Rights Act had generally followed the model of the earliest Ontario legislation, which has been described thus:

> The principal defect of the fair employment and accommodations legislation was the lack of full-time staff to administer and enforce it... [I]t still continued, as Professor W.S. Tarnopolsky has pointed out: "...to place the whole emphasis of promoting human rights upon the individual who has suffered most, and who is therefore in the least advantageous position to help himself. It places the administrative machinery of the State at the disposal of the victim of discrimination but it approaches the whole problem as if it was wholly his problem and his responsibility. The result is that very few complaints were made, and little enforcement was achieved.[8]

Ironically, lack of staff, lack of enforcement machinery and reliance upon the individual are precisely the results of the July 1983 budget and its aftermath. The Speech from the Throne of February 13, 1984 states:

> British Columbia is entering a new era in human rights, where a greater emphasis will be placed on individual responsibility for eliminating discrimination. The government will be introducing legislation supporting the fundamental principle.

We have come full circle.

Human Rights Code of 1973

The Human Rights Code of 1973 prohibited discrimination with respect to race, religion, colour,

sex, ancestry, place of origin or marital status. The
Code was unique in Canada in two ways. First,
individuals were protected from *discrimination without reasonable cause* with respect to accommodation,
services and facilities. Similarly, discrimination in
respect of employment was prohibited "unless
reasonable cause exists" for the discrimination. As a
result, groups that were not specifically mentioned in
the Code were protected unless, for instance, a
landlord or an employer could justify the discrimination.

Second, under the Code the provincial cabinet
appointed members to a Human Rights Commission.
The Commission had certain educative functions and
could also approve affirmative action programmes.
In addition, the Minister of Labour appointed a
Director of the Human Rights Branch. This individual served not only as chief executive officer of
the Commission, but also as the senior public servant
responsible for enforcing the Code. If settlement was
not reached, a board of inquiry could be appointed
by the minister of labour. The final determination of
the merits of a complaint was made by this board of
inquiry, although appeals to the B.C. Supreme Court
could be launched on certain grounds.

The "reasonable cause" section of the Code provided a wide ambit of discretionary authority to
boards of inquiry unknown in other Canadian human
rights legislation — the board was empowered to
decide whether certain kinds of discrimination were
reasonable in the circumstances. Boards of inquiry
discovered that "reasonable cause" acted as a bas-
ket, in which certain categories of discrimination not
specifically listed in the Code could be treated:
discrimination on the grounds of physical or mental
conditions, sexual orientation, family status, age (if
over 45 and under 64), sexual harassment, racial
harassment or pregnancy could all be classified as
unjustified, even though the Code did not specifically
mention them.[9] But certain "reasonable" forms of

discrimination — "maintenance of public decency", freedom of opinion, seniority — were allowed.

Under the Code, the board of inquiry could dismiss the allegation of discrimination if it concluded that it was not justified by the facts. If the board of inquiry believed that the allegation was well founded, it was to order the person or organization doing the discriminating to stop. It could order compensation for the victim of discrimination for wages and salary lost, incidental expenses incurred and, in certain circumstances, could order up to $5,000 additional damages for hurt feelings or loss of self-respect.

Restrictions in Bills 27 and 11

The list of activities subject to the Human Rights Code's prohibition of discrimination was changed in Bill 27 and Bill 11 in one important instance. Section 7 of the 1973 Code prohibited discrimination in employment advertisements. A prospective employer could not express "any limitation, specification or preference as to the race, religion, colour, sex, marital status, age, ancestry or place of origin" of a prospective employee. Moreover, the employer could not require any information from the candidate concerning his or her "race, religion, colour, ancestry, place of origin or political belief". Bill 27 would have eliminated the Code's protection against discriminatory advertisements and application forms completely. And although Bill 11 prohibits discriminatory advertisements, it permits application *forms* to discriminate. Job applicants can be required to answer questions about their race, religion or political beliefs.

The most significant change in Bill 27 was the elimination of the "reasonable cause" provision, and Bill 11 does not restore this provision of the 1973 Code. The clause has certain advantages. Intentional as well as unintentional discriminations are covered.

For example, height and weight requirements for certain jobs often exclude a high proportion of women or members of ethnic minorities. A stairway may have the effect of excluding potential employees in wheelchairs. There may not have been an intention to discriminate in either case. Under the 1973 Human Rights Code, a board of inquiry could act to remedy such discrimination if it considered the requirement or barrier to be unreasonable.[10] Most human rights experts agree that unintentional discrimination is much more significant to disadvantaged groups than intentional discrimination.

Bill 27 and Bill 11 provide a definitive list of grounds of unjustified discrimination, thereby eliminating flexibility enjoyed by boards of inquiry in the past. These bills have added a prohibition against discrimination on the grounds of mental or physical disability. This amendment seems praiseworthy; however, the use of the "reasonable cause" provision in the 1973 Code already put British Columbia in the forefront of protection for these groups in Canada.[11] By adding physical and mental disability to the list of prohibited grounds of discrimination, the government indicates that in its view the handicapped community deserves protection. Is it the government's intent *not* to protect other disadvantaged minorities? With so many competing demands on legislative time, it may be that any protection gained by other minorities would not be legislated for many years to come. Therefore, by any standard, eliminating the "reasonable cause" provision causes immediate concern to minorities such as the gay community. The government did not explicitly indicate why it eliminated this crucial clause.

Despite its flexibility, the "reasonable cause" provision had not received universal acclaim. Employers argued that they could not plan their affairs to respect human rights guarantees when the ambit of human rights was so unclear. They asked why appointed boards of inquiry, not directly accountable to anyone for their decisions, should be allowed to define new grounds. Others, however, argued that the 1973 B.C. Code was responsive to changing public concerns; it did not require amendment by an over-burdened legislative assembly to reflect changing social circumstances.[12]

The Ontario Court of Appeal ruled recently that that province's human rights legislation covers only cases where the individual *intends* to discriminate, or possesses the requisite evil mind (*mens rea*) to discriminate.[13] (An appeal of that decision is pending in the Supreme Court of Canada.) As we've just seen, an important feature of the eliminated "reasonable cause" clause of the old Code was that it did cover unintentional discrimination; the Human Rights Act of 1984 that replaced it has the same wording as the Ontario legislation in question. In other words, victims of discrimination may now be forced to prove that the person or organization that allegedly discriminated against them did so *intentionally*.

The B.C. government was well aware of this important decision in Ontario at the time it drafted the new human rights law for this province. By failing to address the problem of intention, the B.C. legislators may have turned the clock back to the 1940s. At the very least, British Columbia should have stated unambiguously in the new legislation whether or not practices that have an unintended discriminatory effect are to be covered by the human rights legislation. There should be some remedy for unintentional discrimination.

Certain grounds, such as discrimination based on pregnancy and sexual harassment, were implicitly added to the list of prohibited grounds by various boards of inquiry who relied upon the "reasonable cause" section of the Code.[14] In other words, the human rights "jurisprudence" in British Columbia has recognized that pregnancy and sexual harassment are normally prohibited grounds of discrimination. Neither of these grounds is found in Bill 27's and Bill

11's list. Are they now covered in British Columbia? By one interpretation, the explicit removal of the "reasonable cause" provision could be evidence that the government intends *not* to include these matters. If that is the case, then British Columbia clearly has regressed in the human rights field.

Administration and Procedure

Bill 11 replaces the Human Rights Commission and the Human Rights Branch of the Ministry of Labour with the British Columbia Council of Human Rights, consisting of five members appointed by cabinet. Like Bill 27, Bill 11 fails to ensure the Council's independence from the government of the day; Council members may be fired by cabinet at any time, for any reason.

One difficulty with the new approach is that the Council has no explicit statutory power to hire staff. Instead of combining the responsibilities of the former Commission and Branch, both bills simply eliminate the Branch. Moreover, the all-important educative role of the Commission is not transferred to the Council. With no authority to hire staff, it seems obvious that complaints will take much longer to process. The minister of labour has indicated that the ministry's industrial relations officers will perform the conciliation and settlement functions of the Branch's human rights officers. But they are not likely to be familiar with the particularities of human rights matters. Their training is largely directed at achieving settlements and they may dissuade or discourage complainants from proceeding further. They may not have the time to take on additional responsibilities for human rights, even if they do receive retraining.

Under the 1973 Code complaints were filed with the Council and the Director and his or her Branch were expected to investigate and to attempt to effect a settlement. In Bill 11, the Council is empowered to decide whether or not a complaint is "trivial, frivolous, vexatious or made in bad faith;" whether it is beyond the jurisdiction of the Council or is untimely. Although a preliminary screening by the Council is sensible, it is disturbing that there are no criteria set out to assist the Council in deciding whether to refer a complaint to the minister. Under Bill 11, the Council may have one of its members conduct an inquiry without referring a case to the minister for his or her decision on appointing a board of inquiry. The consequences of this new provision are unclear.

Upon receipt of the complaint the Council must first decide whether it should be investigated or dismissed. Unlike the Code, the bill does not stipulate that the Council "shall at once" inquire into the matter. In addition, there is no requirement in the bill to attempt to reach a settlement. The Council has the explicit discretion to dismiss complaints, a power which the Branch did not have. There are no guidelines for the exercise of the Council's discretion to discontinue complaints. The bill seems to remove the conciliation role played by the Branch; no similar role is assigned to the Council.

Procedures before the boards of inquiry have been changed under Bill 27 and Bill 11. Under the 1973 Human Rights Code, a lawyer representing the complainant's interest was normally supplied to the complainant for free. Bill 27 and Bill 11 make no such provision and few members of those groups most likely to be the victims of discrimination can afford to pay legal fees. The board of inquiry may even award costs against the complainant. Legitimate complaints will not be pursued because the complainant doesn't have the money. Bill 27 and Bill 11 reflect a much more adversarial stance in human rights matters, although some would regard the "self-help" attitude here as a triumph of individualism over collectivism. It is an approach which largely ignores the impact of discrimination on disadvantaged groups and upon the community at large.

Under Bill 27 boards of inquiries could no longer award damages for humiliation or loss of self-respect. Boards could only order compensation for all or part of wages lost or expenses incurred by the discrimination. Other Canadian human rights statutes provide very wide remedial discretion.[15] In some cases, there would be little or no direct financial harm caused to a complainant, even in clear instances of discrimination. For example, refusing to permit a physically handicapped person or an Indian to have a cup of coffee in a restaurant results in very little financial loss — but should such blatant cases of discrimination carry no financial consequences?[16]

Also unlike the 1973 Code, Bill 27 and Bill 11 contain no right of appeal from a decision of the board of inquiry.[17] Especially as there is no requirement that members of boards of inquiry in human rights matters be legally trained, it is lamentable that their decisions cannot be appealed.

Conclusion

Although Bill 27 was included in the initial "restraint" package of legislation, even a cursory examination of the Social Credit government's own budget estimates reveals that the bill had almost nothing to do with government cost-cutting. The elimination of the Human Rights Commission and the decimation of the Human Rights Branch result in rather insignificant savings. When the minorities and disadvantaged groups realized the consequences of the Social Credit's "reform" of human rights legislation in B.C., their vocal support for the Solidarity Coalition became a vital part of the general resistance movement to the "restraint" programme. The Solidarity Coalition could not be dismissed as merely an economic protest group fueled by trade unions; the active involvement of racial minorities, women's groups and gay activists gave Solidarity a much broader perspective.

Why then was Bill 27 introduced? Did the Social Credit government not foresee the widespread resistance it would create? After a promise to reconsider the ill-fated "reform", the Social Credit government merely replaced Bill 27 with another human rights "reform" bill, introduced in April 1984, which is fundamentally the same. The administration and enforcement of anti-discrimination measures in B.C. effectively are now "privatized"; a more adversarial approach will place greater reliance on individual victims of discrimination to vindicate their rights. The more sophisticated and more affluent in the community may succeed in their self-defence; the weaker will have only a weakened Human Rights Council and ill-equipped Ministry of Labour employees to turn to. The deliberate requirement that complainants prove that they have been the victims of *intentional* discrimination will mean that subtler, yet often more significant forms of workplace discrimination will persist in British Columbia.

Perhaps Social Credit is indebted to the Fraser Institute for the ideological underpinning of this move to greater "privatization" of human rights administration. Perhaps they hope that by minimizing the government's role, the "invisible hand of the market" would somehow rectify the problems of discrimination in this society. Bill 27 may represent a deliberate attack upon disadvantaged groups by a callous government which calculated that it would have support from the majority of citizens for its legislation. On the other hand, the government may have considered Bill 27 as simply another "restraint" measure, albeit a minor one. But because Bill 11 simply re-enacts many of the worst features of Bill 27, it is difficult to avoid cynical conclusions, given the apparent decision to ignore both widespread concern for strong human rights legislation and reasoned critiques of Bill 27.

Women's Rights:
An Impediment
to Recovery?
Stella Lord

WOMEN'S GROUPS in British Columbia have long known that the Social Credit government is not particularly sensitive or committed to women's issues, and feminists were unanimous in condemning the July 1983 "restraint" package as being particularly damaging to women. One of the first groups to form in opposition to the July 7, 1983 package was Women Against the Budget, one of the mainstays of the Solidarity Coalition which fought the legislation throughout the fall of 1983. The budget and legislation have also been opposed by many other women's groups in the province, including the Vancouver Status of Women, the Victoria Status of Women Action Group, and the North Shore Women's Centre.

The government's programme is likely to affect all women to one degree or another, especially in the areas of employment, education and social services. But some women will bear more of the cost than others. Most severely at risk are those who, either out of choice or circumstance, are single parents, not dependent on any male for support.

Human Rights Legislation

For almost two decades the women's movement has been fighting for a change in women's status in the workplace. Lately this has taken the form of the campaign for "equal pay for work of equal value" clauses in provincial and federal human rights laws. The principle of equal pay for equal work is, at last, now generally conceded (if not always followed by employers). But men's wages are still much higher than women's wages because the type of work men typically do is "worth" more than the work women typically do. "Equal pay for work of equal value" means that dissimilar work — for example, a laundry worker's job and a labourer's job — are compared in terms of skill, effort and responsibility required, and judgements of comparative "worth" are made on that basis. This concept was adopted by the International Labour Organization in 1951 and ratified by the Canadian government in 1972. In 1977, "equal pay for work of equal value" was enshrined in the federal Human Rights Act. But that law covers only workers within the federal jurisdiction.

In British Columbia, women's groups have long argued that the province's human rights laws should include an equal pay for work of equal value clause. It was also argued that the laws should deal specifically with the increasing number of complaints about sexual harassment.

The Social Credit government's new Human Rights Act, which replaced the Human Rights Code in May 1984, ignores both these concerns. Moreover, the Act eliminates the old Code's clause which protected individuals from "discrimination without reasonable cause," by which sexual harassment cases could previously be dealt with. It is not clear whether such cases can be pursued at all under the new Act.

The new Act seriously undermines the legal protection for women and minority groups against discrimination, and it opens the door to more blatant forms of discrimination against women — particularly in the area of employment — which it was thought were part of a by-gone era. It is now permissible for employers to seek information on marital status, maternity plans and sexual orientation. The old Human Rights Code was flexible enough to take into account unintentional forms of discrimination which are often the root of discrimination against women in the labour force. With the "discrimination without cause" clause omitted from the new Act it is easier for employers to exclude women from certain jobs on the basis of such criteria as height, strength or weight. Moreover, pregnant women may no longer be protected from employment discrimination. For victims of discrimination, the emphasis will now be on proving that the other side *intended* to discriminate against them.

Finally, with no investigative staff and without a guarantee of paid legal counsel, women will be reluctant to press their cases. The new Human Rights Act is not designed to be a legal and educational tool for change, as the old one was. It will tend to entrench the status quo and eliminate human rights legislation as a vehicle for change in both legal and educational terms.

Public Sector Wage Controls and the Employment Standards Amendment Act

Another route to equality for women in the workplace has been via the negotiating table. Over the past five years many unions have taken this route. In B.C., the Hospital Employees' Union, the Canadian Union of Public Employees, the Vancouver Regional and Municipal Employees' Union, and the B.C. Government Employees Union have all fought for collective agreements that attempt to close the wage differentials between male and female employees. Because women are over-represented in the public sector and are concentrated into lower-paid jobs in service and clerical occupations, this was an important new development in the struggle for women's equality. It was thought that the new emphasis on equal pay within the highly unionized public sector might influence women's pay scales in the non-unionized and private sector as well.

But that strategy is directly affected by the Compensation Stabilization Amendment Act, passed in the fall of 1983. That act, part of the "restraint" package, extends public sector wage controls indefinitely (and, in certain circumstances, to the private sector) and makes the employer's "ability to pay" (since the employer is the government, "willingness to pay" would be more accurate) a paramount consideration in bargaining. Wage increases are now limited to a maximum of 5%. In a situation where a 5% increase (or less) in the total wage bill must be shared by all workers, it will be very difficult for unions to continue to pursue equal pay goals. It gives unions less room to bargain the issue before some workers are forced to take increases considerably lower than the rate of inflation.

It is also feared that maternity leave protection may be threatened by the fact that under the new Employment Standards Amendment Act employers can negotiate working conditions which do not conform to the minimum requirements of the law. Further, it is feared that employers may press for a lowering of the standards on maternity leave in union contracts.

Layoffs in the public sector may also affect women more than men, since women typically do not accumulate as much seniority as men, due to time taken out of the workforce to raise children. Inasmuch as the focus of the "restraint" measures has been the public sector, and this is where a large proportion of women work, cutbacks in the public sector will seriously affect women's employment security and future job prospects.

Education

Budget cutbacks in education affect all students and teachers, but they are particularly punitive to women. Women at home with children often take the opportunity to upgrade their skills at universities or colleges with a view to entering the job market at a later date. Because of childcare expenses and responsibilities most women have tended to choose part-time programmes or off-campus courses.[1] Severe budget restrictions are forcing universities and colleges to eliminate "peripheral" programmes and in many instances to raise fees significantly. Because they are said to be less cost-effective, there is a tendency for more cuts to be made in part-time and off-campus programmes.

Women's Access Programs, designed to teach women (mostly single parents) on income assistance basic job skills to help them gain access to the labour market, are now in jeopardy because government funding for programme co-ordinators has been eliminated. The government has also eliminated the educational subsidy granted to individuals on income assistance. Many of those taking advantage of this were single mothers seeking to upgrade their education.[2]

Layoffs due to education cutbacks will also affect women more than men. The British Columbia Teachers' Federation reports that 71% of termination notices in 1982 were given to women, even though women represented only 53.7% of teachers in British Columbia. The current layoffs are likely to continue this trend. In post-secondary education women teachers are more vulnerable to layoffs because they generally have less seniority, are in lower-level positions and, in universities, often hold non-tenured appointments.[3]

The cumulative effects of the legislation and budget on women's equality in the workplace are serious setbacks to the limited progress which had been made in this area. The full effects may not be evident for a number of years and might forever elude quantitative measurement. Yet the high cost of lost opportunities will certainly be experienced in human lives.

Social Services: The Plight of Single Parents

While one of the major effects of the "restraint" programme has been to stall women's attempts to gain equality at work, another has been to erode important cushions of basic survival support for many women, in particular single parents.

In British Columbia, more than 80% of single parents, an estimated 60,000, are women. It has been well documented that single women, and in particular single mothers, run a very high risk of poverty. Many subsist on welfare or the kind of low-income jobs which are typical of occupations women hold.[4]

In these circumstances the incidence of family stress is likely to be high, with an increased need for family support services. The effects of budget cuts on these programmes and on children in this province are documented in Marilyn Callahan's chapter in Part IV. They will not be dealt with here, except to point out that women as parents will also be affected by the stress of coping without support, or the emotional trauma of seeing children put into care.

Women as single parents are being affected in other ways too. The erosion of the welfare system which began over two years ago with the introduction of the GAIN programme has been continued in the new budget. In January 1984 welfare payments were frozen for most and cut for those 25 and under.[5] In this situation of dismally low welfare payments and high unemployment, many single parents, whether they are on welfare or employed, face the threat of increased living expenses as a direct result of government policy. These increases encompass housing, day-care and legal assistance.

The $2,500 Provincial Cooperative Housing Home Purchase Assistance Grant, which was one avenue of housing for single parents, was discontinued along with the Renters' Tax Credit in July 1983. The 1984 Residential Tenancy Act also has serious implications for single mothers. It abolishes the Rentalsman's Office and rent controls. These changes will undoubtedly create serious difficulties for tenants in the Lower Mainland. And in 1986, when Expo 86 is expected to attract millions of visitors to Vancouver, unscrupulous landlords will be able to take advantage of the influx of visitors — and the abolition of the tenant's right to appeal to the Rentalsman — to create short-term tourist accommodation by evicting tenants. This is likely to cause serious shortages of low-rent housing. In addition, the new act makes no provision for mediation of cases but instead provides an arbitration service for which a $30 fee will be charged. The government argues that no legal counsel will be required and has made no provision to aid complainants in making their cases.

These changes will result in the likelihood of higher rents and the possibility of eviction without adequate means of appeal or redress. In these circumstances, single mothers who already face difficulties finding low-cost rental accommodation where landlords will accept children will be the people most seriously affected by the new act.

If they are fortunate enough to have gained the

training, found a job and kept it, single mothers who work outside the home often face the problem of expensive daycare. The daycare subsidy, which has not been increased for two years and was once based on income plus expenses or need, is now subject to a stringent means test based only on income.[6] Women who were previously eligible for daycare subsidy may no longer be eligible even though living expenses are rising. They will have to foot the daycare bill out of their income or make alternative childcare arrangements.

Finally, legal aid services are being cut back. The Legal Services Society, which administers legal aid under the Legal Services Society Act (1979) estimates that there is now about an $8 million difference between the amount needed to provide legal aid to all who need it and the amount the provincial government is allocating. Consequently many appeals for legal aid are being turned away even though many of those asking for help are below the Statistics Canada poverty line. Cuts in legal aid are a further setback for women faced with child custody or maintenance problems.

Family service cases, particularly maintenance and custody cases, are a large proportion of the cases dealt with by legal aid. About 90% of requests for this type of help come from women. Although they may be suffering real financial need, budget cuts and an amendment to the Legal Services Society Act priorizing eligibility for services have forced Legal Services to consider only those cases where there is immediate substantial threat to the physical or emotional well-being of the client.

The cumulative effects of the "restraint" programme fall most strongly on those who can least afford them; the economic, social and emotional costs for many single mothers will be especially high. Why is the government pursuing this course, and why has there not been more public outcry?

The Justification — and
Motives — for "Restraint"

The Bennett government has justified the undermining of human rights and basic social services by appeals to "overburdened taxpayers" in the name of economic "restraint" in a period of recession. A strong appeal has been made to the need to promote the value of self-reliance and the resources of individuals. This in turn, it is argued, will reduce the need for government intervention and thus create a favourable climate for private investment in the province. The result will be a restoration of efficiency and a "trickle-down" prosperity for all. That has been the ideological justification for welfare cuts and for "encouraging" single mothers to seek work under the GAIN programme. This ideological pitch makes sense to those who believe that welfare creates a dependency on state help and a lack of motivation to get off welfare.

To reassure the skeptical and to satisfy the very evident social need, it has been argued that individuals, churches and community organizations are available and willing to take up the slack — much of it presumably on a volunteer basis. Thus Transition House for battered women in Vancouver, once directly staffed and funded by the government, is now being turned over to a private group.

The government's justification of its policy reveals a number of contradictions, leading one to suspect that there may be an underlying and unspoken motivation for "restraint". The government's policy seems to be radically out of tune with social reality and in particular with the changes which have taken place in the social aspirations and needs of women.

Today, more than 59% of the women in the labour force are married. The women's labour force participation rate has increased steadily since the early sixties. Increasingly it is women with children under 6 years of age who are looking for jobs. While many women work for pay because they want to, most do it because they *need* to.[7]

Unemployed women are being encouraged to volunteer for social service agencies as a means of securing permanent employment. For example, the Volunteer Bureau of Victoria estimates that a third of the people it interviews for volunteer positions are unemployed. The executive director was quoted as saying that "volunteering builds up references, experiences and self-esteem, and the volunteers often establish contacts that lead them into paid employment."[8] In the past, volunteers for social service activities were usually middle-class women who no longer had young children at home, and for whom working for pay was socially unacceptable. Is it possible that, even though the government's policies do not respond to the needs of women, the government will be in a position to capitalize on higher rates of unemployment and the motivation of women to work outside the home, to staff needed social services with volunteers?

It is tempting to ask to what degree the government is aware of the effects of its policies on women. Are these policies symptomatic of a government which does not understand the position of most women in our society, or is it a conscious attempt to undermine progress on women's equality? Why are single mothers in particular being told to bear the brunt of the costs of "restraint"?

The answer lies in the government's openness to neo-conservative economic philosophy and an ideological swing to the right. It is apparent that the Bennett government has been strongly influenced by the Fraser Institute. This government is oblivious to the fact that history has shown the notion of "trickle-down" prosperity to be a myth. One suspects that it is less a question of ignorance than a commitment to the business elite which underlies the government's adherence to this myth. The same can be said for

Social Credit's support of the market system as a whole. Its commitment to the business elite prevents the government from acknowledging that the so-called competitive, free market is in fact sustained by a whole variety of government measures ranging from massive tax shelters and government subsidization of risk ventures to the prevention of corporate bankruptcies.

Finally, it is worth noting that the qualities most valued in this allegedly free market system are unlikely to be those associated with the work of reproducing, nurturing, or caring for those who cannot care for themselves — children, the sick, the elderly. Those qualities are typically qualities associated with women.

Conclusion

The liberalism of the 20th century has been an attempt to balance the most inhumane effects of the market system through state intervention in social services and support for the family. Women have, in many respects, benefited from this. The Bennett government's new set of policies, however, represents a shift from liberal concepts toward neo-conservatism. The emphasis on competitiveness, individual responsibility and cutbacks in social service spending ushers in an ideological justification for the adverse effects the "restraint" measures will have on those least able to compete in the market system.

Most women, through no fault of their own, do not compete on an equal basis with men. In what amounts to a sex-segregated labour market, more than 60% of women work in just three occupational categories: sales, service and clerical occupations. These jobs tend to be characterized by low pay and few prospects for promotion, and in part account for the fact that women, on average, earn only 60% of what men earn.[9] This means that without male support most women, even those employed in the labour force, now find themselves at the bottom of the socio-economic ladder. One of the main goals of the women's movement has been to change this kind of structural inequality to allow women to become economically independent. For women with dependent children this also means ensuring an adequate support system when and if they need it.

The government, however, is either painfully unaware that its policies will be detrimental to these goals, or it may believe, as the Reagan administration appears to believe, that social change and economic independence for women are too costly for capitalism.[10] If this is the case, the aims of the women's movement are seriously threatened in British Columbia. It means that women will be encouraged to accept the status quo in labour market inequality and to embrace economic dependency and the permanency of marriage within the nuclear family.

There is some evidence that such a regression may be the ideological and political preference of the Social Credit government. Organizations such as Vancouver Status of Women, Planned Parenthood and rape crisis centres — all of which have attempted to combine service with advocacy for change — have seen their government funding seriously threatened or cut completely. Asking churches or community organizations to take up the slack is unrealistic in terms of their ability or willingness to do so. Nevertheless, from the government's perspective, it is probably ideologically and politically safer than to fund troublesome self-help or advocacy groups which seek changes in the status quo.

Taken together, the legislative changes and budget cutbacks represent a new direction in social policy in British Columbia. It is an agenda for change in which women's struggle for equality is viewed as a political impediment to "recovery". It is a new direction toward "recovery" in which the work most women do will not only continue to be unrecognized and unrewarded, but in which the price of non-conformity will be high.

Downsizing the
Unemployment Problem
Stan Persky
and Lanny Beckman

*"You never feel good about laying anyone
off. When I was in the private sector and
had to lay someone off, I'd lay awake
worrying about it at night."*
— Premier Bill Bennett, 1983

IF BILL BENNETT is to be believed, then the premier of
British Columbia has hardly slept a wink in the last
two years. Since Bennett's first dramatic declaration
on "restraint" in February 1982, the former small
businessman who once agonized over laying off a few
employees has been directly or indirectly responsible
for firing about 15,000 public sector workers and
throwing thousands more out of jobs in the private
sector by dampening the provincial economy.* These
actions have occurred in a period of record high

* Premier Bennett's televised address of February 18, 1982
  is generally considered the official beginning of the
  "restraint" programme, followed up by the budgets of
  1983 and 1984.

Canadian unemployment, rendered even more severe in B.C. by this province's extraordinary dependence on depressed export markets.

The "restraint" programme was supposed to cure the recession and create jobs, but its most visible feature is the thousands it has put out of work. The Bennett regime prefers not to discuss the matter. In early 1984, B.C.'s unemployment rate was 15.2% — 3% above the national average — and a minimum 13% jobless rate was being projected for the next few years. Any reasonable assessment of the situation would have made unemployment the number one problem. Yet in the 15,000-word budget speech delivered by Finance Minister Hugh Curtis on February 20, 1984, the word "unemployment" does not appear once.[1] Before analysing the effects of the "restraint" strategy on the workforce, as well as the government's curiously muted response to the unemployment problem, the situation must be placed within what, by any standard, is an alarming context.

Labour force statistics clearly display the severity of the recession in B.C. From 90,000 unemployed in 1981, the number surged to 163,000 in 1982, an increase of more than 80%. The jump in B.C. from a rate of 6.7% in 1981 to 12.1% in 1982 was the largest in the country, matched only by the increase in Alberta. (See Tables 1 and 2.)

Table 1: **Summary of Labour Force Statistics, British Columbia**

	1980	1981	1982	1983	May 1984
Labour force ('000s)	1,278	1,337	1,346	1,389	1,413
Employed ('000s)	1,191	1,247	1,183	1,172	1,193
Unemployed ('000s)	87	90	163	192	220
Unemployment rate (%)	6.8	6.7	12.1	13.8	15.6

Source: *Labour Force Survey*, Statistics Canada

Table 2: **Provincial Unemployment Rates (%)**

	B.C.	Alta.	Sask.	Man.	Ont.	Que.	N.B.	N.S.	P.E.I.	Nfld.	Can.
1980	6.8	3.7	4.4	5.5	6.9	9.9	11.2	9.9	10.9	13.7	7.5
1981	6.7	3.8	4.7	6.0	6.6	10.4	11.7	10.2	11.5	14.2	7.6
1982	12.1	7.5	6.2	8.5	9.8	13.8	14.2	13.2	13.1	16.9	11.0
1983	13.8	10.8	7.4	9.4	10.4	13.9	14.8	13.2	12.2	18.8	11.9
May 1984	15.6	12.0	8.0	7.8	9.3	13.2	14.9	12.2	14.2	21.1	11.7

Source: *Labour Force Survey*, Statistics Canada

More distressing still is the comparison to be made between unemployment rates in 1982, in the depth of the recession, and those of May 1984. In the intervening period a much-publicized economic recovery allegedly occurred. One standard measure of such a recovery is growth of the Gross Domestic Product (GDP). And indeed, in B.C., after a precipitous 7% decline in the GDP in 1982, there was a slight increase in 1983 to $16.1 billion from $15.8 billion the previous year, though the GDP had yet to recover to the nearly $17 billion figure of 1981. However, if the unemployed do not benefit, "recovery" means no more than the recovery of profit rates. While the unemployment rate between 1982 and May 1984 did in fact decline in Manitoba, Ontario, Quebec and Nova Scotia, it continued to increase substantially in B.C. In 1983, the year of recovery, gross employment in B.C. decreased, as it had done in 1982, and the number of those out of work grew. By May 1984, 220,000 people were officially unemployed in the province.

The official figures do not tell the entire story. The B.C. Central Credit Union's estimate of the "invisible unemployed" (including those euphemistically referred to as "discouraged workers") during the first quarter of 1984 raises the actual unemployment rate in B.C. to 17.7%.[2] Tabulated by age group, the credit union's calculations emphasize not only the severity of youth unemployment but also the fact that this is the age group most likely to be under-

counted in official samples. (See Table 3.) Although
the statistics are suggestive rather than conclusive, it
is also safe to say that in addition to the young,
women and ethnic minorities are among the prominent victims of current conditions. In the late 1970s
and early 1980s, with B.C. unemployment relatively
stable at about 7%, the fastest growing segment of
the labour force was female workers. With the onset
of the recession, not only did female unemployment
increase in proportions equivalent to that of males,
but participation of women in the labour force
ceased to grow as it became apparent to prospective
women workers that their job prospects were bleak.
Further, given that women and ethnic minorities are
"late" entrants into the labour force, the bitter adage
"last hired, first fired" no doubt applies.

Clearly, the government that brought B.C.
"restraint" offers little hope to the unemployed.
However, until people recognize that "restraint" is
part of the problem, and not part of the solution, it is
unlikely that conditions will improve. So far, the
Social Credit government has managed to downsize
unemployment as a political problem by privatizing
responsibility for it, blaming its victims, and obscur-
ing the intent and effect of "restraint". Each of these
strategic moves requires closer scrutiny.

Table 3: **Actual Versus Reported Unemployment**
(First Quarter, 1984)

Age Group	Reported unemployment ('000s)	Rate %	Actual unemployment ('000s)	Rate %
15-19	25	24.5	50	39.5
20-24	46	24.4	50	25.9
25-44	102	14.2	102	14.2
45-64	38	10.9	42	12.0
Total	**211**	**15.4**	**245**	**17.7**

Restraining Employment

The most obvious effect of "restraint" is that it adds directly to unemployment by *dis*employing public sector workers, either by firing them outright from government service or by forcing subsidiary public bodies (school boards, hospital boards, municipalities) to do so through budget cutbacks. As early as 1982, long before restraint had been raised to a concept of totemic significance, the B.C. Health Association reported that budgetary restraint was responsible for some 2,000 layoffs of hospital workers; 600 teaching positions were eliminated that year; as well, the government maintained a hiring freeze in the public service, using "attrition" to eliminate a job every time someone quit or retired.[3]

As restraint evolved from the relatively limited notion of "wage restraint" in 1982 to a full-blown ideology by the time of the 1983 and 1984 budgets, the brunt of the firings were borne by government workers.[4] As economist William Schworm argues, "Perhaps the worst aspect of the two restraint budgets is the reduction of public sector employment. The provincial government's direct employment was reduced by over 6,000 full-time employees in 1983 and is to be reduced by almost 4,500 in 1984. This is a 24 per cent decline in a two year period during which over 190,000 persons in B.C. were already unemployed."[5] By spring 1984, Provincial Secretary Jim Chabot was claiming victory in the government's two-year drive to "downsize" the civil service.[6] The government had succeeded as promised, said Chabot, in cutting the civil service payroll by 25%, from 46,000 in 1982 to 35,000 in early 1984.

As with most other pronouncements on restraint, it is necessary to separate reality from ideological advertisements. Certainly, the government had succeeded in disrupting the lives of thousands of workers; in many cases, however, by "privatizing" the work being done, the jobs had been shifted to other workers. As George Reamsbottom, spokesman for the 40,000-member B.C. Government Employees Union, noted, ''The government has a political objective to show they've reduced the number of people on the payroll by a substantial number. The reality is, many of those services have been taken over by someone else and the government is still paying for them.''[7] One of the more surreal examples of this aspect of the ''new reality'' was the decision to privatize services provided by government chaplains to inmates of provincial jails. While the cabinet hummed ''Nearer My Privatized God to Thee,'' the chaplains were bidding for a contract to pray. Some of the reasons behind the strategy of playing musical chairs with people's jobs will be considered below.

In the case of teachers, one of the public sector groups hardest hit by cutbacks, the jobs were simply eliminated. Reduced services are now being provided in more crowded classrooms. The B.C. Teachers' Federation estimates that at least 2,500 teaching positions have vanished (900 in 1981/82, 150 during 1982/83, and 1,600 in 1983/84).[8] The assault on education, a relatively late phase of the restraint programme, is expected to continue: 1,600 teaching positions are slated to by chopped in autumn 1984.[9]

Beyond direct disemployment, the restraint programme also contributes to unemployment indirectly. The fired workers stop buying goods and services. Other worried workers, believing their own job security to be tenuous, become hesitant about making big-ticket purchases. Depressed consumer purchasing power and lower consumer confidence lead to further layoffs in the private sector, often related to business and personal bankruptcies. In fact, according to figures contained in the 1983 and 1984 provincial budgets, bankruptcies in B.C. jumped from 501 in 1981 to more than 1,000 in 1982 and climbed again in 1983 to 1,279. Conversely, new incorporations in B.C., which stood at 23,368 in 1981, sagged to 11,432 in 1982, climbing slightly in 1983. "Provincial restraint programs have dampened economic activity through staff cuts," observed the Conference Board of Canada in February 1984.[10] "Wage restraint has resulted in less spending in other areas of the economy, namely, wholesale and retail trade," said the conservative, privately-funded forecasting group. Ironically, such a situation further erodes investor confidence, the very thing the restraint programme was designed to bolster, thereby indirectly worsening the already severe unemployment problem.

It is impossible to determine the precise amount the government has added to the unemployment rate through direct and indirect disemployment. Since the beginning of the restraint programme in 1982, there has been a net increase of 57,000 people added to the unemployment rolls. We cannot begin to estimate what proportion of this figure is a consequence of restraint. However, given the factors already cited, it is clear that restraint has contributed some significant amount. Even if we take a figure of 15,000 direct layoffs of government workers as a benchmark, it would mean that the programme has exacerbated the unemployment rate by between one and two percentage points, a not inconsiderable increase. Put another way, the 15,000 jobs Bennett's government has eliminated is equivalent to more than a quarter of the net increase in the number of those unemployed. Whatever else proponents of the restraint programme might wish to claim, alleviation of unemployment has not been one of its accomplishments.

Downsizing the Unemployment Problem

Of course, the Bennett government, so quick to boast of other achievements, has been uncharacteristically timid about discussing the unemployment issue. As Pat Marchak comments in Part I on the substance and rhetoric of Social Credit's "new reality", the word *unemployment* is no longer in the government's vocabulary. Further, the emphasis on "restraint" has the effect of *displacing* attention from unemployment, and more particularly, from solutions to unemployment. Although some groups, such as trade unions, recognize that unemployment is an important social problem (perhaps the most important), their voices are drowned out by official propaganda. Many institutions, including the media, have adjusted easily to the new reality of double-digit jobless rates.

The last semi-serious discussion of solutions to unemployment occurred during the 1983 provincial election. The New Democratic Party contenders proposed a $650 million programme to create 90,000 jobs.[11] But this call to work by NDP leader Dave Barrett was promptly lost in the noisy dynamics of the campaign. Late in the race, Barrett made what many subsequently considered to be the fatal mistake of blurting out that should he win, the Social Credit wage restraint programme would be scrapped.[12] The ensuring uproar produced what the defeated NDP called a "scare campaign", but what might more formally be described as a co-ordinated public indoctrination on behalf of the restraint ideology. Premier Bennett called the NDP leader's proposal to end restraint "the most blatant and irresponsible statement of policy I have ever seen" and predicted that unimaginable chaos would follow; the Vancouver *Sun* rushed in to help voters think the unthinkable: "We now know where Mr. Barrett stands on the issue of restraint in government. He would throw open the public purse..." For those slow on the uptake, the *Sun*'s post-election headline drove the lesson home. "Voters spellbound by r-e-s-t-r-a-i-n-t," declared the paper, recalling the Rolaids ad that "spelled relief" for other kinds of indigestion.[13]

When NDP pollsters questioned potential voters in a federal by-election later that summer (after the celebrated July 1983 restraint budget had been brought down), they discovered that the electorate was readily willing to identify unemployment as the number one problem. However, when it came to solutions, the same voters rejected taxpayer-sponsored job creation programmes. This provides one interesting measure of the success with which the restraint ideology has penetrated public consciousness.[14] Of course, this leaves us with a logical and practical dilemma. If our number one problem should not be resolved through government action, as the poll reports, who will provide a solution? Perhaps big business, but it is supposedly mired in recession. Or perhaps the problem is unsolvable and, like an unpleasant illness, is best not discussed. In any case, as the ideology of restraint — daily reinforced by media and political authority figures — is internalized by the public, it has a further function of demobilizing its very victims. Many of those most adversely affected by the programme join the chorus of its implementers, with responses ranging from fatalism to the espousal of further "sacrifice".

Privatizing the Responsibility

The Bennett government's reluctance to discuss unemployment is not a matter of sheer perversity, but rather reflects its theory of capitalist job creation. Five years before the idea of restraint was elevated to programmatic proportions, then-Finance Minister Evan Wolfe spelled out the Social Credit philosophy in his 1978 budget speech: "Government must restrain spending to facilitate private sector growth which will fund our social programs. The long-term thrust of our government therefore is to promote the province's economic future by providing the opportunity and incentive for private sector growth and expansion."[15] On innumerable occasions since then, Premier Bennett has emphasized the private sector's responsibility for job creation. The role of government, in this theory, is limited to "facilitating" conditions: restraining both public spending and borrowing in order not to "crowd out" private investment borrowing; offering tax breaks to corporations; disciplining the workforce through legislative means; discouraging "exorbitant" wage demands through public sector wage restraint; and paying the infrastructural costs for private sector development.

To date, this economic strategy has yielded few tangible results for potential job-seekers. Recognizing that there is a limit to further resource exploitation and a need to diversify the economy, the government is even trying to lure advanced technology — the current panacea to all economic dilemmas — to Lotusland. But in fact, the one concrete proposal to diversify the economy in this way, Dynatek Electronic's plans for a 770-job microchip plant in Victoria, has only produced two years of frustrated expectations. Although the project has been repeatedly hailed as B.C.'s entry into "high tech" production, the solicitous efforts of the Social Credit government, including offers of $11 million in grants and loans from two levels of government, have yet to yield a single integrated circuit. If one goal of restraint is to soften up the workforce for the new "high tech" reality, the government has yet to demonstrate its ability to generate a single job, much less bring this glamorous future into being.

Though the belief that the private sector is the vanguard of job creation is basic to Social Credit philosophy, the premier nonetheless is selective. When the private sector dismally fails to generate jobs (as it has), or when Social Credit is attacked for its financially questionable megaprojects such as Northeast Coal, Expo 86 or rapid transit, then the government which eschews job creation as a proper function of government is quick to pat itself on the back. At such moments it cites, in proudly parental tones, the thousands of days of employment it is providing for everyone from rock and tunnel workers blasting the railroad through mountains, to souvenir hawkers at world fairs. In fact, when Bennett is cornered on the problem of unemployment, he cites these very jobs as proof of his government's commitment to a solution. It does not seem to bother the premier that, on the one hand, he is doggedly attached to the idea of free enterprise as the saviour of the unemployed and, on the other, claims credit for public sector job creation as the sole sign of employment optimism. His is a government hard to embarrass on such slender grounds as logical consistency.

Besides the large net loss of government jobs, there have also been increases in many forms of public employment since the 1983 budget. While some government workers were being fired (or pastured out to "privatization" schemes), other workers were being hired to work on highways and construction projects. Similarly, although teachers were being fired in 1984, builders were being employed with public monies at Expo 86, a project that would also eventually employ thousands of concessions salespeople, groundskeepers and others. Why the government prefers souvenir hawkers to teachers has yet to be revealed, but overall shifts in publicly supported employment tend to be disadvantageous to politically outspoken groups. Teachers and social workers, who have a record of criticizing government programmes and priorities, have fared badly under the restraint programme compared to more quiescent workers such as those in the tourist industry. It might be asked whether the government has selectively manipulated the restraint programme to attack its political opponents. While the evidence is not definitive, Social Credit's lengthy history of political vindictiveness at least makes the theory plausible.

Blaming the Victims

In what is by now an almost classic ideological twist, the government has justified its restraint programme in part by blaming the victims of the recession. Thus, it is not simply the case that capitalist recession has produced widespread unemployment — in the Bennett government's version, it is the workforce itself that is responsible for being out of work. In moralizing tones the premier, pre-empting a spot on prime-time television, has repeatedly pointed out that if only the workers had been less greedy and more productive, we would not be in the present fix. Since, however, the workers persist in childish unruliness (especially those organized in unions, which are sometimes likened to adolescent gangs of vandals), then someone (in this instance, the state) must step in and exercise parental control for everyone's own good.

While the restraint programme has had an undeniable impact on unemployment, its effects on the employed portion of the workforce are no less important. The programme employs a variety of methods to restructure the relations of production, or the conditions under which work is carried out. However diligently the government goes about reducing the income of the disabled and cutting back on social services in general, what is at the heart of its restraint programme is the goal of diminishing the power of labour.

A docile labour force is seen as essential to the strategy of attracting private investment. B.C.'s intransigent workforce, in Social Credit's view, is the chief obstacle to capitalist growth and the resurrection of the economy. The workers, in the government's simplistic perspective, are over-unionized, over-endowed with rights, and overpaid. Consequently, as the functionaries of the government keep chanting, labour is "pricing itself" and the province's products out of the "competitive world market". The draconian measures required to re-enter that market appear to constitute a significant proportion of the "new reality" invoked by the premier. If only B.C. workers could be made to moderate their demands, investment would pour into the province and the very structure of the economy would be favourably altered and diversified: B.C. could become "another Philippines", "another Californian Silicon Valley", or as one trade unionist suggested, "another New Brunswick — a resource-based, cheap labour, high unemployment economy with high rates of profit for a few capitalist families."[16]

The restraint programme has employed diverse methods to achieve such docility. Most directly, legislative means have been used in an attempt to reorder existing relations of production so that employers would have more power to dictate the character of relationships with their workers. The 1983 budgetary and legislative package contained a number of such measures, including a bid to eliminate seniority rights in the public sector and to weaken collective bargaining procedures. While the latter measure was dropped in the face of popular resistance offered by the Solidarity Coalition of trade unions and community groups, the former was enacted into law. Most groups affected by the legislation, however, were ultimately able to negotiate an exemption from seniority elimination — again, largely due to the pressure of political protest. Still, many unions found the obstacle course toward seniority protection was time-consuming, enervating and ultimately only partially successful. Job security had been eroded, albeit to a lesser degree than originally intended by the government.[17]

The 1984 restraint package featured extensive revisions to the B.C. Labour Code. Without reciting the details, their general direction was to make union organizing more difficult, union decertification easier, and to restrict the right of workers to engage in political protest, while centralizing decision-making power in Victoria at the expense of relatively impartial bodies such as the Labour Relations Board. One of the law's more extreme measures gave the government the right to designate particular worksites as "special economic recovery projects" at which the relations of production would be determined at the whim of the government.

A second method of creating a more pliant, investor-attractive workforce has been simply to lower wages. In addition to overt wage restraint legislation, two less direct methods have been utilized. In the field of construction work, lower wages have been achieved by government sponsorship of non-union construction firms, who pay building trades workers an average of $5 per hour less than their union firm counterparts. As one of the province's major employers, disclaimers to the contrary notwithstanding, the government has exercised considerable leverage in helping non-union firms to secure a foothold. However, as subsequent construction labour disputes and protests demonstrated, this course is not without its drawbacks.

Another means of lowering wages has been through privatization of services. While in some cases workers who were formerly in government service have simply been transformed into contracted workers receiving the same wages as before, in other instances unionized government workers have been fired and the services they provided have been contracted out to other workers competitively bidding for the jobs. Ironically, in the latter case, the process has not necessarily produced any savings in public expenditures. The increased costs associated with less efficient workers, and the need to hire additional administrative and supervisory staff, generally offset whatever cost-benefits have been achieved through reduced wages.

Finally, and more generally, the extensive firings have increased job insecurity throughout the workforce, thus tending to create a situation in which it is more possible to exact worker obedience. The spectre of unemployment, viewed by many workers as the ultimate personal catastrophe, often sets up a disposition to accept lower wages, poorer working conditions, and fewer benefits. Furthermore, these sacrifices are often coupled with feelings of gratitude for being "lucky enough to have any job." On the other side of the coin, however, government firings and erosion of workers' rights can boomerang. Lowered morale commonly leads to lower productivity, and worker resentment ultimately leads to an assault on "labour peace", thereby threatening to upset the apple cart of restraint.

Help Wanted

Depictions of the human costs of unemployment have become something of a staple of the daily press, often at the expense of analyses locating the source of the misery.[18] For laid-off workers it is this costly experience that constitutes the "new reality". In even a casual survey intended to garner the cold statistics of the government's failed restraint programme, one encounters the despair of the programme's actual victims. As Mel Lehan, co-ordinator of the Unemployed Teachers Action Centre is pointing out that "the Bennett policies have condemned a lot of dedicated teachers to welfare," a middle-aged woman is weeping a short distance away. "She's taught for years and now she has no choice but welfare," Lehan explains.[19] It is a scene countlessly repeated at B.C. Federation of Labour-sponsored unemployed action centres and in the lineups at the province's numerous food banks, which themselves report a supply crisis.[20] For the laid-off worker the day-to-day structure and rhythm of life falls apart. Work friendships slip away; the sense of doing necessary work erodes along with feelings of self-worth; hours of boredom, aimlessness and depression need filling; the dignity that goes with a decent standard of living and "paying your own way" collapses. As an unemployed man in a food bank lineup recounts to a television interviewer how his circumstances are growing worse and worse, what is shocking is the casual and rational tone in which he offhandedly considers the possibility of suicide.[21]

The combination of such painful human moments and the alarming succession of unemployment figures renders the need for remedy increasingly urgent. Yet the "No Help Wanted" sign seems securely affixed to the entrance of B.C. workplaces. As early as September 1983, almost in the same breath in which it heralded the recovery, the Conference Board of Canada warned that "the best of the current economic recovery may already be over, and the growth in the economy will be sluggish for the rest of the 1980s."[22] By May 1984, the Board had revised its estimate of B.C. growth downward from 2.5% for 1984 to a meagre 0.7%. Unemployment, predicted the Board, would average 14.3% in B.C. in 1984, up from the previous year's 13.8%, even as national unemployment was expected to slightly decline to 11.4%.[23] Given that B.C. unemployment has been running at over 15% for the first half of 1984, the Board's revised prediction of 14.3% may turn out to be optimistic.

Said syndicated economics columnist Don McGillivray in June 1984, "We seem to be within a few months of a new recession...New hiring has almost stopped as companies try to keep staffs small to avoid the spectre of bankruptcy many faced in the 1981-82 recession. After 18 months of 'recovery' the total number of jobs is still about 120,000 less than in mid-1981."[24] As job-seeking students were being told what they already knew — "this summer's student job hunt is even tougher than last" — Statistics Canada reported that the B.C. unemployment rate in

June 1984 rose to 15.7%, the province's highest since the agency began its monthly survey in 1945.[25]

The chief ideologues and advisers associated with the Bennett government might be expected to urge the unemployed to hang in there until the restraint programme generates jobs. Instead, Human Resources Minister Grace McCarthy tells those seeking relief to go to Brandon, Manitoba to find it; B.C. Employers' Council president Jim Matkin suggests military conscription for unemployed youth; and Fraser Institute director Michael Walker, one of the prominent architects of the restraint programme, simply advises, "Go east, young man."[26] Unlike the sometimes insomnia-ridden premier, who in a 1983 "lean, not mean" plea assured British Columbians, "I can tell you from personal experience, no one likes to lay off people," his colleagues and advisers appeared to be sleeping soundly.[27]

Part IV
Services Under Attack

Introduction

WHAT SOCIAL CREDIT *has described as a benign "downsizing" of government has a certain appeal to people who instinctively distrust bureaucracy, especially its tendency to sustain and enlarge its own growth. Reducing the size of government departments and programmes seems a good way to save taxpayers' money and ensure close examination of economic priorities. But things are more complicated. Social Credit may be promising to "get government off our backs," but in fact it is "downsizing" the services that help people get on with their lives.*

The most important (and costly) of these services are in health, education and welfare. They are essential to the quality of our lives — and the productivity of our economy. The government's cutbacks in education and welfare services have been severe, as Warren Magnusson and Monika Langer, Gordon Shrimpton, and Marilyn Callahan show. What is happening in the health care field is a shade less discouraging, and its financing problems cannot

*be made entirely the responsibility of the provincial
government. But the ideal of medicare, of a universally accessible tax-funded health care system, is
certainly being undermined (and likely to be further
undermined) by Social Credit's ideological commitment to privatization. With regard to such ideology,
one need only take a cautionary look at the largely
privatized — and, to many, inaccessible — United
States health care system.*

Some of the cutbacks yield only miniscule monetary relief, and some services are disappearing even
though they are demonstrably cost-effective. Such
cutbacks and programme cancellations are occuring
at the same time as a $806 million budget is slated for
Expo 86 and (worse still) $500,000 is spent on a
public relations exercise boosting Northeast Coal,
amid rumours that this megaproject's only known
customer, Japan, is already seeking a price reduction
of about 25% to bring the B.C. coal into line with
prevailing world prices.

Amid these heavy megaproject expenditures, welfare payments are being reduced and made harder to
get. In a grim parody of its own philosophy of
"privatization", the Social Credit government has
appealed several times to church and charitable
organizations to fill the vacuum left by withdrawn
government assistance. What had come to be
regarded as a human right — minimum subsistence
without affront to personal dignity — is now to be
relegated to the realm of charity, of hand-outs.

But this insulting "solution" cannot work for
long. In Victoria alone in the past year, several
charitable agencies have at one time or another been
cleaned out of resources because of the heavy
demand. One such agency, which for years served
twelve or fifteen clients a day, is now being appealed
to by 100-plus every day. In the first few months of
1984, this agency spent well over $100,000 on its
work. As of June 1 it had a working balance of $6!

In the field of education, where B.C. has long been

the worst-funded province in proportion to per capita income, school boards have over the years made resourceful use of shrinking funds (there has been a drop of approximately 20% in provincial share of school costs since 1976), but nonetheless local autonomy is being reduced in favour of a ministry which has shown itself capable of crass and insensitive policy decisions.

Both in education and welfare, a series of hasty and sometimes ill-considered actions are undermining services without showing evidence that this can be justified even by economic gains.

What are the reasons for it all? Is the objective to be "lean, but not mean," as Premier Bennett claims? Does less government necessarily mean more freedom? Not if you are poor and left to the mercies of the "free market"; not if you are sick and cannot afford the necessary health care "co-payments"; not if the quality of your education leaves you unqualified for the few promising job opportunities likely to arise in a province with an unemployment rate of 15.6%. Then what are the reasons for "restraint", B.C. Social Credit version? We would do well to take a long hard look at that question; most of us do not stand to benefit from the government's answers.

Medicare at Risk
William K. Carroll, Charles Doyle and Noel Schacter

A GLANCE AT the 1984 B.C. provincial budget leaves the impression that health care has been spared from Social Credit austerity. Finance Minister Hugh Curtis claims to have treated health care "most generously",[1] increasing its budget by 2% while other services continue to be substantially cut back. The government's largesse in this regard must, of course be, measured against an inflation rate hovering around 5%, and an even higher rate of price increases within the health care sector.

There seem to be two main reasons for the government's apparent moderation. First, since its introduction, the Canadian system of publicly funded health care has been one whose basic premises apply to all provinces and territories. Under the Medical Care Act (1966), funding is shared by federal and provincial governments on the understanding that each province will maintain a system that is (1) available to every resident; (2) comprehensive in services; (3) accessible to all insured persons; (4)

portable from province to province; and (5) admin-istered on a non-profit basis.[2] The obligation to abide by the programme's five premises has limited each province's ability to dismantle the system to suit budgetary or ideological preferences.

A second, and more cynical reason for Social Credit's apparent moderation may be read in Health Minister Jim Nielson's observation that "no one wants to go on record as being against motherhood and medicare"[3] — least of all, we might add, poli-ticians manoeuvring for re-election. Medicare has proved to be an extremely popular programme which few Canadians would wish to see eliminated. In short, the constraints of federal-provincial arrange-ments appear to have coincided with a certain political acumen to temper the government's "restraint" on health care.

But behind the reassurance that health care remains "our most essential service"[4] are ominous pointers to what Social Credit plans for our health care system. In the Canada Health Act (April 1984), the federal government has attempted to save medicare by penalizing provinces which apply user fees. B.C. Health Minister Nielson responded that the province would seek "ways around the stupid act." Such an attitude could have been anticipated by anyone familiar with the province's 1983 budget, with its hints of a Social Credit health care strategy: first, in the stated commitment to privatization generally; second, in the presentation of budget figures to make it appear that public health costs are rising beyond reasonable bounds; third, in raising the specific question of "user fees" by announcing that "health co-insurance charges" would be increased in September 1983.

What all this amounts to is a policy of increasing "privatization" of medical services, an undermining of the universal medicare system established in 1968, and the danger of moving back a considerable distance toward pre-1957 conditions of health care, lowering quality and narrowing accessibility.

What would be sacrificed in such a move? A good indication is given in the federal health services review *Canada's National-Provincial Health Services Program for the 1980s*. Commissioned by the federal government and written by Emmett Hall, the judge whose report in the 1960s laid the foundations of medicare, the review found that individuals, organizations, medical professionals, and governments, all favoured medicare.[5] It found also that Canadian health services today, though not free of "serious difficulties", are among "the very best" in the world.

Before Canada's two-stage adoption of a national health insurance programme (provincial hospital insurance and, later, provincial insurance for doctors' services) the standard of care depended on the individual's ability to pay, with some charity medical services available for low-income families. Prior to medicare fewer than 40% of Canadians had private health insurance protection. "For all but the most affluent, a serious illness — especially one that required a lengthy stay in hospital — could be a passport to destitution."[6] Even Canadians fortunate enough to have some form of health insurance were not fully protected against hospital and medical expenses. Private health insurance resembled automobile insurance plans: patients were required to pay an initial fixed amount out of pocket before the insurance plan took over, and if too many claims were made premium rates would go up.[7] The most intolerable contradiction of this system of "cash-register medicine" was that those who faced the highest health risks — the poor, the elderly, the chronically ill — could least afford health care.[8] The great achievement of medicare was a health care system organized around human needs, not purchasing power.

Its very principles, however, have been jeopardized

by recent government policy in B.C. and elsewhere. The threat to medicare has taken several forms, including budget cutbacks and the privatization of health care through user fees and for-profit care facilities.

A Problem of Rising Costs?

In the 1983 budget Finance Minister Hugh Curtis lamented the fact that allocations to health care had risen from 24.2% of total provincial government expenditure in 1976/77 to 29%, leaving the impression that medicare costs have gotten seriously out of hand. Yet just the opposite is true. When health care costs are assessed as a percentage of the total value of goods and services produced in the economy — the Gross National Product — the cost of Canada's health care system is actually lower than in other western countries. Since public insurance programmes were introduced in Canada, health care costs have been a stable proportion of GNP, between 7% and 7½%. B.C. costs, although they have risen somewhat more steeply, are within this range.[9] In comparison, Sweden and Australia spend 8% of GNP on health care, while in West Germany the proportion is 9%.

The United States — the only major western country without public health insurance — furnishes a revealing contrast to Canadian medicare. Before the introduction of medicare, total health expenditures in Canada formed a slightly higher fraction of GNP than expenditures in the U.S..[10] By 1981 U.S. health care spending had risen above 9% of GNP, while Canadian spending remained in the range of 7 to 7½%, demonstrating quite clearly that "public funding of health care does not lead to cost escalation."[11] Not only is medicare a fairer and more accessible system than the private form of health care that prevails in the U.S., "the Canadian form of funding — universal, comprehensive, and public insurance — has made cost control possible.''[12] By implication, increasing privatization of the health care delivery system in B.C. can be expected to bring diminished accessibility and higher costs.

The Threat of Privatization

Any public health care system can be gradually privatized in two main ways: first, by shifting the source of its funding from general taxes to private fees for service; second, by shifting services from public, community-oriented organizations to for-profit establishments. Although the basic structure of medicare remains intact in B.C., both these forms of privatization are evident in recent government policies.

Originally medicare was intended to be tax-funded, and direct personal payments for health care were supposed to be eliminated. But B.C. has long been one of a minority of provinces which charge monthly premiums. At family level, B.C. levies the second-highest premiums after Ontario (in 1982 the full rate for a family of four was $385 per year). B.C. is also the only province which charges premiums to the elderly.[13] Low-income individuals and families can apply for lower premium payments, but — largely because they don't know this — many who are eligible do not do so. In any event, when premiums were raised in September 1983, subsidies for low income people were not raised to nearly the same extent, worsening the burden on the poor. Because of the premiums system alone, lower-income residents of B.C. pay more for health care than their counterparts in most other provinces.

More controversial still are the "user fees", in effect a form of privatization. In its 1982 report, *Medicare: the Public Good and Private Practice*, the National Council of Welfare called user fees "the

Achilles heel of our health care system."[14]   Emmett Hall also rejects user fees: "this policy and practice of imposing hospital ward charges is an application of the 'user pay' concept which is contrary to the principle and spirit of the *National Health Program* advocated by the Royal Commission in 1964 and legislated into being by the Medical Care Act of 1966."[15]

An excuse offered for user fees is that most people must be reminded of the costs of medical care or else they will abuse it. Yet an extensive international review of the effects of user fees concludes that *"There is no evidence that copayment results in substantial decline in the unnecessary use of hospital and medical services."*[16] This finding is not surprising. Use of most medical services is under the control of doctors and medical authorities rather than potential patients. Moreover, people do not consume medical services as they do other commodities. Few people would *choose* to be "sick" as a pastime or in an attempt to get a "free" benefit. In the final analysis, user fees act not as a deterrent against abuse of medicare, but as "a regressive tax on the sick."[17]

Though among the highest in Canada, user fees in B.C. are relatively small (and therefore their immediate effect is likely to be on the poorest families), but they are increasing and are likely to increase further. Since 1981 user fees for long-term care residents, to take one example, have grown by 56% (from $8.50 to $13.25 per day). Pensioners' incomes in the same period have increased by only 26%. The present user fee thus represents 80% of a minimum pension. B.C. applies user fees more than any other province,[18] yet as long ago as 1977 the federal Parliamentary Task Force on Federal-Provincial Fiscal Arrangements urged that they be stopped, stating, "User charges that are high enough to serve as deterrents, deter the wrong people, the old and the poor, while user charges that are low enough to be acceptable on distributional grounds are too low to be worth collecting."

In contrast to regular income taxation, both premiums and user fees are regressive methods of charging for health care. Yet another such method has been recently introduced in the Health Care Maintenance Tax Act (Bill 2), seemingly in the form of two taxes, one of which is described in the 1984 budget as an income surtax necessitated by "federal underfunding". However, UBC economist Robert Evans, in his recent paper "Hiding Behind Medicare", notes that "The Health Care Maintenance tax is in no way earmarked for health, but will instead flow directly into general revenue." Evans maintains that in light of Social Credit's record of dubious investments in money-losing megaprojects and the like, this surcharge could be more accurately labelled a Northeast Coal or B.C. Railway tax.

The second tax was intended to be a single tax based on family size and collected through the federal tax system. The ostensible purpose of this tax was to provide funds "in an amount equal to the federal penalty" for continuing user fees.[19] The intention of Bill 2 appears to be — like the imposition of user fees themselves — to support Social Credit's "free market", "pay-as-you-go" ideology. If so, it may be seen as making political capital out of people's sickness.

Although user fees raise the spectre of privatization and of limiting accessibility of medical care, the threat they pose is minor compared to the growing practice of for-profit medical services. Again in this respect, B.C. is not unique but seems to be following the pattern of Ontario and other provinces, where large multinational corporations such as Extendicare and American Medical International, as well as smaller, local companies, have been taking over management of debt-burdened hospitals. These arrangements are in clear violation of the Medical Care Act, which requires non-profit health care administration.[20]

The attraction of for-profit facilities lies in their

offer to provide inexpensive but adequate service at a profit to the providers, due to their managerial expertise. Yet "their chief ways of making money are by reducing staff, keeping the wages of hospital workers down, overusing and overcharging for special services, and turning away patients with low incomes or 'unprofitable' diseases," according to one study.[21] The implications of this sort of "expertise" in health care administration are illustrated in a 1981 survey of hospital workers at 82 long-term care facilities in B.C., and a 1984 follow-up study of four facilities. According to both reports, for-profit care units provide lower-quality service than their non-profit counterparts across a whole array of areas such as physical health, emotional well-being, and safety. Further, the private facilities surveyed tended to be run less efficiently than the nonprofit units; indeed in some cases they delivered lower-quality service at a higher cost.[22]

The Burden of "Restraint"

Privatization is not the only threat to the quality of health care service in British Columbia. Budgetary pressure on hospitals and funding cuts to community-oriented and preventive medical services have been gradually taking their toll over the past few years. In 1982 government cutbacks created an $84 million shortfall in hospital budgets. Simultaneously, the longstanding government practice of covering hospital deficits was abolished. Hospitals were forced to make drastic adjustments. By March 1983, 93 acute-care hospitals had closed 1,228 beds and eliminated over 3,000 staff positions;[23] and 53 hospitals had introduced user fees for non-emergency use of their emergency departments. The Public Commission on Social and Community Service Cutbacks, which was holding province-wide hearings at the time, gave the following description:

Every day brought more news of beds being closed, operating rooms being shut down, specialized programs and diagnostic services limited, patients being turned away from emergency wards, even deaths occurring as a result of budget restraints.[24]

Since that time some beds have been restored and positions refilled, but budgetary "restraint" continues to be the order of the day. At the University of B.C.'s Health Sciences Centre, 52 beds and 44 positions were eliminated in 1983 alone; at Victoria's Royal Jubilee Hospital another 19 full-time equivalent positions will disappear in 1984.

Funding reductions to community health clinics are also worrisome. Recently the James Bay Health Clinic in Victoria had its provincial grant cut by 27%. Community control of this integrated health and human resource centre is presently being abolished, and the Ministry of Health is taking over. This is both a move toward centralized control and a reduction of democratic participation. The Reach Clinic in Vancouver's East End has been likewise hit with a 29% reduction and told that the government will no longer cover the costs of salaried physicians employed there; doctors will now be paid on the basis of a fee per insured patient treated. This has effectively eliminated access to the clinic for many of its 8,000 patients who, because they are recent immigrants or are impoverished but not on the welfare rolls, remain uninsured by the Medical Services Plan.

Centres such as these are for the present continuing to function but with a narrowing range of services, particularly in the area of preventive medicine. Nutrition, health education, and counselling programmes are being curtailed as clinics direct their diminishing resources to the most pressing health problems. The elimination of grants to community-oriented services such as Planned Parenthood and the Vancouver Women's Health Collective have similar implications.

In the meantime, in another area of health-care, the government's recent initiatives concerning the Workers' Compensation Board are cause for immediate concern. Mandated to prevent work-related injuries and to care for injured workers, the WCB was the subject of legitimate criticism for some of its practices and decisions even before Social Credit brought in "restraint".[25] Since December 1983 matters have taken a sharp turn for the worse. In that month the government appointed as WCB chairman Walter Flesher, a former corporate lawyer whose previous experience in health and safety was confined to helping employers appeal WCB decisions. Flesher in turn appointed Bill Greer, formerly the employers' council safety officer, as executive director of the WCB's industrial health and safety department.[26]

This tilt toward a corporate-minded adminstration was matched in January when employers' assessment rates for 1984 were frozen at the 1983 level. To defray the costs of this bonus to employers, Flesher eliminated more than 40 staff positions in the WCB claims and accident prevention departments and closed entirely the Prince Rupert regional office.[27]

Finally, in the crucial area of accident prevention, the WCB has recently shelved proposed safety regulations for farmworkers and abolished two of its safety inspection sections, including the hearing branch which monitored noise levels on the job and aided workers afflicted with hearing loss.[28]

The "restraint" policies actually free employers to neglect on-the-job safety in favour of lowered production costs and higher profits. Like so much of Social Credit's austerity programme, the long-term effects of these measures will in all likelihood *increase* costs (of both workers' compensation and medical care) while creating unnecessary hardship for the victims of "restraint".

Conclusion

Contrary to Social Credit's claims, health care has been seriously cut back.[29] Reckoned in constant dollars, there has been a net decrease of at least 3% in health ministry expenditures (1% should also be deducted to take into account population growth). This shortfall in funding has already resulted in the closing of hospital beds and community-based health facilities, and in the laying off of many health care workers.

The major justification for cutting back health care has been the claim that costs have increased dramatically over the past decade — with the implication that increases have been too great. But as we have seen, health care costs are not increasing as a percentage of our total economic output, which is the most realistic yardstick for measuring health care costs because it reflects our ability to pay.

While health care expenditures are being reduced, British Columbians are paying more than ever before in "health care" taxes. The amount of health care money made available for other purposes when the government increases health revenues while decreasing expenditures is not small: $100 million is being "saved" by their not bothering to keep pace with inflation and population growth, and the new Health Care Maintenance Tax will pump $91 million into general revenues this fiscal year and $166 million next year.

What is happening to this money? Under a guise of "restraint", the Social Credit government has chosen to take money intended for health care and use it to finance its megaprojects. What has falsely been labelled "restraint" is more accurately described as redistribution. The majority of British Columbians are losing valuable health care services and decent job opportunities in medical care while employers and investors have their profits subsidized through government expenditures.

Given this government's preoccupation with helping the private sector, they probably consider health care expenditures too high simply because the money could be used to help profit-hungry industries. Seen from this viewpoint it is easy to understand why the new Canada Health Act would anger B.C. Health Minister Jim Nielson, because it restricts the fiscal flexibility required for redistribution. True medicare,[30] with its commitment to universal accessibility, cannot allow for user fees or extra-billing and thus becomes a threat to Social Credit's reverse-Robin Hood philosophy.

Because the population as a whole is growing older, medical care demands will continue to grow in the coming decades. This trend will create further fiscal pressure: tax dollars will be required for health care, reducing the potential for government subsidy of the private sector. Faced with this fiscal dilemma and a conservative-minded government in Ottawa, Social Credit may see the destruction of medicare as a realistic long-run goal. Continued underfunding of health care may well be coupled with increased reliance upon fee-for-service payments and privatization of services.

Far from a return to the bad old days of cash-register medicine, what is needed is a strengthening of medicare and a return to full commitment to its basic principles.

In fact, medicare should be broader. Its major deficiency is its prevailing narrow concept of personal health as a private affair. Overlooked is the fact that large numbers of people seeking health care suffer from diseases which originate in whole or in part in environmental and working conditions: over-processed or under-nutritive foods, industrial accidents, environmental pollution, etc.[31] More needs to be done to eradicate the conditions which contribute to disease, and preventive medicine should be developed and applied. The fairest and most efficient way of tackling these problems is through social planning and co-operation. Matters of such widespread consequence cannot be left to the vagaries of the profit-oriented "free" market.

The Human Costs of "Restraint"
Marilyn Callahan

IN JULY 1983, the Ministry of Human Resources fired 599 of its regular full-time staff and eliminated or reduced several programmes. Almost 90% of the dismissed staff worked directly with children. They included child care counsellors who assisted children with emotional and social problems in school, youth workers who worked primarily in downtown Vancouver with runaways and prostitutes, family support workers who provided counselling and direct assistance to families and children in crisis, the child abuse team which provided consultation to field staff involved in complex cases (frequently regarding sexual abuse), and the 165 staff of more than twenty Lower Mainland group homes and treatment centres for children unsuitable for foster care.

Other cutbacks are slated for 1984/85. Budget estimates indicate a further reduction of 515 full-time staff. Given the decrease in estimated expenditures in the Direct Community Services portion of the budget (from $113 million in 1983/84 down to $97 million in

1984/85) it appears that this staff reduction will take place throughout the province in community offices which deliver family and income services. Although the funds to foster-homes, child care resources and institutions have increased by $6 million, the allocation to voluntary agencies which provide some of the preventive services for families has decreased by $1 million.

Because some of the fired staff will be redeployed in other programmes in the ministry, and some programmes will be transferred to individuals, corporations, or non-profit societies funded in whole or in part by Human Resources, it is very hard to estimate how much money will be saved by these changes. However, in announcing the initial cuts in 1983, Human Resources Minister Grace McCarthy suggested that $16 million a year would be saved. This is a small fraction — less than 2% — of an overall budget of $822 million, but a much larger slice — 16% — of the Family and Children's portion of $102 million.

In the income maintenance program (GAIN*), cutbacks include a freeze on welfare rates for all recipients and a reduction in rates for some people under 25 years. The effects of the welfare freeze on families and children are obvious. The government expects that re-introduction of age categories, a system eliminated in 1982 after complaints from several sources including the provincial Ombudsman, will encourage young people "to relocate for jobs and turn to their families for help." Single persons and childless couples under 25 will receive $25 less per month than other individuals and, unlike some

* GAIN — Guaranteed Annual Income for Need — provides income for the unemployed, those who are unable to work, handicapped adults, and the elderly. You qualify for GAIN by applying to the local Human Resources office; you must meet qualifications that differ according to age and abilities. Although GAIN is a provincial programme, the federal government pays half the costs.

other recipients, will be unable to retain any portion of the money they may earn while on GAIN. Clearly, those most affected by these policies will be unemployed young people with limited job skills and limited family resources. Ironically, when these cutbacks were made, unemployment rates for young people were rising to consistent levels of 25% to 30%.

B.C.'s welfare system is one of Canada's most complicated. With the introduction of yet another category of persons with different rates, there are now 23 separate categories for a two-person family. Welfare payments for most of these range from $570 to $1,001 a month. These categories represent a series of judgements about who deserves government assistance and who does not, and they bear little relationship to the actual living expenses of the people involved.

The ministry has taken other unprecedented measures to restrict eligibility for GAIN. The number of people awaiting unemployment insurance who might qualify for GAIN has been reduced by the new hardship policy. Prior to the changes, those waiting for UIC payments to begin could receive a half-month's GAIN allowance — or more, if their UIC was delayed. B.C. and Ottawa have a long-standing dispute over this issue, but the casualties are the individual recipients rather than the governments. Those awaiting UIC cheques in B.C. will now have to exhaust every possible resource: family, friends, assets, and even potential assets such as credit, before qualifying for a small portion of the GAIN allowance. No other welfare law in Canada insists that applicants must use all available credit before qualifying for benefits. To require that persons undertake debts which they may not be able to repay is unfair to creditors as well as recipients and seriously undermines the purpose of GAIN (which after all stands for Guaranteed Available Income for *Need*).

Probably the most puzzling change relates to

earnings exemptions. People on GAIN have been able to retain some earnings without a reduction in their monthly rate: $50 for singles, $100 for families. These figures have remained the same for years, and the government has stated frequently that this policy provides an incentive for persons on GAIN to find casual jobs. But now, recipients will qualify for this exemption only when they have received GAIN for eight consecutive months: all others will have any earnings taken off their GAIN cheques. Welfare recipients may be ill-advised to accept part-time work, particularly if expenses such as transportation, clothing or childcare are involved. They may also be reluctant to take short-term jobs and return to GAIN in a few months, because they would have to wait a further eight months for an earnings exemption. This policy may cost many more dollars than it saves.

Effects of Cutbacks

In summary, B.C. has taken four approaches to cutting social services and income programmes: eliminating some; transferring others to voluntary or profit-making organizations; tightening up the eligibility requirements; and reducing benefits. At least 115,500, or 14%, of all children in B.C. are directly affected by these changes. These are children in families on welfare; children in foster homes, group homes or institutions; or children with physical or mental handicaps whose families need extra help to care for them. In fact, this is probably a conservative estimate; it doesn't include those children and families who receive assistance from the 127 family service, crisis line and youth projects funded in whole or in part by Human Resources. What is likely to happen to these children?

1. *The numbers of children coming into care will probably increase.* According to the latest annual report from the Ministry of Human Resources, the

number of reported cases of child abuse in B.C. has risen from 987 cases of probable abuse in 1980 to 1,536 in 1982. Fewer child welfare workers will mean fewer and more superficial investigations of these complaints. The choices for workers when children are in need of care are greatly reduced. In some communities, there will be few options other than removing children from their homes.

2. *Seriously neglected or abused children are more likely to receive inadequate attention or none at all.* Fewer workers means a slower response to complaints. The recent case of 13-month-old Deirdre Bohnenkamp of Cranbrook is an example. In her short lifetime, Deirdre was severely abused physically and sexually. In spite of complaints, ministry staff were unable to offer help soon enough to prevent her death. Occasional tragedies are unavoidable. However, if their frequency increases, social workers will feel pressure to remove children from their homes even if they don't appear to be in immediate danger and in spite of the painful consequences of separation for the children and their families. In addition to there being fewer workers in Ministry of Human Resources offices, some of the remaining workers will have limited experience in child abuse and neglect and will not have the support and guidance of child abuse teams. Because of "bumping procedures", several social work positions have recently been filled by persons without formal training or experience in social work. These replacements have included nutritionists, financial workers and others.

3. *Children will remain in care for longer periods.* In spite of laws that require child protection hearings to start within 45 days of the child's separation from his or her family, in some communities it takes eight or nine months. More cases will result in an even longer backlog in court schedules. Children often remain in receiving homes or foster homes during this time. Moreover, the combination of fewer staff with less training and experience in family work, and

of families with more severe problems, will result in fewer reconciliations. The longer family members remain separated, the less likely it is that they will reunite.

4. *Pressures on Ministry of Human Resources staff will greatly increase.* In some ministry offices in rural communities, staff has been reduced by 50% with the loss of family support workers. In addition to cancellation of the child abuse teams, the staff development programme has been drastically reduced, leaving workers with fewer resources for consultation and skill development. Workers will be under conflicting pressures: on the one hand they will have few options besides removing children from their families and on the other hand circumstances will be pressuring them to avoid apprehensions.

5. *Child welfare services will vary greatly in accessibility and quality throughout the province.* In announcing the cutbacks, Grace McCarthy said she expects churches and voluntary organizations to provide the necessary services to families and children. A number of organizations already exist to assist families: for single parents, sexual abuse victims, handicapped children, teenagers, and so forth. The strength of these services is their capacity to respond flexibly and immediately to needs and to provide services less expensively than government. However, most services in such organizations are provided by volunteers and they are often unprepared to deal with serious emotional or family difficulties. The programmes "transferred" to the voluntary sector were those for children already in government care, many of whom require professional services. Voluntary organizations can rarely afford salaries for professionals. Furthermore, and particularly in rural or economically depressed areas, many communities cannot provide a full range of voluntary services for families.

An effective child welfare system is one that creates a strong partnership between voluntary and government services. In Ontario, for example, where Childrens' Aid Societies deliver all child welfare programmes, the government has maintained a major role in funding, planning and evaluating services. In contrast, at the point when the B.C. government should be taking an active role in stimulating the development of quality voluntary services, particularly in rural communities, field staff here have been greatly reduced and those remaining have limited responsibility for working with voluntary organizations. Family and childrens' co-ordinators in each region who might have undertaken such tasks have been fired.

Human Resources has also transferred some child welfare services to individuals and corporations who intend to make a profit providing such services. When this has happened in other areas of care such as nursing homes and psychiatric programmes, a predictable series of events has occurred. Entrepreneurs have started out to provide a reasonable level of service and yet make a profit. But these two objectives are often contradictory and the result is increasing user fees and/or a declining quality of service. For example, some private psychiatric services cost $200 per day. Only the very rich, or children in government care, can afford them.

Services in the profit-making sector could remain accountable and competitive if a large section of the public used them; this is true for human services as well as for hamburgers. But when the services are provided for a relatively small number of powerless consumers — in this case children and families in crisis — low-quality services will remain virtually unnoticed and tolerated as long as cost and user fees are not too high. If, on the other hand, services reach a sufficiently low level, the government would be forced to develop standards, hire inspectors and, as is not infrequently the case, to assume full control of the services. This is a very expensive way to get back to square one.

6. *The public attitude toward children and families in crisis may change.* As a result of recent policy changes, many members of the general public may come to accept the proposition that families should care for their own children and that most have the resources to do so. Golding calls this shift "domestication of the social services," adding: "The caring professions and the services they provide are seen as an unnecessary state appropriation of the proper functions of the home and family."[1] More attempts may be made to discourage women from working outside the home, not just as a means to curb unemployment but also to reduce social service expenditures.

On the other hand, more community members will be involved in child welfare organizations and will realize the need for adequate preventive services for children and families. They may form much-needed lobby groups to advocate improved funding and service.

7. *Costs for children in care will rise.* More children in care for greater lengths of time and with fewer local resources will lead to increasing costs in the Family and Childrens' Services category of the budget. As noted, this category (which includes foster homes and institutions) was the only one where the budget increased for 1984/85. Although B.C. appears to spend less than other provinces on child welfare, it would be unfortunate to increase spending only in the child welfare services which least benefit children. Several eliminated programmes in the child welfare area were cost-effective. For example, foster care costs $3,600 to $7,200 a year per child, depending upon age and behaviour. The eliminated Family Support Worker programme, designed to assist families to care for their own children, cost only $1,000 to $1,250 a year per child.[2]

8. *B.C. will fall further behind other provinces in terms of overall performance in child welfare.* Prior to cutbacks, B.C. had an improving but nonetheless

dismal record in child welfare. B.C. has had a consistently higher percentage of children in foster or institutional care than any other province except Quebec, Newfoundland and the Northwest Territories.* The difference is substantial. Ontario, Prince Edward Island and Nova Scotia have one half the rate of children in care that B.C. has. The remaining provinces have 30% to 40% less.[3] Comparing B.C. and Ontario shows that once in government care, B.C. children stay there longer.[4]

Many factors besides the functioning of the child welfare system can account for the percentage of children in care. Some provinces may have higher percentages of poor families, or they may simply have a higher proportion of young people in their populations. But there is no evidence that B.C. has a disproportionate number of poor or young people. A study by the National Council of Welfare concludes that, along with Ontario and the Yukon Territories, B.C. has the lowest percentage of children living in poverty.[5] The 1981 census also shows that preschoolers and adolescents — groups especially likely to come into contact with the system — form a smaller percentage of all children in B.C. than in any other province. The facts simply do not support the explanation that B.C. has more children in government care because we have, as a province, more vulnerable children.[6]

A more convincing explanation for problems in the B.C. child welfare system is the system itself. Even before cutbacks, B.C. spent considerably less money per child receiving government welfare services than did other provinces. For example, when we compare B.C. expenditures on child welfare with those of two provinces with similar reporting systems we find that

---

* The stated goal of every child welfare system in the country is to reunite children with their families. Therefore a high rate of children in care indicates a low rate of success in this goal.

B.C.'s record prior to cutbacks was about a third lower than either Ontario or Manitoba.[7]

Comparative examination of the federal government's share of child welfare expenditures in each province is most revealing. For example, Ron Yzerman, the Director of Welfare Services, Health and Welfare Canada, stated recently that although Alberta (for example) had about 3,000 fewer children in care than B.C. in 1981-82, it received over $10 million more from the Canada Assistance plan funds.[8] Because Ottawa matches provincial spending dollar for dollar, this means Alberta spent more on child welfare than B.C. did.

Reasons for Cutbacks

Government officials have stated that cost savings were the major reasons for the cutbacks. However, programmes eliminated or shifted to voluntary or profit-making organizations had several characteristics in common.

1. *Eliminated programmes were labour-intensive.* The Family Support Programme, the most important one abolished, provided skilled counselling for a relatively few children and families in serious crisis. A Family Support worker spent three to four hours a week with a family, in contrast to social workers who usually visit children in foster homes once a month at best. Moreover, Family Support Workers carried small caseloads — about eight to ten — whereas social workers can carry 40 to 50 families. Like Family Support Workers, street workers, home aides and group home workers dealt with a relatively small number of clients.

2. *They encouraged professional autonomy.* Much work in these programmes was carried out in one-to-one private sessions, usually away from the office and frequently after office hours. No doubt

this conflicted with the increasing demand for "accountability" at all levels of government.

3. *They lacked a powerful constituency.* Their relatively small numbers and the highly sensitive nature of their problems make it unlikely that children and families in crisis could or would take political action on their own behalf. Most policymakers in child welfare are far removed in age, economic status and social experience from the families and children involved in these services. Professionals who lobby on behalf of their clients can appear self-protective. At the same time, voluntary family agencies risk retribution if they vigorously oppose the policies of the government which funds them. Finally, the public is generally unconcerned about child welfare matters unless a poignant case is highlighted in the media.

4. *They were recently developed.* All the abolished child welfare programmes had been introduced within the last decade and did not have enough time to demonstrate their effectiveness or establish themselves firmly in the power structure of Human Resources. With the exception of the child abuse teams, where highly experienced child welfare workers competed for positions, workers in these programmes usually had less seniority than other staff.

5. *They lacked a firm legislative mandate.* Unlike other programmes where eligibility is clearly defined by law, the eliminated services were *authorized* under the GAIN Act, but there was no *requirement* that they be provided. Unlike financial assistance programmes, there is usually no appeal if an applicant is turned down for these services.

In announcing the cuts, McCarthy stated: "Social workers, financial assistance workers and clerical staff will continue to provide the basic social services, financial services and child protection services required by statute in British Columbia." But it is misleading to imply, as McCarthy does, that the eliminated programmes were not fundamental child welfare services. All other provinces identify these services in their child welfare legislation, and three jurisdictions (New Brunswick, Yukon and Quebec) require that these services should be provided, if possible, prior to any apprehension of the children. The eliminated B.C. programmes were, however, different from those required in B.C. by statute: they were designed for families at risk of family breakdown but nonetheless still together as a family (or for children coping, at least marginally, on their own).

The cancelled programmes were those which would save maximum amounts of government staff salaries and yet involved a minimum degree of legislative and organizational complication. In selecting the programmes it did for cutbacks, the government was able without creating a major public uproar to make another statement about its commitment to a philosophy of individual responsibility. This time, the individuals expected to be responsible for themselves are poor families, abandoned and neglected children, and those with special needs or disabilities. Throughout the process, the power of professional workers has been severely reduced.

Some Suggestions for Improving Child Welfare

A government genuinely concerned about fiscal responsibility and quality services to children and families could have made other choices:

1. *Eliminate services in Human Resources which overlap with the functions of other ministries.* The ministry inspectors who investigate possible welfare fraud and help staff prevent such situations would be more appropriately transferred to the Ministry of Finance or the Attorney-General's office. This would enable them to deal with similar matters in other ministries. In 1981/82 Human Resources spent $845,076 on the ministry inspectors programme. An

integrated service responsible for monitoring abuse in several ministries would probably be cheaper. Similarly, it would make sense to transfer the employment-related programmes of the Human Resources Ministry to the Ministry of Labour.

2. *Institute new programmes and redesign present ones to reduce the number of children requiring foster or institutional care.* After reviewing hundreds of family support programmes to evaluate their effectiveness, the authors of a major Canadian study conclude that helping families in crisis involves offering a range of services from one-to-one counselling to concrete help, informal community programmes and parent training. The Family Support Worker programme in B.C. tended to focus on short-term intensive counselling and practical assistance to families on a case-by-case basis. Rather than discontinuing the programme, the ministry could have redeployed some Family Support Workers to develop self-help groups and informal supports in communities with high rates of child abuse. For example, workers could have developed a corps of volunteer home-visitors to visit regularly with troubled families to provide encouragement and training. In an Ontario project of this kind, the use of lay visitors resulted in reduction in violence in families and in no repeated cases of serious abuse. Parents in Crisis, a self-help organization for abusive parents, has chapters in only a few communities in B.C. Family support workers could have organized others.

One area where a community support approach is essential is with Native Indians living on reserves. In B.C., there are several examples of possible programmes. With the support of Human Resources staff, the Stoney Creek band south of Vanderhoof has developed a child welfare committee which reviews cases of potential family concerns prior to apprehension and tries to develop alternative care plans on the reserve. Apprehensions have decreased markedly since the programme's inception. In the

Okanagan, the Spallumcheen band has undertaken
to deliver its own child welfare services on the
reserve.[10] To reduce the disproportionate number of
Native Indian children in care, it is essential to
develop similar strategies throughout the province.
Funds and staff allocated by Human Resources to
work in partnership with Native People would be a
sound measure. Manitoba and Saskatchewan have
fewer Native Indian children in care, very likely
because of their pioneer work in such programmes.[11]

3. *Eliminate programmes in other ministries which
serve more advantaged children and families.* The
Ministry of Education provides $16 million to
separate (i.e., private) schools in B.C., which is the
precise amount of savings from cutbacks to family
and children's services in Human Resources. This
figure is increased to $22 million in the 1984/85
budget. All taxpayers have the right to send their
children to private schools but they do so voluntarily
and have no right to be subsidized by the taxpayer. It
is ironic that a government which professes to
promote rugged individualism gives aid to the wealthy
but denies basic services to children of lower income
groups.

These are some alternatives which could have been
chosen within a few ministries serving children.
However, other more fundamental choices must be
examined. There is widespread belief that funds
directed to economic projects will reap future economic benefits for all citizens, whereas spending on
children, particularly disadvantaged ones, merely
produces ungrateful and less-motivated young people
and the prospect of more such spending in future.
Faith in economic engineering far exceeds faith in
creating social change. Even during buoyant economic times, B.C. had an undistinguished record of
funding child welfare services. Just as our record
began to improve, programmes which appeared to be
responsible for the improvement were eliminated.
Even if cost savings were the primary motive, it

would be difficult to mount a case for these eliminations. Instead, supposed fiscal responsibility was put forward to cloud the real reasons for the cutbacks: the lack of value the government places on children and families who need help to survive in an increasingly complex and unresponsive society.

This chapter has examined changes in one area of child welfare — policies and services for children and families in crisis. Many other changes affecting children have occurred in other ministries: in elementary and secondary school funding, in family planning services, in summer works programmes, student loans and legal aid. These new policies may well produce a generation of young people who have been excluded from the opportunities necessary for their development into full human beings and productive citizens. Need anyone be surprised if these young people have little faith that such inequities can be redressed by the political process?

The "New Reality" in Education
Warren Magnusson and Monika Langer

MANY WERE startled when most of the province's teachers joined in the November 1983 job action to protest the government's "restraint" policies. The teachers had always been denied the right to strike, and they risked being fired by absenting themselves from work. Nevertheless, almost 60% of them had voted in favour of the job action, and about 90% stayed out when the time came. Like other workers in the public sector, the teachers were threatened by Bill 3's provisions for arbitrary dismissal and by Bill 11's public sector wage controls. More fundamental to the teachers, however, was the government's threat to the public school system itself — a threat that had become apparent in early 1982 and that had been intensified by the measures in the July 1983 package.

In its six-point list of objectives for the job action, the B.C. Teachers' Federation called not only for a restoration of collective bargaining rights and a return to fair lay-off procedures, but also for the maintenance of school services at present levels until

1986, a halt to the centralization of educational decision-making, guarantees of access to post-secondary education for all qualified students, and the "restoration of social, democratic and human rights for all British Columbians."[1]

Some school boards were sympathetic to the teachers' job action. Others — mainly those dominated by Social Credit — were vigorous in their efforts to force the teachers back to work. However, even the boards which fought the strike criticized the province's actions. In July, the B.C. School Trustees Association had registered its "shock" at Social Credit's latest measures; President Joy Leach said that the "real tragedy" would be "the hurt inflicted on the education of children, the loss of citizen control in education and the spectre of thousands of employees left jobless."[2] The Association of B.C. School Superintendents echoed these sentiments in a "Statement of Concern" issued in March 1984. The superintendents complained about the "unprecedented stresses" and "the erosion of public confidence in the public school system" caused by the government's actions:

> [I]t is wrongheaded to believe that B.C.'s public school system is fat and extravagant. It is clear that prolonged imposition of economies will impose severe hardship upon many children, particularly those whose circumstances already make them vulnerable.[3]

It was not just the government's assault on education spending that caused this virtually unanimous criticism. Social Credit had practically destroyed the autonomy of the school boards and usurped the authority of education administrators, while overthrowing the collective agreements of the teachers and subjecting them to new controls. This seizure of the public school system by the government in Victoria was carried out in the name of "restraint", but its clear intent was to forestall democratic opposition to the "new reality" in education. That "new reality" is an impoverished school system.

The Loss of Local Autonomy

The most drastic measure introduced by the government was the Education (Interim) Finance Act of April 1982. Its main effects are to give the minister of education control over the size of the budget for each local board and the portion allocated for special education programmes, and to deprive local school boards of their right to levy taxes on non-residential property. The elected local school boards have thus been deprived of their major revenue source, and stripped of the power to spend their own money on educational services beyond the levels approved by the minister in Victoria. This has made a mockery of the long-established principle of local decision-making in education — a principle until recently accepted by conservatives, liberals and socialists alike, and now rejected, the superintendants say, without any "compelling rationale [or] supporting evidence."[4]

The struggle for responsible government in the early 19th century was bound up with the demand for local control of the public schools, and this right was eventually recognized in all the Canadian provinces. Although ministries of education took responsibility for establishing curricula, accrediting teachers, etc., locally-elected boards administered the schools and raised the taxes to support them. To alleviate the pressure on local property taxes as public school systems expanded in the 20th century, the provinces made grants out of general revenue to support the schools. In most provinces, such grants now provide the major portion of education revenues, but until recently school boards have remained free to set their own budgets and determine their own educational programmes. Such latitude not only conforms to the tradition of local autonomy in school administration, but it also makes sense in terms of the principles of fiscal responsibility. Any education spending beyond the bare minimum is the responsibility of the local board, and it is financed out of local property taxes for which the board must account to the local voters. If a board chooses to spend more on education than its counterparts elsewhere — and the local voters are prepared to accept the taxes — neither the provincial government nor anyone outside the community has any reason to complain

In B.C., however, the provincial government stepped in to prevent local boards from spending more on education than Social Credit wanted them to. Under the old system of funding for the schools, provincial support was tied to the levels of spending determined by the local boards. Under the new law, the minister of education can reduce any school board's budget to the level he chooses, and so determine total spending on schools within the province as a whole and within each particular district. Thus, NDP-dominated school boards can be brought into line with Social Credit policy.

The province's seizure of control over spending was matched by its seizure of local revenue sources. In 1982, 58% of the total assessed value of real property in the province was in the non-residential category.[6] Taxes on non-residential property were the largest single revenue source for school boards and had grown from 32.4% of their total revenues in 1978 to 39.3% in 1983. The 1982 act allowed the province to expropriate *all* local revenues from taxes on non-residential property, ostensibly for "school purposes", but in reality the money went into general revenues. The school boards had to make do with "restrained" provincial grants in lieu of their lost tax revenues. The seizure of non-residential taxes denied local authorities access to taxes on business — since non-residential tax is a business tax. Consequently, school boards were left with "access" to *residential* taxes only, and any tax increases they wanted were thus politically much more difficult to impose.[7] In addition, this measure ensures that provincial efforts to reduce business taxes are not undermined by local decisions to increase them.[8]

The government's drive to cut education spending gathered momentum in 1982 and 1983. The Education (Interim) Finance Act was amended to make its controls more stringent, and the government proceeded to develop a new formula-based "fiscal framework" to govern the budgets of school boards. In typical fashion, the province moved in fits and starts, changing its policy every few months without warning or consultation. The general movement was toward tighter fiscal control, but the school boards were never sure until the last moment how much money they would have: the allowable figure for 1983 changed *seven times*.[9] It is easy to imagine the effects of provincial caprice on school board efficiency. There was no way of telling how severe the cuts would be, or where or when they would come. As the superintendents noted, the effects on morale — and hence on the *efficiency* of a labour-intensive system — were devastating.

The government's stated objective was to roll back education services in the province to the level they were when Social Credit resumed office a decade before. This meant reducing spending at both the local and provincial levels, in actual as well as "deflated" dollars, between 1983 and 1986.[10] School boards have been forced to cut back a range of services, including various special education programmes established at local discretion to meet local needs. There has been a downgrading of art, physical education, shop facilities and the like, as well as a reduction in teaching staff and a general increase in class sizes.

Rolling back education services has also meant losing teachers' aides integral to special education, reducing provisions for substitute teachers, paring budgets for transportation and utilities, reducing building and ground maintenance, and significantly cutting materials and supplies. The resulting costs to the children of British Columbia are attributed to financial "necessities". As other chapters have shown, these necessities are mythical; and, as we shall see, the government's case for "restraint" in education is based on misleading data.

The Myth of Overspending

The B.C. government has justified its assault on local autonomy by playing up recent increases in education spending:

> Between 1975/76 and the 1982/83 school years, the number of pupils declined from 524,152 to 482,255. The number of employed teachers rose from 27,184 to 28,184. *Expenditure per pupil ran 29.7% ahead of inflation.* From 1976 to 1982 the total cost of school district budgets in B.C. rose by 19.34% in real terms. Spending increases have run ahead of inflation by almost 20% over the six years prior to restraint.[11]

We are meant to be shocked by such figures, but should we be? Over the last decade, schools have increased their responsibilities and their services by serving a more diverse student population, developing alternate programmes for potential drop-outs, offering more subjects in secondary schools, increasing specialized programmes, providing services for physically and mentally handicapped students, strengthening fine arts and performing arts programmes, improving library services, providing for pre-school and kindergarten programmes, and improving counselling services and career preparation programmes. Obviously, these improvements mean increased spending. Still, there are constant complaints from the public about the inadequacies of our current education system. How can these inadequacies be corrected without devoting more resources to the schools? Might the increase in spending since the mid-1970s not reflect society's desire — expressed through locally-elected school boards — for more and better education? (It should also be pointed out that part of the increase is the result of the provincial government's decision to close down or cut back schools for special needs children — such as Jericho Hill School for the Deaf — and "mainstream" as many of their students as possible in the regular school sytems, which is an expensive undertaking.)

The government itself admits that spending increases are the result of improvements in the school system. It attributes these increases to

> more elaborate school programs with more course options; intensification of special education efforts such as integration of visually impaired students into regular classes; reduction of class sizes; relatively rapid growth in teachers' salaries; reluctance of school districts with declining enrollments to reduce staff, and higher percentages of students in the more expensive secondary (high school) grades.[12]

As University of B.C. economist Robert Allen says, the remarkable feature of this list is that these are "either unavoidable, or, on the face of it desirable developments."[13] Programmes for all students have been enriched, opportunities for the handicapped or learning disabled have been greatly improved, and pupils generally have benefited from reduction in class sizes. These are reasons for pride in our public education system, not for dismay — unless, of course, we think that only the children of the rich deserve a quality education.

The reference to the "relatively rapid growth in teachers' salaries" requires further comment, as it was the 17.3% increase in teachers' pay in the fall of 1981 (for the 1982 calendar year) which brought the issue of "restraint" in education to a head. Under Education Minister Bill Vander Zalm, reference to this pay increase became virtually synonymous with the characterization of the public school system as fat, extravagant and over-funded. Since almost two thirds of public school expenditures go to teachers' salaries, either salary increases or salary controls have direct and immediate implications for the whole budgetary process and for school district efforts to live within prescribed budgets. It is hardly surprising, therefore, that much of the government's initial assault on spending came in the form of an attack on teachers' salaries via the closure of schools, the inclusion of increment costs in calculating pay increases, and attempts through March 1983 to peg budget levels to teachers' agreeing to a pay freeze.

It is true that *average* salaries have increased at a pace exceeding the rate of inflation over the past decade, but this increase is due to an upgrading of average teachers' educational qualifications and an increase in the tenure or seniority of the average teacher. In the mid-1970s when more teachers were hired to staff an overall expansion in educational services and programmes, they were naturally hired at the lower end of the salary scale. As they accumulated experience, their salaries went up. In effect, an attack on average salaries is an attack on the concept that teachers or employees in general are entitled to raises as they gain experience and upgrade their qualifications. Moreover, if one looks at salary *scales*, the following picture emerges: between 1977 and 1983, pay scales for B.C. teachers increased by 83.2% while the Canadian Consumer Price Index increased 86.3%. Salary *scales* have only just managed to keep pace with inflation. And with teachers getting no raise in 1984 while inflation is projected at 5%, *scales* will fall behind the rising cost of living.

The government implies that its own resources have been strained by extravagant spending at the local level. The fact is that school boards have been doing more with less in recent years. As John Malcolmson notes in a report to the B.C. Teachers' Federation:

> Between the years 1980 and 1982, provincial funding support increased by a factor of 23.9 per cent. Over the same period the Vancouver CPI increased by 26.3 per cent reflecting inflation's impact. Yet Statistics Canada's Education Price Index for B.C. increased by a full 34.5 per cent. What this means is that provincial funding support lagged a full 8.6 per cent behind the most objective measure of real cost increases in the system.[14]

There are two points to be noted. The first is that school boards have had to cope with a higher rate of inflation than the general public: prices of the things they buy have been going up much more quickly than other prices. This means that the government's claims about "real" increases in education spending are much exaggerated, because no account is taken of the exceptional increases in the costs of goods and services school boards have to buy. The second point to note is that local school boards — *not* the provincial government — have borne most of the costs of improving the education system in a period of high inflation. If the province is faced with a fiscal crisis, it is not because of its generosity to the schools.

Malcolmson provides data that show a persistent *decline* in provincial support for public school education during the period in question[15] (see Table 1). Social Credit's lack of enthusiasm for education is

Table 1: Cost Shares for Public School Education

Year	Net budget (in millions)	Provincial %	Local %	Local (after HOG) %
1971	403.8	46.7	53.3	37.0
1972	442.3	46.0	54.0	35.7
1973	503.5	47.2	52.8	32.2
1974	605.5	45.0	55.0	39.1
1975	765.7	45.0	55.0	38.8
1976	896.5	44.2	55.8	39.4
1977	972.4	45.3	54.7	38.5
1978	1,077.8	42.5	57.5	41.6
1979	1,089.3	39.8	60.2	39.4
1980	1,208.5	38.8	61.2	41.2
1981	1,443.5	34.5	65.5	48.1
1982	1,673.4*	34.7	65.3	49.9
1983	1,698.3	36.0	64.0	48.8

* Includes cut of $37.5 million to provincial school budget (July, 1982)

Source: calculated from B.C. School Trustees Association, *Analysis of School District Budgets* (various years) and Ministry of Education *Comparative and Analytical Data* (various years).

reflected in an almost 20% drop in the provincial share of school costs since the defeat of the NDP in December 1975. The government's stinginess is hidden in its accounts because funds from the levy on non-residential property and from the Home Owner Grants to offset residential property taxes are both counted as provincial contributions to the schools. Neither, in fact, is. As we have seen, the non-residential property tax was seized from the school boards, ostensibly as a temporary measure, in 1982. The revenues it generates used to be purely local. The government now takes the revenues, allocates them among the school boards, and claims thereby to be making a "contribution" to school finance. This is pure deception. Home Owner Grants *do* come out of ordinary provincial revenues, but they are (as their title implies) grants to homeowners and not to schools. They are a popular "perq" for the middle classes. They are designed, it is true, to offset local taxes on residential property, but whatever the government pretends, those taxes are used for many other purposes besides schools. Only by an accounting (and public relations) trick are the Home Owner Grants attributed to the schools. Besides, as Malcolmson's table shows, the provincial share of school spending has been declining *even if* the Home Owner Grants are counted as a contribution to education.

The reality, then, is that school boards have had to cope with a relative decline in provincial funding during a period of general inflation in which goods and services for schools have been rising faster in price than ordinary consumer goods. That the boards have nonetheless been able to make significant improvements in the school system in this period is testimony to their efficiency. As the school trustees themselves have noted, they are under strong pressure to economize because their only source of revenue (other than provincial grants) is the property tax, and the property tax is highly visible and highly unpopular.[16] Fiscal conservatives, concerned about rising property taxes, have won their share of elections for local school boards, and have enforced some stringent economies. Their political opponents have also had to be extremely cost-conscious because of the burden the provincial government has placed upon local property taxes. Despite these pressures toward fiscal conservatism at the local level, the government remains unsatisfied. It is not prepared to allow local communities to spend more for schooling than Social Credit ideology finds acceptable.

One gets the impression from government propaganda that B.C.'s school system is lavishly funded by Canadian standards. Just the opposite is true. As Robert Allen shows, in B.C. a smaller share of personal income goes to education than in *any other* Canadian province.[17] By this measure, B.C. already has the worst-funded education system in the country — and the province proposes to cut it back even further. As a proportion of the total provincial budget, public school spending has fallen from 14.7% in 1977/78 to 11.2% in 1983/84.[18] The latest round of cuts come at a time of *increasing* school enrolments. The government's own projections are that the number of school children will rise from 478,545 in 1983/84 to 485,386 in 1987/88.[19] This is of major significance, for the government has complained loud and long about the school boards' reluctance to dismiss teachers during the recent period of declining enrolments. As enrolments begin to move upward again, the boards might be credited with foresight for having retained experienced teachers who would be needed in the future. Instead, the government is continuing to malign the boards while forcing them to push 3,000 teachers out of the system.[20]

The Quality of Education

There is little doubt that the government's measures will reduce the quality of education in British Columbia — what other effect can a rollback of educational services have? Nevertheless, the government is making an appeal to those who believe, mainly on the basis of American horror stories, that the quality of education has been deteriorating and that something must be done to stiffen the system. That stiffening seems to involve a reduction in school services, a narrowing of educational opportunities, and a neglect of children with particular needs. It also involves capricious intervention by politicians in a school system they barely understand.

Typical was Education Minister Jack Heinrich's announcement on August 31, 1983 that as of January

1984, Grade 12 students would be required to write provincial examinations which would count for 50% of their marks. Heinrich declared that this measure would "respond to strong public concerns for improved standards in education."[21] Uniform exams obviously have their uses, and the old provincial examination had its appeal to people concerned about "standards", but this system was abandoned more than a decade ago for sound educational reasons. To return to it suddenly — without consulting parents, teachers, principals or school boards (let alone the students involved) and without considering any of the alternatives — is simply to opt for a politically fashionable solution to complex educational problems. The main effect will be to disrupt ongoing efforts to improve the quality of high school education.

The government has adopted the same approach toward revising the high school curriculum. On March 13, 1984 the Ministry of Education released *Secondary School Graduation Requirements: A Discussion Paper*. Despite its title, the paper was clearly *not* intended as a basis for meaningful discussion with the professional community and public. Responses were required by May 31, 1984, and the paper stated that they were being sought merely as "part of the refinement of this proposal."[22] In effect, the programme is a *fait accompli*: "revised graduation requirements will begin an implementation pattern in September of 1984."[23]

The proposed restructuring of the Grade 11 and 12 curriculum requires students to select one of three programmes of study: Arts and Science, Applied Arts and Science, or Career Preparation. Additional changes include an increase in the number of required courses as well as a stipulation that all students must complete at least one mathematics and one science course during their senior secondary years.[24] According to Heinrich, these changes will enhance the quality of education and "meet the needs of a changing society."[25]

In the education community, however, many have expressed concern about the substance of these proposals and the manner in which they were presented. The three-track streaming is widely "viewed as a major flaw, a throwback to the 1950s and an inadequate, woefully outdated prescription for education in the 21st century."[26] This streaming threatens to re-establish a hierarchy of students and, in conjunction with the other requirements, will undermine a whole range of electives such as "visual and performing arts, home economics, industrial and business education."[27] In addition, a variety of locally developed courses will suffer. Referring to the proposed curriculum changes, the Native Indian Education Council of Greater Victoria, for example, states that it is "deeply disturbed by [the White Paper's] implications for the future of Indian education and the future of [the] Indian students in the public schools of British Columbia."[28] The council goes on to point out that the education ministry's proposal further erodes the autonomy and flexibility which school districts require to respond to local education needs.[29]

Research indicates that improvements in education require policies directly opposite to those adopted by Social Credit:

> Those who seek quality through tighter and tighter control of schools and teaching are pursuing phantoms through a haze...In contrast to attempts at tight quality control, a burgeoning body of evidence now emerging from the study of effective schools indicates that concentration on conditions supportive of teaching at the school and district level are most likely to yield the desired results.[30]

Increased centralization and standardization undermine the flexibility and professional discretion which are so vital for an effective education programme. There has been no major review of the B.C. education system since the 1961 Chant Royal Commission on Education — yet the intervening 23 years have been a time of dramatic social change in B.C. Instead of undertaking the in-depth study and consultation needed to deal with the complex problems of education in the 1980s, the government has opted for sweeping changes without prior input from trustees, superintendents, teachers, parents or community groups. The result is a programme which will make B.C.'s education more rigid, more restrictive, less able to adjust to local needs and changing circumstances, and less capable of meeting the needs of all children. Only by the crassest doubletalk can this be called an improvement in education.

Conclusion

In the name of "restraint", Social Credit has renounced longstanding democratic principles and practices in education. As we have seen, the government's rhetoric in no way reflects the reality of B.C.'s public school system. Far from being fat and extravagant, that system has been receiving a smaller share of personal income than any other province and has had to manage on persistently declining provincial support. Local school boards have shown efficiency and foresight in contending with these problems and have paid the lion's share of improvements. Clearly, "restraint" is a cover for policies that have little to do with economy and efficiency.

As part of its general effort to centralize decision-making and thus facilitate the implementation of neo-conservative economics, Social Credit has created a "new reality" in education. This "new reality" is unsound educationally *and* economically. Not only does it undermine the very conditions which are necessary for a quality education, but by attacking B.C.'s human resources, "restraint" in education is sacrificing tomorrow's workforce. Considered purely in cost-benefit terms, the cuts in education spending can only harm B.C.'s economy. Considered more broadly in human terms, the cost of current policies is incalculable. Unless the present trend is reversed, British Columbians will pay dearly for Social Credit's assault on education.

A Decade of Restraint: The Economics of B.C. Universities
Gordon Shrimpton

UNIVERSITIES are investments. Unfortunately, some provincial governments in this country tend to regard post-secondary institutions as luxuries to be sacrificed in order to divert money to sectors which, they believe, generate wealth more effectively. In this view, the university is a consumer, not a supplier of wealth, and in difficult times the only way to save such "expensive" educational programmes is to build up the corporate, industrial and agricultural production side of the economy. Eventually, the argument goes, the increased profits will generate taxes and make possible a return to healthier funding for social services and higher education.

The above is a view of economic policy often called "supply-side" economics. It can be refuted by exposing its internal logical flaws, but also simply by asserting its opposite, "demand-side" economics, which questions whether it really makes sense to increase productivity at the expense of impoverishing the buyer. If widgets can be produced 2 cents cheaper with government incentives, how does that help if the average purchaser is made 5 cents poorer? The product is rendered effectively more expensive despite the drop in price. In fact, the supplier is helped by enriching the consumer. That may sound obvious, but it isn't to everyone — otherwise there would be no Bennetts, Reagans or Thatchers.

This is not intended as a lesson in economic theory. Instead, the following argument shows that even the supply-side economist should *not* be starving universities. Universities are not luxuries. They aid all sides of the economy, but make a significant contribution on the "supply-side", a contribution that the Bennetts of this world are unwise to ignore.

The University and Society

Misinformation or ignorance about higher education makes it easy for the public to accept the deterioration of colleges and universities. Despite warnings from the past, we can get so used to the advantages of education that we forget the evils of ignorance. Most people know that research goes on at universities but, paradoxically, will ask a faculty member if he or she is "off" for the summer when classes are over, or will wonder why the professor gets a year "off" every seven years. The professor is not just a conveyor of knowledge to students, but participates in generating new knowledge. This is research, a fundamental component of his or her job. Research involves scrutinizing received information and passing on that which stands up to critical examination. Students must learn similar techniques. The professor teaches methods, and the art of generating new ones.

Perhaps the pragmatic political economist will remain unmoved by these facts. For him, the real question is what does the university offer to improve the economy. This question is not easily answered because the questioner is acting like an owner of an apartment building who won't collect rents — and then concludes that apartments are a bad investment. His, or her, disappointment with the investment stems from a personal attitude. The public, government and industry could make better use of colleges and universities, and learn much more from them.

Most people can see the immediate advantages of applied science. For example, chemicals are components of fertilizers and insecticides that increase agricultural production and efficiency. Chemical and physical research makes possible the development of the various electronic and automotive marvels we take for granted. Today, our tinkering with our environment through chemicals and pollutants has reached unprecedented levels. We also need science to help us improve and even reverse the effects of science on the environment over the past half-century or more. Today we have entered a world that ignores or wishes to forget where such things as scientific discoveries, medical improvements and advances in computer design often originate — in those so-called "ivory towers" whose budgets it is fashionable to slash.

Because universities are committed to research, they need a reliable source of funds. Research often spans many years and relies on the future availability of support staff, equipment and supplies. The scientist cannot do tomorrow's experiments with yesterday's equipment. The social scientist cannot pursue his studies without data, journals and reference works. To be a pioneer one must be at the frontier, not six months or a year behind it. Yet in 1982, the B.C. government announced a 12% increase for universities — only to take back 3.8% three months into the fiscal year. There was no 1983 increase on the reduced 1982 allocation. In 1984, universities and colleges were forced to absorb a 5% cut. All this while enrolment and inflation were steadily increasing, and after a decade of dwindling support (see Figure 1).

Many are suggesting that universities eliminate or cut back programmes that do not respond to the economy's or society's immediate needs. It is dangerously easy to oppose theoretical, abstract, or "basic" research on the grounds that it is irrelevant to our needs. Its "irrelevance" has proved again and again to be its redeeming quality:

> Applied research can provide a large immediate pay-off....But what is not fully appreciated

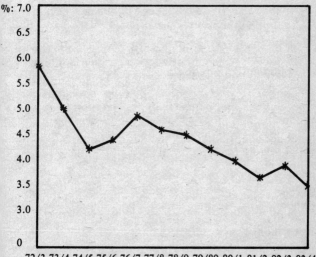

Figure 1: University Operating Grants as a Percentage of Provincial Government Expenditure*

* Consolidated revenue fund.

Source: Institutional Analysis, University of Victoria, October 18, 1983.

is the importance of basic research. University research often appears unrelated to current industrial needs. Douglas, in his 1969 article in *Science Forum*, pointed out that if universities in 1900 had worked only on current national needs, they would have been working on breeds of horses suitable to Canadian needs, the design of river boats, the production of telegraph wires, and so forth.[1]

Capitalist society demands profits, but true civilization is impossible without those activities we call culture. Nevertheless, the graduate from "liberal arts" is more than a mere jewel on society's earlobe. The liberal arts (philosophy, history, literature and

---

Table 1: Educational Attainment of the Adult Population, 1981

The table shows the proportion of the population 15 years and over with some university education and with some nonuniversity post-secondary education.

	Some university education	Some nonuniversity post-secondary education
Newfoundland	12.1%	20.0%
Prince Edward Island	16.0	23.8
Nova Scotia	15.4	24.0
New Brunswick	13.3	20.5
Quebec	13.5	27.6
Ontario	16.9	26.1
Manitoba	16.0	23.2
Saskatchewan	15.3	22.7
Alberta	18.4	29.8
British Columbia	18.6	29.7
Canada	**16.0**	**26.6**

Source: Statistics Canada, *Update from the 1981 Census*, March 1, 1983, p. 17.

From: Robert Allen, "Investment and Education."

---

the like) can give us adaptable and trainable people of the sort most needed. For example, one New York investment firm hired a liberal arts major to run its computer network. He identified and solved a great number of the firm's problems. The arrangement proved so successful, at least from the company's perspective, that it "now fills all its back-office jobs with liberal-arts grads."[2] The personnel officer or industrialist who finds this story surprising should ask whether he or she has not been acting like the property owner mentioned above who refused to collect the rents.

Universities also provide a range of professional trainees: engineers, school teachers, lawyers, doctors, nurses and so on. B.C. takes full advantage of the availability of these people: Table 2 shows the extent to which the province makes use of people with some higher education. In 1981, only Alberta had more people with some college or university training.

The Underfunding of B.C. Universities

However, if B.C. is Canada's second greatest "consumer" of highly educated people, it is also Canada's second poorest supplier (see Table 2). In the words of Robert Allen:

> B.C.'s economy generates an unusually high demand for highly educated workers, but B.C.'s education system produces a disproportionately small number of suitable graduates. As a result, B.C. firms hire many professionals and managers from out of the province.[3]

The pragmatic economist may be more elated than distressed by these figures. Superficially, it looks cheaper for B.C. to hire from outside the province if it can avoid the cost of educating its own people. Not only is this not even good "supply-side" economics,

Table 2: **Post-Secondary Enrolment**

The table shows (as a percentage) total full time post secondary enrollment divided by population for each age, 1981-2.

Age:	19	20	21
Newfoundland	14.5%	10.1%	8.3%
Prince Edward Island	21.1	16.1	14.2
Nova Scotia	24.0	21.4	17.7
New Brunswick	20.4	15.9	13.9
Quebec	26.3	21.3	16.1
Ontario	30.1	27.4	17.1
Manitoba	19.3	16.8	9.6
Saskatchewan	16.9	15.4	8.3
Alberta	18.0	14.5	8.5
British Columbia	15.8	13.5	9.3
Canada	**24.4**	**21.0**	**17.1**

Source: Statistics Canada, *Education in Canada: A Statistical Review*, catalogue no. 81-229, for 1981-2, 1982.

From: Robert Allen, "Investment and Education."

it is irresponsible: *of course* you save money when you refuse to pay for commodities you use.

There seems little doubt that the B.C. treasury has experienced a significant decline in revenue over the past year or two. Yet Figure 1 shows that the steady decline in B.C. university operating grants began much earlier. They fell from nearly 6% of total government spending in 1972/73 to less than 4% in 1983/84. However, this only tells part of the story. The 1983 and 1984 provincial budgets first slashed student aid, then eliminated it, ultimately replacing it with a dubious loan programme. It's ironic that a government that preaches debt retirement and constantly excoriates Ottawa for the size of the federal debt forces its students (who currently suffer the highest unemployment rate in Canada) to finance their education by going into debt.

The real or net cost of higher education to this

province is actually negligible. In 1983, more than 75% of the provincial operating grant to colleges and universities came from Ottawa through cash transfers and tax credits.[4] Every dollar the province gave to colleges and universities in 1983 for operating funds cost the province only about 25 cents. Nor does the money disappear when it has reached the college or university. About 85% of it goes into salaries and wages, and much of the rest is spent locally for purchase of goods, services and supplies. About 30% to 35% of the salaries and wages will be withheld for income tax and most of the rest flows into the urban economies of Victoria and Vancouver. Recent studies have shown the effect of this money on those economies.[5] Dollars flow through the cash registers of local shops to enrich the community's merchants, to provide more taxes to all levels of government, and to be spent and re-spent in the economy. It has been shown that the spending and re-spending effect roughly doubles the value of a dollar as a stimulus to the local economy and a consequent generator of tax revenue. In other words, money spent on higher education is a cheap investment in urban prosperity. Each dollar invested in 1983 cost the province only about 25 cents (reduced to between 15 and 20 cents in 1984). This dollar flows through the city economy, ultimately enriching it to the value of about $1.15.[6] From this, the province reaps about 15% as taxes.[7] This means that B.C. is making *no significant net investment* in the operation of universities and colleges in 1984, since the tax return is just about covering the provincial outlay.

It would be a shame to see higher education only through the eyes of a pragmatic economist. The benefit of higher education is measured in values other than dollars. Society benefits immeasurably from the intellectual energy, improvement in self-esteem, and flexibility of those who increase self-growth through education. Conversely, it suffers immeasurable shock and hardship when educational

Figure 2: **Unemployment by Education**

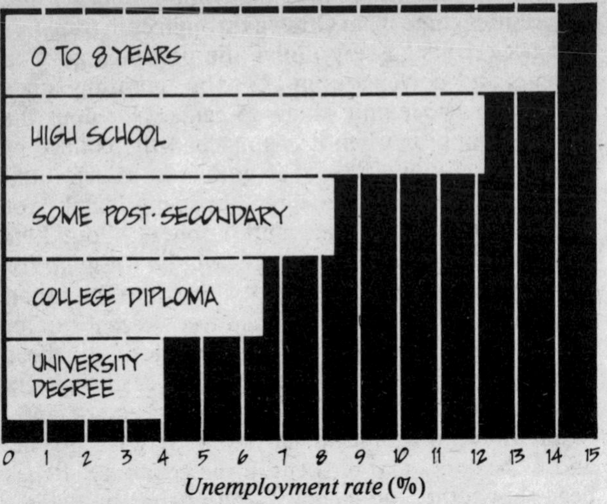

Source: Statistics Canada 71-001, April 1982.

opportunities are withheld. Figures 2 and 3 together are a sobering illustration of this. Participation in the workforce declines dramatically with the decline in educational achievement, while employability increases as the level of education improves.

Beyond the Ledger: The Social Benefits of Post-Secondary Education

Universities and colleges offer opportunities for self-improvement and access to new levels of employment for both young and old. Unfortunately, university education is beyond the reach of many British Columbians. One reason is geography. Our three universities are all nestled together in the lower left-hand corner of the province, far from the interior and northern cities and towns.[8] David

Thompson University Centre in the west Kootenays was until recently a university entry point. Now it is gone, student aid is gone, and, from the perspective of lower income families in the interior of the province, a university education has become the privilege of the wealthier and more fortunately located, particularly the inhabitants of Victoria and Vancouver. This year, the Governor General's medal — awarded to the graduating student with the highest marks — at the University of Victoria was won by Susan Hykin, who also received a special M.A. scholarship from the Social Sciences and Humanities Research Council of Canada. She began her higher education at David Thompson. She said, on graduation:

> I feel quite strongly about what's happened at DTUC, and all of the students growing up there. In these times... families won't be able to move

Figure 3: Labour Force Participation by Education

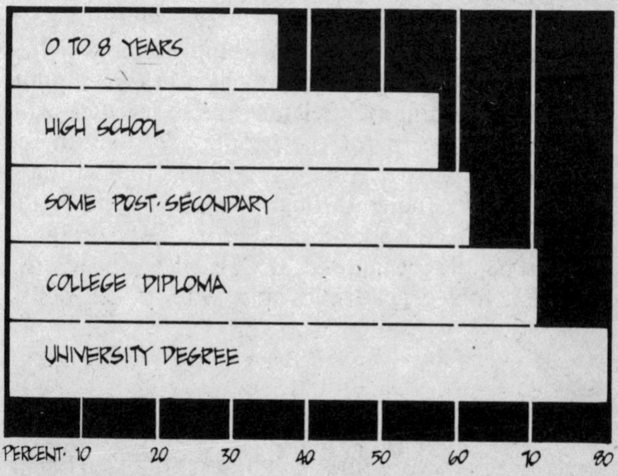

0 TO 8 YEARS							
HIGH SCHOOL							
SOME POST-SECONDARY							
COLLEGE DIPLOMA							
UNIVERSITY DEGREE							

PERCENT: 10   20   30   40   50   60   70   80

Source: Statistics Canada 71-001, April 1982.

to large centres. Three per cent of students in the area go on to university in the first place. Of those who go away from the local area, one-half drop out in the first year. The total number of university-trained students in the West Kootenays is less than 1% of the high school graduating class. DTUC was a real effort to change that. It's a tremendous loss.

Universities and colleges do have an economic contribution to make to society, but their best and greatest accomplishments are harder to measure. When an adult goes to a community college and learns to read or write and begins to appreciate the pleasure of literature, for instance, the psychological change that person undergoes has a value beyond dollars to the student, and also to the teacher. Faculty in post-secondary institutions see clearly that they have something vital to contribute directly to the world around them. Sociologists, economists and political scientists rarely withdraw into worlds of abstract theory, but often study current trends and events. Schools of human and social development spring up to study and improve techniques in such things as childcare, social work and nursing. While the academic becomes more involved in the community, the governing politician seems to legislate with little or no concern for the people affected. In the legislature, "debate" follows rigid ideological lines. Legislation is rammed through, with no regard to the criticisms of the opposition. The protests of thousands of people are ignored. B.C. is becoming a province of involved academics and ivory-tower politicians.

Conclusion:
Beyond "Restraint"

FOR MORE THAN a decade the Western world has been in an economic crisis. The long post-war period of steady growth, high employment and stable prices drew to an end in the early 1970s. What had been relatively effective instruments of economic management no longer seemed to work. Prices kept rising, even as rates of growth declined and unemployment increased. When governments committed themselves to the war against inflation, they squeezed more of the life out of their economies and drove unemployment to levels unheard of since the Great Depression. Peoples and governments cast around for scapegoats, and friendly trading partners began to bar one another's goods. The North Americans and West Europeans who had so completely dominated the world economy, were challenged first by the Japanese, then by OPEC, and finally by an array of newly industrializing states. The economic affairs of the world could no longer be managed by a cosy club of like-minded states. Indeed, it seemed that they could no longer be managed at all.

The men who dominated post-war politics in the West — nominally liberals, conservatives or social democrats, but all "moderates" committed to the mixed economy, the welfare state and Keynesian economic management — no longer had the answers. They could not promise that things would get better or even that they would not get worse. This opened the way for the New Right, which did not promise to improve things immediately but had, they said, the *structural* solutions to our problems — not just our economic problems, but the social, political and even moral problems that also seemed involved in the present decay.

The 1980s have brought the New Right to power in Washington, London, Victoria and elsewhere. It has set the tone for political debate, defined the political agenda and induced its political opponents to deal with issues in reactionary terms. The effects on the political imagination and on the course of public policy are everywhere apparent. What the New Right has done is to reduce the standards of living of ordinary people, curb their rights and impair their security as workers and citizens. Reaganomics, in particular, has worsened almost every problem in the global economy, and heightened the political tensions that impede international co-operation. And yet for many people Reagan and his ilk remain political heroes. In Canada, millions await the new messiah with the strong chin who will bring them their own brand of neo-conservatism.

The policies of the New Right appeal to what is worst within us. Many will accept the reasoned criticisms we offer here — nod sombrely at the deterioration of services, sigh at the loss of rights, shake their heads at the mistakes of economic policy — and yet somehow feel that the neo-conservatives have got the principles right. There is a crisis: something must be done. And there is a voice within us that tells us to slash at the comforts we have accumulated, to attack those who have not yet suffered enough from the new order, to purge ourselves of the rot within. How can we deserve recovery unless we suffer the pain of restraint? There is no easy answer to this, except to say that sado-masochism is no more healthy in public life than it is in private.

To the extent that the global economic crisis is connected to a lack of restraint, the real excesses are not the ones the New Right has identified. We are depleting the world's resources at an alarming rate; we are poisoning the air, the water, the earth and even our own bodies; we are wasting what wealth we have on destructive arms and senseless luxuries; and we are feeding our excesses from the labour of the world's poor. The New Right is not concerned about such matters. It does not preach restraint for the sake of the poor or for the good of our souls. "Restraint" is the price demanded of us in return for another orgy of economic expansion, for the luxuries we still hope to acquire. This is the ultimate source of its political appeal.

The Real Restraints

The B.C. government has responded to the global economic crisis with a programme of "restraint". This has not been a programme of frugality: Expo 86 would hardly be going ahead if it were. Instead, it has been designed to put restraints on services to ordinary people, to limit the rights of workers and consumers, to curb the trade unions and other groups that represent the disadvantaged, and to free business and the government that supports it from the restraints of responsibility to the people as a whole. The "new reality" is not one where the cabinet ministers have to take the ferry to Vancouver, or where the corporations have to give up their tax breaks.

Instead, the "new reality", its features familiar from the social experiments of Margaret Thatcher and Ronald Reagan, involves a fundamental restructuring of our economy, a redistribution of wealth, and a reconstruction of our political and social life. And all this has one simple objective: to make it easier for business to make money. The new culture heroes are the "risk takers", those with too much money who invest some of it to make even more. The man and woman on the picket line are not risk takers.

Of course, we are supposed to believe that more money for business means more jobs for the rest of us. The theory seems to be that if we impoverish ourselves enough — accept lower pay, give up our fringe benefits, weaken our unions, lift our environmental regulations, etc. — those nice men in Tokyo and New York will start investing their money here again. Then, perhaps, we can be fully employed, albeit at a fraction of our present standard of living.

The fact is that even the promised increase in jobs has not occurred. In B.C., the full effects of restraint have not yet been felt. We only know that unemployment, bankruptcies and foreclosures have been going up while real wages have been falling. So far, so bad. In Britain, which has had five years of Margaret Thatcher's policies, the effects have been far worse: de-industrialization, massive unemployment, increasing social tensions. The British economy is in worse shape than it was five years ago. The American experience under Ronald Reagan has been rather similar, except that the Reagan administration has been much less faithful to the "restraint" philosophy. Thanks to its devotion to military expenditures, it has been stimulating the American economy, albeit in a perverse way. With its "beggar-my-neighbour" trade and interest rate policies, it has also been exporting American economic problems to other countries, including Canada. The effects on the global economy as a whole have been disastrous, but Ronald Reagan boasts that the United States is now doing relatively better than its allies in coping with the economic mess he has created.

The Canadian government can do little to alter the rhythms of the global economy; the B.C. government is in a weaker position still. Nevertheless, it can improve the province's prospects by developing its internal resources. Premier Bennett is so concerned to remind us of the excesses of our past that it is perhaps worth reminding *him* that he was premier for eight full years before 1983, and that he and his father have led this province for 29 of the last 32 years. If bad government has gotten us in an economic mess, Social Credit had better take the blame.

The truth is that Social Credit policies have continually exacerbated the structural problems of the B.C. economy. By pouring money into one big resource development after another, the government has increased the province's dependency on volatile export markets for raw materials. Our resources have been mined for corporate profit at huge public expense, and we are left with a depleted fishery, depleted forests, and huge surpluses of coal and hydro-electricity. So much for wise management in the past. It would be nice to think that the new economic policies of Social Credit were based on a different investment strategy, but we see the same old ideas at work. The infrastructure for manufacturing is being neglected and our human and social capital is being run down to save money for big — and hopelessly *unprofitable* — resource investments like Northeast Coal. The only nod toward something new is Expo 86: an extravaganza we may enjoy enough to forget that it does nothing to overcome the basic deficiencies of the B.C. economy.

"Pacific Rim" development models are much in vogue in B.C. It seems forgotten — or is it? — that the Philippines, South Korea and Taiwan are developing rapidly because they have repressive governments prepared to keep their people desperately poor to attract multinational capital looking for docile, low-paid labour. Whatever we think of this development strategy for poor countries, there is no way that it could work in Canada. Ours is a high-wage country and a liberal democracy: it will remain so, despite Premier Bennett. More relevant development models are to be found in the developed West rather than in the impoverished East.

Which have been the most successful of the Western economies over the years? Not the American — with its small public sector, poor social services, weak business regulations and declining unions — but the West German, the Scandinavian, the Swiss, the Benelux. These countries of northern and central Europe have *larger* public sectors, *better* social services, *stronger* business regulations and more *powerful* unions than the U.S. and Canada. In other words, they have more of what Premier Bennett likes to call "socialism". These are the countries with the highest rates of economic growth, the lowest levels of unemployment, the most stable prices, the best labour productivity. These are the ones with the highest standards of living in the world. Isn't there something we could learn from them? But the premier, as his education policies show, is not in the learning business.

If there is a key to the success of these European economies, it is that they have developed their own resources, especially their human resources. Moreover, they are countries where "labour" has been recognized as an estate of the realm, not treated as an enemy within. They are countries where an array of social services has been steadily developed, and where businesses have been obliged to accept social responsibilities. "Creeping socialism" has been recognized as a condition for economic growth and social stability, not as an obstacle to them.

This is not to suggest that the answers to our problems are all to be found in Europe, or to deny that there have been failures there as well. However, we would be wise to keep these other models in mind when we are told that Ronald Reagan's or Bill Bennett's is the only way to recovery. In fact, as we have seen, the short-term economic effects of Social Credit's programme in B.C. have been perverse. Stimulative Keynesian fiscal policies, although they would have worked no magic, would have eased the pain of the recession and might have speeded economic recovery. Moreover, policies of this kind could have been combined with public investment strategies that would have begun to rectify rather than exacerbate the structural problems of the B.C. economy. That such obvious options have been rejected suggests that Social Credit has been less concerned with genuine economic recovery than with turning the present crisis to its own advantage and to the advantage of corporations.

"Restraint" has been an excuse to abuse democracy, restrict rights and increase inequality. The attack on social justice is almost explicit. The ethic, it seems, is of the "survival of the fittest"; and what is fittest, apparently, is to do your neighbour down. This is hidden by the rhetoric of "free enterprise" and "individual initiative". The irony is that there will be little scope for individual initiative or free enterprise in a society dominated by huge corporations, backed by a government that seals itself off from popular influence. Under the New Right, ordinary people will have less opportunity to develop themselves, less freedom to live as they choose, less control over government and business, less security for themselves and their families, less equality, less justice and certain less fraternity. This is the new reality behind the slogans that suggest that *we* are the beneficiaries of "restraint". Let us not be fooled. The big companies will profit. The banks will profit. Bill Bennett and his friends will profit. The rest of us will pay.

Toward Genuine Recovery

It is clear by now that the right has abandoned the great consensus of the post-war period, leaving a fragile and diminished alliance of liberals and social democrats to hold the centre. Whether it is espoused by John Turner or Brian Mulroney, the neo-conservative drift in national politics is unmistakable. In B.C. as elsewhere, rights and welfare services established in the post-war era must be protected against this threat, but the left cannot be content with defending a betrayed consensus whose mechanisms of socioeconomic fine-tuning are unequal to the challenge of the 1980s.

There is, then, a need for new approaches to policy, indeed for a renewal of left politics itself. In Western Europe the process of renewal has already begun in the spirited debates over industrial strategy within Britain's Labour Party, in the Reds-Greens debate in West Germany, and so on. In Canada, James Laxer's recent critique of federal NDP policies — however wrongheaded in itself — has at least raised some of the issues that bear upon political renewal. In British Columbia the ironic but welcome legacy of Social Credit "restraint" may well be a hastening of regeneration on the left. The Solidarity Coalition, with its grassroots orientation, extra-parliamentary tactics and commitment to advancing real alternatives to austerity, is one hopeful development. Another is the recent election of a provincial NDP leader, Robert Skelly, who has promised a needed rebuilding of the party as a broadly participatory socialist movement.

Social Credit and governments of its kind have certainly grasped one essential truth: the "new reality" of economic crisis and capitalist restructuring is indeed *global*. Its very pervasiveness narrows the policy alternatives of any national government, and much more so a provincial one. Unfortunately, the breadth and depth of the crisis have provided Social Credit with the opportunity to peddle its brutal policies as the only rational and socially responsible solution to a situation which seems to be well beyond anyone's control. The attraction of this idea rests in the subordination of politics to the dictates of what is euphemistically called "free enterprise". As long as we are held fast to the premises of the latter — the priority of profit, the vagaries of allocation in the market — the political rhetoric of "restraint" may seem to have a certain logical appeal. International credit ratings and international competitiveness remain political priorities in Paris and Bonn no less than in Victoria. Governments feel they must spend within their means, fostering an investment climate that is attractive to international and local capitalists alike.

But if the constraints imposed by the global economic malaise have given the right certain opportunities, they may also hold promise for the left. In less developed countries such as Argentina and Mexico, years of externally imposed austerity — similar in spirit to the Social Credit programme for B.C. — have provoked massive popular opposition, and governments have been obliged to respond with neo-nationalist challenges to the existing world economic order. B.C., of course, is not Brazil. Our austerity is "voluntary" and the popular resistance that it provokes may be more easily contained. Yet the broad parallels are evident, and they only underscore the need both for critical analysis at the international level and for solidarity across national borders.

Local as well as global developments give rise to opportunities for political action. Increasing militarization and increasingly monolithic and doctrinaire capitalism are being met both here and abroad by a growing number of grassroots protest movements. These movements are cutting across traditional boundaries of age, sex, political persuasion and

nationality; they are drawing upon larger segments of
the population and are more consciously linked to
similar movements in other countries than ever
before. Moreover, the various particular protest
groups are increasingly discovering common fundamental values which transcend their own specific
concerns and facilitate joint action. Peace activists,
feminists and environmentalists provide the clearest
example. The common values challenge the priorities
of establishment politics and its restriction of
decision-making to so-called experts.

The grassroots movements thus call for a radical
shift in values and reorganization of existing structures to allow for effective participation at every level
and by all those affected. This widespread call for
genuine participatory democracy is healthy, both
ethically and economically. Democratic restructuring
would promote recovery more effectively than
supply-side, monetarist or corporatist programmes.
"A more democratic and egalitarian economy has
economic promise because people want it, and it
costs less to put people in charge than it does to keep
them down."[1] Ours is still a rich country in every
way. The resources, capital, technology, aspirations
and skills are available to build what the Canadian
Conference of Catholic Bishops calls "an alternative
economic future",[2] but deployment is impeded by
the restraints of capitalism. To overcome those
restraints and build a future in which the emphasis
would be on a fully human life for all rather than a
maximization of profits for some, we must develop
new modes of production — co-operative, community-based, worker-controlled. What we must seek
are the political means for realizing these practical
possibilities.

In British Columbia, the Solidarity Coalition
provides an excellent example of co-operation among
diverse groups in calling for a reconsideration of
government priorities and implementation of genuinely participatory democratic processes. The forms

of such processes will depend on the needs and the human and material resources of particular communities. A crucial prerequisite for such a shift in values and structural reorganization is the transcending of rigid modes of thought, the desire for greater ideological openness, and the development of more imaginative social and economic alternatives.

Our aim in this book has been to expose the policies of the Social Credit government, to indicate the repressive nature of its "new reality", and to stimulate the creative thinking essential if we are to climb out of the morass which, in our own corner of the world, has been made stickier. We believe that there is a better way, and that a critical assessment of the present is the best starting point from which to construct the positive human community British Columbia can become.

Appendix A
The "Restraint" Package

THE LEGISLATIVE PACKAGE
OF JULY 7, 1983

Legislation Attacking Labour

Bill 2 — Public Service Labour Relations Amendment Act. Removes government employees' rights to negotiate job security, promotion, job reclassification, transfer, work hours and other working conditions. Died on order paper (part of Kelowna Accord).

Bill 3 — Public Sector Restraint Act. Enables public sector employers to fire employees without cause upon expiry of collective agreement. "Without cause" phrase later removed but very broad termination conditions remain. Became law October 21, 1983; major public sector unions negotiated exemptions.

Bill 11 — Compensation Stabilization Amendment Act. Extends indefinitely public sector wage controls; makes employer's ability to pay paramount; establishes new guidelines of minus-5% to plus-5%. Became law October 21, 1983.

Bill 26 — Employment Standards Amendment Act.

Undermines labour standards in areas such as pregnancy leave and safety on the job by removing minimum employment standards from all collective agreements. Abolishes Employment Standards Board. Became law October 21, 1983.

Bill 18 — Pension (Public Service) Amendment Act. Abolishes terminal funding for public service pension plan and increases unfunded liability. Became law September 23, 1983.

Legislation Attacking Rights

Bill 27 — Human Rights Act. Repeals Human Rights Code; abolishes Human Rights Branch and Commission. Narrows definition of discrimination and limits compensation. Died on order paper; replaced in 1984 by Bill 11, essentially the same, which became law May 16, 1984.

Bill 5 — Residential Tenancy Act. Abolishes Rentalsman's Office and rent controls. Died on order paper; replaced in 1984 by Bill 19, essentially the same, which became law May 1, 1984.

Legislation Attacking Services

Bill 24 — Medical Services Act. Enables doctors to opt out of medicare and empowers Medical Services Commission to issue and restrict billing numbers. Died on order paper.

Bill 6 — Education (Interim) Finance Amendment Act. Like the April 1982 act, this amended act deprives local school boards of their right to levy taxes on non-residential property and gives the minister of education control over the size of the budget for each local board. Also extends the "sunset" provision of the 1982 act to the end of 1986. Became law October 21, 1983.

Bill 19 — Institute of Technology Amendment Act. Tightens government control over British Columbia Institute of Technology, eliminating community, faculty, staff and student representation. Minister of education must approve all courses and programmes. Became law October 21, 1983.

Bill 20 — College and Institute Amendment Act. Gives

minister of education control over courses and budgets and eliminates local representation on college boards; abolishes Academic Council, Management Advisory Council, Occupational Training Council. Became law September 23, 1983.

Bill 23 — Motor Vehicle Amendment Act. Closes motor vehicle testing branches; eliminates mandatory vehicle inspection. Became law October 21, 1983.

Bill 8 — Alcohol and Drug Commission Repeal Act. Dissolves Alcohol and Drug Commission, an educational rehabilitative and research agency. Became law October 21, 1983.

Legislation Centralizing Power

Bill 9 — Municipal Amendment Act. Declares null and void all regional plans; removes regional districts' right to plan for the region as a whole. Became law October 21, 1983.

Bill 21 — Crown Corporation Reporting Repeal Act. Eliminates the Legislative Committee on Crown Corporations, thereby reducing parliamentary control. Died on order paper.

Bill 28 — Provincial Treasury Financing Amendment Act. Provides for direct borrowing for crown corporations by the central government. Became law October 21, 1983.

Legislation Concerning Taxation

Bill 4 — Income Tax Amendment Act. Repeals personal income tax credit and renters' tax credit. Became law October 21, 1983.

Bill 17 — Miscellaneous Statutes (Finance Measures) Amendment Act. Allows government to increase minimum property tax, increases government's power to collect taxes owing. Became law September 23, 1983.

Bill 15 — Social Service Tax Amendment Act. Increases sales tax and extends it to restaurant meals over $7 and to long-distance telephone calls. Became law October 21, 1983.

Bill 13 — Tobacco Tax Amendment Act. Increases tobacco tax by 25%. Became law September 23, 1983.

Bill 7 — Property Tax Reform Act (No. 1). Introduces the variable mill rate system that allows municipalities to levy different rates on different classes of property. Became law October 21, 1983.

Bill 12 — Property Tax Reform Act (No. 2). Extends the variable mill rate system to other areas. Became law October 21, 1983.

Bill 22 — Assessment Amendment Act. Provides for biennial property assessment. Died on order paper, but Assessment Amendment Act 1984 (Bill 7) enacted May 1, 1984.

Bill 14 — Gasoline (Coloured) Tax Amendment Act. Establishes new pricing formula and clarifies tax application for bunker fuel. Became law October 21, 1983.

Other Legislation

Bill 16 — Employment Development Act. Authorizes $415 million for capital investment in 1983/84. (These funds were contained in existing departmental estimates.) Became law October 21, 1983.

Bill 25 — Harbour Board Repeal Act. Abolishes the Harbour Board, terminates all employees and transfers the assets to B.C. Development Corporation and B.C. Railway Co. Became law September 23, 1983.

SUBSEQUENT LEGISLATION, FEBRUARY-MAY 1984

Legislation Attacking Labour

Bill 28 — Labour Code Amendment Act. Limits political protests involving job action; outlaws secondary picketing; enables cabinet to set regulations for all voting (certifications, strikes, lockouts, decertifications); empowers cabinet to designate "Economic Development Projects" open to non-union labour and exempt from strikes; limits unions' power over discipline and membership matters. Became law May 16, 1984.

Bill 18 — Pulp and Paper Collective Bargaining Assistance Act. Lifts lockout in pulp and paper industry; outlaws strikes; extends indefinitely previous contract and empowers cabinet to impose a collective agreement. Became law April 3, 1984.

Legislation Attacking Rights

Bill 11 — Human Rights Act. Replaces Bill 27 of 1983; substantially the same. Became law May 16, 1984.

Bill 19 — Residential Tenancy Act. Abolishes rent controls; replaces Rentalsman's Office by government-appointed arbitrator charging for service. Became law May 1, 1984.

Appendix B
Solidarity Coalition's Declaration of the Rights of the People of B.C.

A Declaration of the Rights of the People of British Columbia

We believe that the measure of a society's humanity is the degree to which it provides rights that protect all its participants, its minorities no less than its majorities;

We believe that the substance of justice in a society is the degree to which rights are accorded to the poor and the powerless, and not simply to the rich and the strong;

And we believe that the test of a society's commitment to democracy is its resolve to guarantee those rights even in the face of hardship and adversity;

Therefore we declare that in a democratic, just and humane British Columbia every person has these fundamental rights which no government may justifiably extinguish:

- The right to protection from all forms of unreasonable discrimination, by legislation that ensures human rights and programs that confront prejudice.
- The right to freedom of expression and opinion without fear of reprisal.

- The right to universally accessible, comprehensive and confidential medical care.
- The right to a public school system that allows all children to develop to the full extent of their potential, and to post-secondary education that is accessible to all.
- The right of senior citizens, disabled persons and visible minorities to participate fully and equally in society.
- The right of every woman, in fact as well as in principle, to a full and equal place in society.
- The right to receive adequate social services and assistance.
- The right to freedom from arbitrary or unjustified eviction or increase in rents.
- The right to universal accessibility of necessary legal assistance.
- The right to local powers of decision-making about the provision of social services, and effective regional planning of the development of our communities.
- The right of all employees to negotiate freely and collectively with their employer all the terms and conditions under which they work.
- The right to freedom from arbitrary or unjustified termination of employment.
- The right to open and democratic government, scrutiny of government actions, due process of law, full parliamentary debate and consultation with affected groups on all legislative proposals, and express submission of fundamental changes in law or rights to the electors.

This declaration is made in the face of an unprecedented legislative assault that seeks to eliminate or subvert existing rights and protections. This cannot be allowed. We also assert, therefore, that the people of this province have the right and the responsibility to resist. We shall do so with all of our strength.

Solidarity Coalition

Notes

The New Economic Reality:
Substance and Rhetoric

1. This paper is based on several speeches given at UBC, Langara College, Malaspina College, Simon Fraser University, the University of Toronto, Carleton University and for teachers' associations in Kelowna and North Surrey, under the titles "Rise and Fall of the Peripheral State," "The Ideology of Restraint," and "B.C. Under Restraint." I have attempted to include contributions from audiences in this version, and am grateful for them.

2. Detailed in Patricia Marchak, *Green Gold. The Forest Industry in British Columbia*. (Vancouver: The UBC Press, 1983), chapters 3 and 4, and "The Rise and Fall of the Peripheral State," forthcoming in Robert S. Brym, ed., *Regionalism in Canada: Marxism versus Dependency Theory,* (Toronto: Clarke Irwin).

3. Quesnel Forest Products, co-owned by Daishawa Marubeni and West Fraser (Seattle).

4. I am indebted to Jacqueline Maund for this information, contained in "The Implications of the Japanese

Resource Procurement Strategy," MA thesis (Geography), UBC, 1984.

5. No requirements for preference going to B.C. contractors were written into contracts. Among them were: two ships to be built in Korea and Belgium at a cost of $170 million; Mitsubishi for coal handling machinery ($20 million); two large contracts for tunnels on the Anzac line worth $54.6 million, and $39.4 million for a conveyor belt to Five Cail Babcock of France. In total, some $300 million worth of contracts have gone to companies owned and resident outside B.C.

6. Gideon Rosenbluth and William Schworm, "The Illusion of the Provincial Deficit," in this volume, p. 56; B.C. Central Credit Union, *Economic Analysis of British Columbia* 3:4, August 1983; Gideon Rosenbluth and William Schworm, "The New Priorities of the Social Credit Government of British Columbia," B.C. Economic Policy Institute, UBC, 1984; and Jonathan R. Kesselman, "Revenue Sources for Maintaining Social Services in B.C.," B.C. Economic Policy Institute, UBC, 1984.

7. Since 1977, the provincial government has used the funds transferred under the Established Program Financing formula for purposes other than higher education and simultaneously reduced provincial grants. Estimates by Gideon Rosenbluth and by Philip Resnick based on federal government budget estimates indicate an increase in federal funds in 1983/84 of $33.6 million not passed on to the institutions, plus a drop of $13.9 million in provincial government funding, for a total reduction of $47.5 million (representing a 21.3% drop in funding from the previous year). For cuts in public education, the study by the Canadian Teachers' Federation, *Economic Recession and the Quality of Education: Some Threatening Trends, 1984*, argues that education has deteriorated more in B.C. than in any other province.

8. Patrick McGeer, quoted in *B.C. Business* 10:3 (March-April, 1982), p. 10.

9. Ian Mulgrew, "No one laughs about class war," *Globe and Mail*, March 21, 1984, p. 3. See also Mulgrew, "One of five in B.C. lives on welfare, UI," *Globe and Mail*, April 5, 1984, p. 1.

10. "Democracy," has recently re-entered the government's vocabulary in relation to the new Labour Code

Amendments. See p. 106.

  11. *Budget, 1984*, pp. 2-3.

Recovery Through Restraint?:
The Budgets of 1983/84 and 1984/85

1. F.A. Hayek, *The Road to Serfdom* (Chicago, University of Chicago Press, 1944).

2. Unless otherwise indicated, data in this paper are taken from OECD, *Main Economic Indicators*, November, 1983, and Province of B.C., *Labour Research Bulletin*, Vol. II, No. 11, 1983.

3. Province of B.C., *Restraint and Recovery* (Victoria: Queen's Printer, 1983).

4. *Macleans,* October 17, 1983.

5. Province of B.C., *Restraint and Recovery*, p. 4.

6. See Gideon Rosenbluth and William Schworm, "The Illusion of the Provincial Deficit," p. 56 of this book.

7. Victoria *Times-Colonist*, November 3, 1983, January 1984.

8. Rosenbluth and Schworm, "The Illusion of the Provincial Deficit."

9. Province of B.C., *Budget 1984* (Victoria: Queen's Printer, 1984), p. 6.

10. T. Siedule, and K. Newton, "The Unemployment Gap in Canada, 1961-78," Discussion Paper No. 145, Economic Council of Canada, 1979.

11. See e.g., A.R. Dobell, "What's the B.C. Spirit? Recent Experience in the Management of Restraint," unpublished paper, Univerity of Victoria, 1983.

12. *Globe and Mail*, January 23, 1984.

13. In B.C. the unemployment rate for people aged 15-24 in October 1983 was over 21% as compared to the provincial average of 12.5% For women over 25 the rate was 10.3% as compared to 9.7% for men over 25. Rates in the resource-based regions of the interior of the province and central Vancouver Island ran as high as 16.3% while in Victoria, heavily dependent on government employment, the rate was 14.6%, the second highest rate for all urban centres across the country.

The Illusion of the Provincial Deficit

1. Province of B.C., *Budget 1983*, p. 9.
2. *Ibid.*, p. 7.
3. Province of B.C., *Budget 1984*, p. 1.
4. *Ibid.*, p. 5.
5. *Public Accounts 1982/83 Vol. I*, pp. C24, C28, C29. Our figure does not include the provincially guaranteed debt of local governments, hospitals, school districts, colleges and universities.
6. *Ibid.*, p. C21.
7. *Ibid.*, p. C17.
8. *Ibid.*, p. C21.
9. The downgrading of B.C. Hydro's rating by Moody's Investors Service from "AAA" to "AA1" in July 1983 meant one-eighth of one per cent more in interest charges. Nevertheless it was cited to government ministers as justifying their budget-slashing (Winnipeg *Free Press*, July 13, 1983, p. 12).

The Hidden Agenda of "Restraint"

1. Jonathan Kesselman, "Revenue Sources for Maintaining Social Services in B.C." B.C. Economic Policy Institute, UBC, 1984.
2. B.C. Ministry of Finance, *Estimates, 1984/85*, p. 234.
3. Examples of the prevailing tendency to analyze the management of provincial austerity measures rather than overall goals and priorities include A.R. Dobell, "What's the B.C. Spirit? Recent Experience in the Management of Restraint," unpublished paper, University of Victoria, 1983; and Richard McLaren and Bruce Welling, "Employee Bashing Under the Dome in British Columbia," in *Business Quarterly*, Fall 1983.
4. Statistics Canada 13-001, *National Income and Expenditure Accounts*, First Quarter, 1981, pp. 28-31; B.C. Ministry of Industry and Small Business Development, *Economic Review and Outlook, 1982-83*, p. 50.
5. B.C. Ministry of Finance, *Financial and Economic Review*, 1976, p. 80; B.C. Ministry of Industry and Small Business Development, *External Trade Report*, 1980, p. 85. Prices are deflated for these calculations using the G.N.E. Implicit Price Index.

6. B.C. Ministry of Finance, *Financial and Economic Review*, 1976, p. 8, and 1981, p. 166.

7. B.C. Ministry of Labour, *Labour Research Bulletin*, Vol. 11, No. 1, January 1983, p. 5, and Vol. 10, No. 2, January 1982, p. 4.

8. *Ibid.*, Vol. 11, No. 1, January 1983, p. 4.

9. B.C. Ministry of Industry and Small Business Development, *B.C. Business Bulletin*, Vol. 1, No. 1, p. 6.

10. B.C. Ministry of Finance, *British Columbia Budget, 1983*, p. 72.

11. B.C. Ministry of Finance, *British Columbia Budget, 1983*, p. 62.

12. B.C. Teachers' Federation, "Education Finance in B.C., 1982," 1982, pp. 6-7.

13. B.C. Ministry of Labour, *Labour Research Bulletin*, Vol. 11, No. 2, p. 3.

14. Vancouver *Sun*, September 7, 1982, p. A1; Vancouver *Province*, October 17, 1982, p. A4.

15. Vancouver *Province*, February 10, 1983, p. B1.

16. B.C. Ministry of Finance, *British Columbia Budget, 1983*, p. 36.

17. C.S.P., "Progress Report No. 35," and Employers' Council of B.C., *Industrial Relations Bulletin*, Vol. 16, No. 2, January 10, 1984.

18. B.C. Ministry of Finance, *Estimates 1983/84*, pp. 105, 120, and *Financial and Economic Review*, 1982/83, pp. 125-26.

19. B.C. Ministry of Finance, *British Columbia Budget, 1983*, p. 30.

20. *Ibid.*, p. 32.

21. B.C. Ministry of Finance, *British Columbia Budget, 1984*, pp. 16-17.

22. See John Malcolmson and Cliff Stainsby, *The Fraser Institute, The Government and a Corporate Free Lunch* (Vancouver: Solidarity Coalition, 1983).

The Solidarity Coalition

1. Thanks are due to Art Kube, John Malcolmson and Renate Shearer for providing documentary records of events.

2. T.H. Marshall, "Citizenship and Social Class," in T.H. Marshall, *Class, Citizenship and Social Development*

(Westport, Connecticut: Greenwood Press, 1973), pp. 65-122.

3. See Goran Therborn, "The Rise of Capitalism and the Rise of Democracy," *New Left Review* 103, 1977, pp. 3-41.

4. It is worth noting, however, that in B.C., Native Indians and certain racial minorities were prohibited from voting in provincial elections until 1949, and that Status Indians were not granted federal voting rights until 1960.

5. Anthony Giddens, "Class Division, Class Conflict and Citizenship Rights," in Anthony Giddens, *Profiles and Critiques in Social Theory* (London: MacMillan, 1982), pp. 164-180, especially p. 174.

6. Granted by the federal government of Canada in 1944. See Paul Phillips, *No Power Greater* (Vancouver: B.C. Federation of Labour, 1967), pp. 129-30.

7. Bob Russell, "The Political Economy of the Social Wage," *Studies in Political Economy* 13, 1984.

8. Ian Mulgrew, "Kinds of Myths Victory's Made Of," *Globe and Mail*, May 11, 1983, p. 8.

9. In particular, the Canadian Union of Public Employees, Canadian Union of Postal Workers, Canadian Association of Industrial, Mechanical and Allied Workers, Independent Canadian Transit Union, and United Brotherhood of Carpenters and Joiners of America.

10. See Jeremy Wilson's chapter in this volume.

11. See for instance Jackie Larkin, "The Generals Didn't Strike," *Canadian Dimension* 18:1, 1984, pp. 3-6, and Bryan Palmer, "A Funny Thing Happened on the Way to Kelowna," *Canadian Dimension* 18:1, 1984, pp. 13-16.

12. For a more general analysis see Francis Fox Piven, "The Social Structuring of Political Protest," *Politics and Society*, 6, 1976, pp. 297-326.

13. Victoria *Times-Colonist*, May 4, 1984, p. A1.

14. Vancouver *Sun*, February 27, 1984, p. 1.

15. Sidney Tafler, "Socreds Outline Major Changes in Labour Code," *Globe and Mail*, May 9, 1984, p. BC1.

16. Sid Tafler, "Law 'Forcing' Defiance: NDP," *Globe and Mail*, May 17, 1984, p. BC3.

17. "Kube Vows Fight Against Labour Bill," *Globe and Mail*, May 17, 1984, p. BC1.

18. *Pacific Tribune*, May 16, 1984, pp. 1, 2, 12.

19. Ian Mulgrew, "No One Laughs About Class War," *Globe and Mail*, March 21, 1984, p. 3.

20. Paul Phillips, *No Power Greater*, pp. 147, 163.

21. See S.M. Miller and Donald Tomaskovic-Devey, "A Framework for New Progressive Coalitions," *Social Policy* 13:3, 1983, pp. 8-14.

22. See Greg M. Nielsen and John D. Jackson, "The Development of Quebec: Class and Nation," in J. Paul Grayson, ed., *Introduction to Sociology* (Toronto: Gage Publishing Limited, 1983), pp. 170-215.

23. David Wallis, "Solidarity Moves Eastward," *Pacific Tribune*, February 29, 1984, p. 5.

24. Claus Offe, "The Separation of Form and Content in Liberal Democratic Politics," *Studies in Political Economy* 3, 1980, pp. 5-16.

25. See Sid Tafler, "Pushing the 'Right' Ideas," *Globe and Mail*, December 10, 1983, p. 8; Cliff Stainsby and John Malcolmson, "The Fraser Institute, the Government and a Corporate Free Lunch," *Canadian Dimension* 18:1, 1984, pp. 19-26; and Ben Swankey, *The Fraser Institute: A Socialist Analysis of the Corporate Drive to the Right* (Vancouver: Centre for Socialist Education, 1984).

The Legislation Under Siege

1. Bernard Crick, *The Reform of Parliament* (New York: Anchor Books, 1965), p. 17.

2. Victoria *Times-Colonist*, October 22, 1983.

3. Vancouver *Sun*, August 10, 1983.

4. Vancouver *Sun*, August 10, 1983.

5. Vancouver *Sun*, September 20, 1983.

6. Crick, pp. 79-80.

7. Vancouver *Sun*, July 16, 1983.

8. Vancouver *Sun*, September 20, 1983.

The Ideology of Neo-Conservatism

1. Michael Crozier, Samuel P. Huntington and J. Watanuki, *The Crisis of Democracy: Report on the Governability of Democracies to the Trilateral Commission* (New York: New York University Press, 1975.)

2. James M. Buchanan and Richard E. Wagner, *Democracy in Deficit: The Political Legacy of Lord Keynes* (New York: Academic Press, 1977), p. 28.

3. Barry Goldwater, *The Conscience of a Conservative* (Shepherdsville, Ky.: Victor Publishing, 1960), pp. 183, 71.

4. Cited in Jonathan Martin Kolkey, *The New Right* (Washington: University Press of America, 1983).

5. Keith Joseph and K. Sumpton, *Equality* (London: J. Murray, 1979), p. 18; Samuel Brittan, *The Economic Consequences of Democracy* (London: Temple Smith, 1977), p. 277.

6. Cited in Kevin P. Phillips, *Post-Conservative America* (New York: Random House, 1982).

7. Cited in Phillips, *op. cit.*, p. 140.

8. David Held and John Keane, "In a Fit State," *New Socialist*, March-April 1984.

9. Bernard Crick, cited in Held and Keane, *op. cit.*

10. For a good discussion of such a sytem, see the recent study by Alec Nove, *The Economics of Feasible Socialism* (London: George Allen and Unwin, 1983).

Social Credit as Employer

1. Vancouver *Province*, April 27, 1983, p. A11.

2. Charles H. Levine, "More on Cutback Management: Hard Questions for Hard Times," in Charles H. Levine, ed., *Managing Fiscal Stress: The Crisis in the Public Sector* (Chatham: Chatham House, 1980), p. 305.

3. *British Columbia Budget: 1983*, p. 63.

4. Job security was not absolute. Employees could be and were fired for cause under the terms of the Public Service Act and their union agreements. It should also be noted that the provincial cabinet has always had an unrestricted authority under the act to remove or dismiss any employee. See Public Service Act, RS 1979, Chap. 343, section 48.

5. James Matkin, Deputy Minister of Intergovernmental Relations, was one of its chief architects. In 1983 he left government to become head of the B.C. Employers' Council.

6. A basic protection factor was set at 10% maximum for 1982/83 with a plus-2% to minus-2% experience adjustment factor (past compensation experience and historical relationships with other groups), and an additional 2% for special circumstances (manpower or skill shortages and labour productivity increases). In the second

year a basic inflation protector equal to the average percentage increase in the Vancouver consumer price index would be applied.

7. Under these May 25 guidelines the three factors remained the same for the first year but the experience factor was now also to apply in the second year.

8. On July 27 the basic income factor in the first year was reduced from 10% to 6% and from a maximum of 8% to 5% in the second year. The experience adjustment factor (recent compensation experience and historical relationships) and the special circumstances factor (labour productivity, compensation for training made necessary by technological change, and the state of the provincial economy) would apply in both years and could now both range from plus-2% to minus-3%.

9. Ros Oberlyn, "Deficit rises; Curtis warns of more cuts," Vancouver *Sun*, February 15, 1983, p. A1.

10. The terms of this part of the settlement were set out in the GERB-BCGEU *Master Agreement*, October 25, 1982, Clause 27.03 and Appendix 5.

11. Compensation Stabilization Amendment Act, 1983, section 5 (new section 12.1 of the Act).

12. The basic income factor was reduced to 1%, and the experience adjustment and special circumstances factors set at plus-2% or minus-3%. The special experience adjustment factor no longer included historical relationships, and productivity was removed from special circumstances to become a separate factor at the discretion of the Commissioner.

13. Compensation Stabilization Program, *British Columbia Institute of Technology and British Columbia Government Employees' Union*, Ruling of the Commissioner No. 2/84, March 8, 1984, p. 12.

14. B.C. Ministry of Finance, *Estimates 1983-84*, Schedule E, and *1984-85*, Schedule D.

15. This type of coalition and politicization of B.C.'s public employees is precisely the kind of development foreseen by James O'Connor in *The Fiscal Crisis of the State* (New York: St. Martin's Press, 1973), chapter 9.

16. As a prelude to a much-needed reform of GERB and the Public Service Commission, Mike Davidson resigned as GERB chairman in June 1984. He received a new appointment as a vice-chairman of the B.C. Labour Relations Board.

17. Herbert Simon, *Administrative Behavior*, 2nd. ed. (New York: Free Press, 1957), p. 65.

Human Rights Under Restraint

1. Victoria *Times-Colonist*, July 9, 1983, p. 1.
2. Victoria *Times-Colonist*, July 15, 1983, p. 1.
3. Victoria *Times-Colonist*, September 29, 1983, p. B1.
4. Victoria *Times-Colonist*, December 9, 1983.
5. Victoria *Times-Colonist*, October 21, 1983.
6. Victoria *Times-Colonist*, December 9, 1983, p. 1.
7. April Katz, "Human Rights and Employment in British Columbia," in *Labour Law and Practice* (Vancouver: Continuing Legal Education Society, 1983), p. 5.1.0.2.
8. Ian A. Hunter, "The Origin, Development and Interpretation of Human Rights Legislation," in R.S. Macdonald and J.P. Humphrey, eds., *The Practice of Freedom* (Toronto: Butterworths, 1979), p. 81. Professor Hunter, of the law faculty at the University of Western Ontario, is a leading expert on human rights legislation.
9. At the time of writing two cases of alleged sexual harassment are pending before boards of inquiry.
10. This means that it was not a necessary condition for performance of the job, or that it was modifiable without undue hardship to a business.
11. See *Jefferson v. Baldwin and the British Columbia Ferry Service* (Report of a Board of Inquiry under the B.C. Human Rights Code, September 29, 1976).
12. See *Insurance Corporation of British Columbia v. Heerspink* (1982) 2 S.C.R. 145.
13. *Ontario Human Rights Commission et al. v. Simpsons-Sears, Ltd.* (1982) 38 O.R. (2d) 423. (O.C.A.)
14. See note 9.
15. See, for example, s.41 of the Canadian Human Rights Act, S.C. 1976-1977, c.33.
16. Bill 11 appears partially to rectify this glaring deficiency with an ambiguous reference to an "award of up to $2000" (s.17(2)(b)). However, the exact impact of this new language is far from clear.
17. The Judicial Review Procedure Act (R.S.B.C. 1979 c.209), however, will still be available to review decisions of the board of inquiry at the Supreme Court level, but in somewhat fewer situations than under the Code.

Women's Rights:
An Impediment to Recovery?

1. According to the Ministry of Education's post-secondary enrolment statistics for 1981/82, there were 17,269 part-time and 9,051 full-time female students in post-secondary non-vocational programmes in community colleges in B.C.

2. Susan Whitter, "B.C. Provincial Restraint Policy and its Effects on Women and Education." *Women's Education* 2:2, December 1983.

3. The information on teacher layoffs was obtained from the B.C. Teachers' Federation's Status of Women office. For the situation facing women academics in Canada, see Dorothy Smith, "An Analysis of Ideological Structures and How Woman are Excluded: Considerations for Academic Women," *Canadian Review of Sociology and Anthropology* 12:4, 1975.

4. National Council of Welfare, Ottawa, *Women and Poverty*, 1979; and *The Working Poor: People and Programs*, 1981.

5. In an effort to "encourage" single mothers to seek employment, GAIN — Guaranteed Annual Income for Need — was introduced in October 1981. Single mothers with one child over six months, or with two children of whom one was over 12 years, were reclassified as "employable". Being classified "employable" reduces your welfare payments by between $55 and $35 a month. Further, GAIN recipients were now forced to reapply every four months. In 1981 a single parent on welfare with one child received $540 a month. The Law Centre, *Fact Sheet*, October 1981; reported in *Status of Women News*, October 1981.

6. It is difficult to get accurate official information on the application of daycare subsidies. This assessment is based on interviews with daycare operators, supervisors and women who have applied for daycare subsidies.

7. See Pat Armstrong and Hugh Armstrong, *The Working Majority*, Canadian Advisory Council on the Status of Women, 1983.

8. *Monday Magazine*, April 26, 1984, p. 4.

9. Pat Armstrong and Hugh Armstrong, *The Double Ghetto* (Toronto: McClelland and Stewart, 1977).

10. Marilyn Power, "Falling Through the 'Safety Net':

Women, Economic Crisis and Reaganomics," *Feminist Studies* 10:1, 1984.

Downsizing the Unemployment Problem

1. Ian Mulgrew, "B.C. budget raises taxes, trims deficit," *Globe and Mail*, February 21, 1984.

2. B.C. Central Credit Union, Economics Department, "B.C.'s Employment Prospects," *Economic Analysis of British Columbia*, May 1984.

3. Vancouver *Sun*, May 12, 1982.

4. The evolution of the concept of restraint is briefly traced in Jill Gibson's unpublished paper, "The Evolution of Restraint Budgeting in B.C., 1975-1983," April 1984.

5. William Schworm, "The Economic Impact of the British Columbia 'Restraint' Budget," B.C. Economic Policy Institute, May 1984.

6. Sid Tafler, "B.C. job cuts partly fake," *Globe and Mail*, March 19, 1984.

7. *Ibid.*

8. Interview with British Columbia Teachers' Federation researcher John Malcolmson, June 22, 1984.

9. Vancouver *Sun*, June 20, 1984.

10. Conference Board of Canada, *Quarterly Provincial Forecast*, February 1984.

11. B.C. New Democratic Party, "Jobs Now," undated [1983].

12. Although this alleged blunder has found a place in B.C. electioneering folklore, there has been no subsequent research to confirm its purported impact on the electorate.

13. Stan Persky, "Pinstripes and Red Underwear," *This Magazine*, August 1983, provides a narrative analysis of the campaign.

14. Personal communication, B.C. Provincial NDP.

15. Vancouver *Sun*, April 10, 1978.

16. Interview with Cliff Andstein, B.C. Government Employees Union negotiator, June 12, 1984.

17. Interview with Gordon Bailey, secretary-treasurer of the Vancouver and Municipal Region Employees' Union, June 22, 1984.

18. The Vancouver *Sun*'s weekend feature of July 8, 1984, observing the first anniversary of the 1983 budget, is a case in point, combining a series of vignettes about how

fired government workers have fared with a lengthy and self-justificatory interview with the premier.

19. Interview with Mel Lehan, June 20, 1984.

20. *Globe and Mail*, July 7, 1984.

21. CBC Television News, July 6, 1984.

22. Peter Cook, "Economic recovery: is it all but over?" *Globe and Mail*, September 29, 1983.

23. *Globe and Mail,* May 17, 1984.

24. Don McGillivray, "Economic upturn aborted," Vancouver *Sun*, June 15, 1984.

25. Brian Lewis, "Student job hunt tougher," Vancouver *Province*, June 10, 1984; *Globe and Mail*, July 7, 1984.

26. Vancouver *Province*, June 10, 1984.

27. Vancouver *Sun*, October 21, 1983.

Medicare at Risk

1. *British Columbia Budget 1984* (Victoria: Queen's Printer, 1984), p. 13.

2. *1979 Annual Report* of the Minister of National Health and Welfare (Ottawa: Supply and Services, 1981), p. 1.

3. Victoria *Times-Colonist*, April 10, 1984.

4. *British Columbia Budget 1984*, p. 13.

5. Emmett M. Hall, *Canada's National-Provincial Health Program for the 1980s* (Ottawa, 1980), p. 2.

6. Ed Finn, *Medi-Care on the Critical List* (Canadian Centre for Policy Alternatives, 1983), p. 5.

7. National Council of Welfare, *Medicare: The Public Good and Private Practice* (Ottawa: Minister of Supply and Services, 1982), pp. 8-9.

8. *Ibid.*, p. 2.

9. R. Evans, "Hiding Behind Medicare: Health Care Funding in the B.C. Budget" (Vancouver: B.C. Economic Policy Institute, Department of Economics, UBC, 1984), p. 8. Evans sees the sharp cost upturn of 1982 as reflecting the impact of what he calls the Great Recession "on total output, not a major change in health costs patterns."

10. Gordon Hatcher, *Universal Free Health Care in Canada 1947-1977* (Washington: U.S. Department of Health and Human Services, 1981), p. 9.

11. Evans, p. 9.

12. Evans, p. 8.

13. National Council of Welfare, p. 38.

14. National Council of Welfare, p. 2.

15. Hall, p. 42.

16. Robin F. Badgley and David R. Smith, *User Charges for Health Services* (Toronto: Ontario Council of Health, 1979), p. 9; emphasis in original.

17. Finn, p. 10.

18. National Council of Welfare, p. 36.

19. Evans, p. 14. In June 1984 the federal government stated its refusal to collect this tax.

20. Victoria Branden, "Medibucks," *Canadian Dimension* 18:2, 1984, pp. 7-8.

21. Finn, p. 13.

22. See *Long Term Care in British Columbia: The Union Members' Perspective* (Vancouver Hospital Employees' Union, 1981), and Noel Schacter, *The Profit Motive and its Impact on Long Term Care Institutions* (Victoria: report submitted to Hospital Employees' Union, 1984).

23. NDP Caucus Research Office, "Acute Hospital Survey" (March 1983).

24. Public Commission on Social and Community Service Cutbacks *Interim Report* (Burnaby, July 1982), p. 38.

25. See Charles Reasons, Lois Ross and Craig Paterson, *Assault on the Worker* (Toronto: Butterworths, 1981).

26. "WCB: Destined for Permanent Disability?" *The Hospital Guardian* 4:2, 1984, p. 16.

27. "WCB: Destined for Permanent Disability?" p. 17.

28. "WCB: Destined for Permanent Disability?" p. 17-18.

29. It is worth re-emphasizing that the Social Credit government got advice on its package of "restraint" legislation from the Fraser Institute, among whose unsound and unseemly publications is a book by Ake Bloomquist titled *The Health Care Business*, which calls for a "market-oriented health system". Many erosions so far experienced in B.C. medicare seem to derive from the kind of regressive thinking promulgated in that book.

30. On the other hand, as Ron Labonte says in "Private Laboratories and the Funding Crisis in Health Care" (Health Sciences Association, December 1982), "'Privatization' transfers the cost from where it can be constrained (hospital programs) to where it is open-ended. Hospitals pay for testing mainly through their global budgets. To

work within budgets, lab services are being cut back, and the tests are being sent to private labs which are reimbursed on a fee-for-service basis by the Medical Services Plan.'' (p. 47).

31. Donald Swartz, ''The Politics of Reform: Conflict and Accommodation in Canadian Health Policy,'' in Leo Panitch, ed., *The Canadian State: Political Economy and Political Power* (Toronto: University of Toronto Press, 1977), p. 335.

The Human Costs of Restraint

1. Peter Golding, ''Rethinking Common Sense About Social Policy,'' in David Bull and Paul Wilding, eds., *Thatcherism and the Poor* (London: Child Poverty Action Group, 1983), p. 10.

2. Janet Currie and Fred Pishalski, *Loosening the Fabric: the Termination of the Family Support Worker Program in B.C.* (Victoria, 1983), p. 5.

3. Figures compiled by the author from the Canada Assistance Plan report, Ron Yzerman, Director, Welfare Services and Work Activity Division, and Canada Census, 1981.

4. Figures taken from *Annual Report, Ministry of Human Resources in B.C., 1980/81*, p. 32, 33, and *Statistical Supplement to 50th Annual Report*, Ministry of Community and Social Services, Ontario, 1981, p. 62.

5. *Poor Kids: A Report by the National Council on Welfare on Children in Poverty in Canada*. Ottawa, 1975.

6. Native Canadians have rightly complained about the disproportionate number of Native children in care. In B.C. almost 40% of the children in care are Natives, one of the highest percentages in Canada. See Patrick Johnson, *Native Children and the Child Welfare System* (Toronto: Canadian Council on Social Development, 1983).

7. Most financial figures were taken from the annual reports of each province. Gross expenditures were used. Daycare, mental health, detention and correction services and residential services for the handicapped were omitted. Additional figures were provided by Philip Hepworth, Policy Development Consultant, Health and Welfare Canada, and by Corrine Robertshaw, *Child Protection in*

Canada (Ottawa: Health and Welfare Canada, 1981), p. 21 (1978 figures).

8. Letter from Ron Yzerman, Director, Welfare Services and Work Activity Division, February 7, 1984.

9. Canadian Sociotelic Limited, *The Nature and Effectiveness of Family Support Measures in Child Welfare*. Prepared for the Ontario Ministry of Community and Social Services, Toronto, August 1983.

10. Jack MacDonald, "The Spallumcheen Indian Band By-Law and its Potential Impact on Native Indian Child Welfare Policy in B.C. (Vancouver: School of Social Work, UBC, April 1981).

11. See for example Len Evans, *Ministerial Statement on Indian Child Welfare Placements* (Winnipeg: Department of Community Services and Corrections, 1982). Manitoba completed an agreement whereby child welfare services were provided by Native Indians in February 1982. Peter Hudson and Brad McKenzie, "Child Welfare and Native People: The Extension of Colonialism," *The Social Worker* 49:2, Summer 1981, p. 65.

The "New Reality" in Education

1. B.C. Teachers' Federation, "This is What We're Fighting For."

2. "People of B.C. to Judge Wisdom of Education Centralization," BCSTA News Release, July 8, 1983.

3. Association of British Columbia School Superintendents, "A Statement of Concern for Public Education in British Columbia," March 1984, pp. 3-4, 17.

4. *Ibid.*, p. 4.

5. 1982 SBC chap. 2.

6. *1983 Education Finance in British Columbia*, Bargaining Division, B.C. Teachers' Federation, August 1983, p. 5.

7. Now even these tax rates are centrally determined so school boards have virtually no latitude in the revenue area.

8. Bills 7 and 12 in the July 1983 package, which introduced the variable mill rate system, were intended to encourage municipalities to offer tax breaks to business as well.

9. *1983 Education Finance*, pp. 6-8.

10. The government's original target was to reduce education spending by 5% in actual dollars — by considerably more in real terms — by 1986. "Changes in Education Financing in B.C.: Details and Implications," BCTF, August 10, 1983.

11. Province of British Columbia, *Restraint and Recovery: The Next Steps*, p. 10.

12. *Ibid.*

13. Robert C. Allen, "Investment and Education in British Columbia: A Review of the Evidence in *Restraint and Recovery*," B.C. Economic Policy Institute, Paper No. P-84, Department of Economics, UBC, p. 7.

14. "School District Budgets: Trends in the Evolution of Funding Responsibility," BCTF, December 1983, p. 6.

15. *Ibid.*, p. 5.

16. See, for example, B.C. School Trustees Association, *A Taxation Report to Business*, 2nd ed., March 1983.

17. "Investment and Education," p. 12.

18. *1983 Education Finance*, p. 32.

19. "Changes in Education Financing," p. 1.

20. B.C. already has a higher than average pupil-teacher ratio. Nonetheless, the government is determined to increase this ratio by two pupils per teacher. Allen, "Investment and Education," p. 13.

21. *Ministry Policy Circular* No. 06 (83.09.02), "Provincial Examinations" (British Columbia Ministry of Education, September 1983), p. 1.

22. Jack Heinrich, *Secondary School Graduation Requirements: A Discussion Paper* (B.C. Ministry of Education, Victoria: Queen's Printer, 1984), p. 12.

23. *Ibid.*

24. The minimum number of Grade 11 and 12 courses to be successfully completed is to increase from twelve to thirteen, and there is to be an increase from three to four in the minimum number of Grade 12-level courses selected from courses that have Grade 11 prerequisites.

25. *Secondary School Graduation Requirements: A Discussion Paper*, "Foreword".

26. "BCTF brief on the White Paper: Public commission on education needed — now," *BCTF Newsletter* 23:13, June 6, 1984, p. 6.

27. *Ibid.*

28. Native Indian Education Council of Greater Victoria, *Statement on Proposed Changes in Secondary*

School Requirements, May 17, 1984, "Introduction".

29. *Ibid.*, pp. 2-3.

30. Association of British Columbia School Superintendents, "A Statement of Concern for Public Education in British Columbia," March 1984, p. 8. The superintendents cite, among others, Herbert J. Walberg, "Educational Climates," in H. Walberg, ed., *Improving Educational Standards and Productivity: The Research Basis for Policy* (Berkeley, Ca.: McCutchan Publishing, 1982), and Eric A. Hanushek, "Throwing Money at Schools," *Journal of Policy Analysis and Management* 1:1, 1981, pp. 19-41. For further discussion of this issue see also the *Brief from Trustee C. Pickup, Greater Victoria School Board, in Response to the Secondary School Graduation Requirements: A Discussion Paper, B.C. Ministry of Education, March, 1984* and the Native Indian Education Council of Greater Victoria, *Statement on Proposed Changes in Secondary School Graduation Requirements*, May 17, 1984. Note also that the British Columbia School Trustees Association has urged the government to establish a royal commission to investigate education in B.C. (BCSTA AGM Resolutions Book, Resolution 8, April 1984). The BCTF, the Association of B.C. School Superintendents and other education professionals have made similar recommendations.

A Decade of Restraint:
The Economics of B.C. Universities

1. *Report of the Committee on the Future Role of Universities in Ontario*, H.K. Fisher, Chairman (August, 1981); A.E. Douglas, "The Soothsayers," *Science Forum*, February 1969, pp. 17-18.

2. *Newsweek*, June 1983, p. 61.

3. Robert C. Allen, "Investment and Education in British Columbia: A Review of the Evidence in *Restraint and Recovery*" (Paper No. P84-4, B.C. Economic Policy Institute, Department of Economics, UBC, 1984), pp. 8-9.

4. The federal government declares a contribution to post-secondary education of $4,496.6 million for 1983. *Support to Education by the Government of Canada* (Ottawa: Office of the Secretary of State, 1983), p. 14. B.C.'s share of this amount would be about 10%

(estimated by population). This would be about $449.6 million. For the year 1983/84, the provincial government gave to colleges and universities $574 million — $300 million to universities and $274 million to colleges (*Estimates 1983/84*, Province of B.C., pp. 61, 66, 190). Therefore, in rough figures, the percentage of university grants that came from federal or federally controlled sources is 78.3%. In the text, we used the rounded figure of 75%.

5. *The Economic Impact of the University of Victoria* (UVic Institutional Analysis, 1978); *The Impact of the University of British Columbia on the Greater Vancouver Regional District* (UBC, Office of Institutional Analysis and Planning, 1982).

6. The rough calculation runs in the following way. About 90% of the operating grant will be spent locally and about 85% through salaries. If the salaries are discounted by about 30% to 35% (income tax withheld), then about 60 cents of every dollar of operating funds will flow into the local economy. In Victoria, the multiplier effect is about 1.9. This makes the 60 cents effectively $1.14 once it has rippled through the local economy. In Vancouver, where the Lower Mainland is much larger and there is more room for the ripple to spread, the multiplier is 1.99. This makes the initial 60 cents effectively $1.19 to the Lower Mainland's economy.

7. After discussions with members of the economics department at UVic, particularly Professor Leonard Laudadio, we arrived at the following estimates. Of the 30 to 35 cents of income tax, about 10 cents goes to the provincial treasury. Of the remaining 65 to 70 cents about half is spent locally and becomes subject to the 7% sales tax plus other hidden taxes on such things as gasoline, alcoholic beverages and the like. This means that about 12 to 13 cents of revenue is generated every time a dollar flows through the provincial economy. The effect of the multiplier mentioned above will obviously increase this amount.

8. C. Gallagher, *A Widening Gap* (University of Victoria, Institutional Analysis, 1982).

Conclusion

1. See Samuel Bowles, David M. Gordon and Thomas E. Weisskopf, *Beyond the Wasteland* (Garden City: Anchor Press, 1983), p. 262. The authors — American economists — argue on the basis of detailed analysis and projections that such restructuring is indispensible for genuine recovery.

2. Canadian Conference of Catholic Bishops, *Ethical Choices and Political Challenges* (Ottawa: Mutual Press, 1984), p. 19. The alternative future proposed by the bishops is remarkably similar to the one advanced by Bowles *et al.*

Notes on Authors

Editors

William K. Carroll, Assistant Professor of Sociology, University of Victoria, specializes in studies of social movements and the political economy of Canada. He is author of a number of articles on corporate power and social class in Canada.

Charles Doyle, Professor of English, University of Victoria, is a poet, critic, editor, anthologist, biographer and author of fourteen books. He is also president of a community association, vice-president of the St. Vincent de Paul Society of Greater Victoria, and president of the University of Victoria Educators for Nuclear Disarmament. In 1974 he was first president of the Confederation of Faculty Associations of British Columbia.

Monika Langer, Assistant Professor of Philosophy, University of Victoria, is a specialist in social and political philosophy, and has written especially on Sartre, Merleau-Ponty and Marx. She has worked for both CBC and Radio-Quebec, and has taught at several universities, including Toronto and Yale.

Warren Magnusson, Assistant Professor of Political

Science, University of Victoria, has written on urban politics and political theory of local government, and is an editor of *City Politics in Canada*. Although he now specializes in political theory he has taught Canadian politics at several universities, including Western Ontario and Toronto.

R.B.J. Walker, Assistant Professor of Political Science, University of Victoria, has written extensively on the political theory of international relations, and is editor of *Culture, Ideology and World Order*. He was formerly a fellow at the Center of International Studies, Princeton University, and has taught at Queen's University and UBC.

Contributors

Lanny Beckman is the publisher of New Star Books.

Marilyn Callahan, Associate Professor of Social Work, University of Victoria, specializes in the study of child welfare, welfare law, and social policy affecting women. She is a former child welfare officer, and is active in various social service organizations, including the Women's Sexual Assault Centre. She is an author of *Welfare Rights and GAIN*.

Stella Lord is a doctoral candidate in sociology at Carleton University and an active member of the Victoria Status of Women Action Group. She specializes in the study of women and work, and has taught sociology in Victoria and at Carleton.

John Malcolmson, research analyst for the B.C. Teachers' Federation and doctoral candidate in sociology at Simon Fraser University, is engaged in a major study of the political economy of restraint in B.C. He has taught sociology at Simon Fraser University and the University of Victoria.

Patricia Marchak, Professor of Sociology, University of British Columbia, is author of *Green Gold: The Forest Industry in Canada*, *In Whose Interests? An Essay on Multinational Corporations in a Canadian Context*, and *Ideological Perspectives on Canada*. She is a director of the Pacific Group for Policy Alternatives.

Stan Persky teaches political science at Capilano College in North Vancouver, and is the author of several books, the most recent being *Bennett II* and *America, the Last Domino*.

T. Murray Rankin, Associate Professor of Law, University of Victoria, is a specialist in both the law of the environment and human rights legislation. Among his scholarly works is the definitive report for the Canadian Bar Association, *Freedom of Information in Canada*.

Philip Resnick, Associate Professor of Political Science, University of British Columbia, has written extensively on the political economy of Canada. He is author of *The Land of Cain: Class and Nationalism in English Canada 1945-1975* and *Parliament vs. People*.

Gideon Rosenbluth, Professor of Economics, University of British Columbia, is a specialist in industrial organization and a founder of the B.C. Economic Policy Institute.

Norman J. Ruff, Assistant Professor of Political Science, University of Victoria, is a former provincial public servant and a specialist in employee-management relations in the public service. He has written extensively on B.C. politics and is an author of *The Reins of Power: Governing British Columbia*.

Noel Schacter, research analyst for the Hospital Employees' Union, Victoria, is a doctoral candidate at the University of California (Santa Barbara), with a special interest in social policy. He has taught at various post-secondary institutions in B.C. and has been a researcher for various community groups and unions.

John Schofield, Associate Professor of Economics, University of Victoria, is a specialist in regional economics and cost-benefit analysis, and is author of numerous scholarly articles in these fields.

Gordon Shrimpton, Associate Professor of Classics, University of Victoria, is an author and editor of numerous works in his field. President of the University of Victoria Faculty Association from 1982 to 1984, he is currently president of the Confederation of University Faculty Associations of British Columbia.

William Schworm, Associate Professor of Economics, University of British Columbia, is a specialist in investment theory and a founder of the B.C. Economic Policy Institute.

R. Jeremy Wilson, Assistant Professor of Political Science, University of Victoria, has written extensively on

B.C. politics and is an author of *The Reins of Power: Governing British Columbia.*

Printed in Canada